Understanding Management

Understanding Management

The Social Science Foundations

Paul Willman

OXFORD

UNIVERSITY PRESS

OXFORD
UNIVERSITY PRESS

Great Clarendon Street, Oxford, OX2 6DP,
United Kingdom

Oxford University Press is a department of the University of Oxford.
It furthers the University's objective of excellence in research, scholarship,
and education by publishing worldwide. Oxford is a registered trade mark of
Oxford University Press in the UK and in certain other countries

Published in the United States of America by Oxford University Press
198 Madison Avenue, New York, NY 10016, United States of America

British Library Cataloguing in Publication Data

Data available

Library of Congress Control Number: 2014935042

ISBN 978–0–19–871691–4 (hbk.)
       978–0–19–871692–1 (pbk.)

Printed and bound by
CPI Group (UK) Ltd, Croydon, CR0 4YY

Acknowledgements

Many people have helped with the material for this book. Ray Loveridge encouraged me to take on the course at Oxford where I first engaged with these ideas and Ted Piepenbrock sat in on it, giving valuable feedback. Yally Avrahampour and Brittany Jones, both MBAs, have taught the Masters course with me at LSE where the materials were developed and helped me think things through. Howard Gospel, Steve New, and several anonymous reviewers for OUP have provided valuable corrections. The manuscript itself has benefitted from detailed comments from Mike Power, Barbara Townley, and David Musson. Helena Caldon did a wonderful job on the manuscript. I bear full responsibility for the remaining defects.

Note to the reader

An objective of this book is to argue that the academic field of management, which is conventionally divided into six sub-disciplines, has common underlying concerns. This argument is presented in Chapter 1 but it is also reflected in the structure of the book. I use chapters to present the content of these sub-disciplines and themes to explore commonalities. This explains the contents page below.

Contents

Contents

List of Figures and Tables

Figures

Tables

While every effort was made to contact the copyright holders of material in this book, in some cases we were unable to do so. If the copyright holders contact the author or publisher, we will be pleased to rectify any omission at the earliest opportunity.

Introduction

This text has developed out of a core management course at Masters level that is intended to introduce the field to students who may have little prior knowledge of management. It is thus extensive in its coverage and integrative in its intent. Management is a quite fragmented area of study with lots of academic branches, but I would argue the tree is narrower at its roots, and these roots are primarily in social science. So a key purpose of the book is to present management theory as applied social science. This is not primarily a book for MBA students, but aims at coverage equivalent to a conventional MBA course; so I am keen to interpret 'management' broadly to embrace the sub-disciplines of strategy, finance, accounting, marketing, organizational behaviour, and operations management. The text tries to show how they arose and how they relate, thus engaging the reader in a little history.

My writing is intended to be critical, in the specific sense that I hold the view that some parts of what is called management theory stand up better to intellectual analysis than others. The book also indicates what academics regard as optimal or best practice in certain fields. However, two sorts of readers may be discouraged by this text.

I have spent over twenty years in business schools and at one, attending one of the many cocktail parties with executives that are the stuff of life there, I was approached by an executive who, having heartily participated in the drinks on offer, asked me 'What should I do about my business?' I asked him what he did, how he saw the problems he faced, and what he had tried to do already to resolve them, to the point where his attention span was stretched. One of my colleagues then arrived and was accosted with the same question. He immediately responded: 'You should identify your core competences, develop your strategic intent and compete for the future.' I thought, 'well, there is that.' But this book is not for those looking for that kind of answer.

LSE has a Latin motto: *Rerum cognoscere causas*—to understand (*cognoscere*) the causes (*causas*) of things (*rerum*). Now in some traditions of social science, academics are worried about whether one can speak of causes, and whether mention of social scientific 'things' is appropriate; in addition, many would not use the verb 'to understand' in such a transitive way; many who believe all of these things in this field study what is called 'critical management'. If any have made it this far, they may wish to avert their gaze now. This text is designed to help students who will be managers understand what may and may not work; and why. In that sense it is critical. But it is the work of a relatively unreconstructed positivist.

The book is extensive, also in a slightly negative way. It tries to deliver a general understanding of the elements of management, not the detailed knowledge necessary for a specialist. So from this book you can, for example, take away a broad understanding of what academic finance theory does and, perhaps, why, but it is not a guide to the pricing of collateralized debt. You will understand the main schools of strategy, but it will not tell you how to do a value chain analysis. It focuses on styles of thought more than plans of action.

The choice and discussion of materials probably reflects a number of biases, and influences of which I am unaware, but here are those I can acknowledge. I was taught social theory by Anthony Giddens and W. G. Runciman at Cambridge University and this affects the ways in which I see the early development of management thinking out of social theory. I was taught industrial relations and industrial sociology by Alan Fox, Rod Martin, and John Goldthorpe at Oxford University and this gives me a particular view on how firms work and employees respond. My first academic post was in Joan Woodward's department at Imperial College (sadly, she was no longer there, but Dorothy Wedderburn was), which left me with a particular respect for empirical studies of organization. Nearly two decades at London Business School—including during the 'big bang' period of the deregulation of financial markets and several merger waves—left me with a slightly cynical view about what modern economics can tell one either about the operation of financial markets or, quite distinctly, the conduct of corporate strategy. The privilege of editing the Tavistock journal, *Human Relations*, opened my eyes to the rich interaction between academic activity and industrial practice; the back catalogue is astonishing. Finally, and this is reflected in the text throughout, being at Oxford and LSE rammed home how much social science there is, often unacknowledged, in the academic study of management. If I picked up half of what was on offer through all of this, I count myself lucky.

Chapter 1

The Management Field

Introduction

Most of the theory we teach on business and management courses emerges from pre-existing and, in some senses, more fundamental academic disciplines. Moreover, this emergence has several broad features. First, the field has the following characteristics: it is derivative, opportunistic, eclectic, and fragmented. Academic and practical knowledge has been mined to deal with specific sets of problems. Second, it has emerged over a relatively short period; most business theory dates from the period since 1890. Third, it has almost all emerged in English, and from English-speaking countries, but it did not all originate there. So, bluntly, we know that we anticipate managing business growth in the early decades of the twenty-first century, much of it in emerging markets, with a conceptual toolkit from developed economies from twentieth century developed economies. It would be useful to understand how much of it might work.

In many cases, the linkages of business theory to mathematics and social science are clear from the management history literature. For example, the lineage of organizational behaviour can be traced back through the 'human relations' movement to the industrial psychology of the 1920s. Arguably, there is a similar line of sight from Taylorism—to which human relations was a reaction—through operations management to operational research. Psychology was mined again to support the rise of consumer marketing in the 1930s, as part of the development of a management discipline that did not find enough in economists' models of price and preference to analyse and understand the development of markets and brands.

Economics has indeed provided a rich vein for the study of management, though often not by the latter field adopting economic models but by turning them around. The entire business discipline of strategy may be understood to have originated as an attempt to advise firms on how to protect the economic rents that efficient markets would naturally erode; strategy is about how *not* to compete in an economic sense. But early twentieth-century economics did not have enough to say about what went on inside the large firms increasingly dominating Western business—how did hierarchies work, what was driving the emergence of multi-divisional organizations and subsequently matrix structures? Organizational sociology initially filled the gap, developing theories of bureaucracy and practices of organizational design, before economists, sensing that much economic activity now took place within firms, developed theories about market failure and hierarchy. Probably the most successful management field and the most recent—academic finance—can also be traced back into the work of economists such as Samuelson, but it required additional insights from operations research—such as the idea of portfolio risk—and from applied mathematics—such as the use of diffusion equations to price options—before the modern body of theory could develop. These are merely examples, but they illustrate a common dynamic of adapting and integrating academic insights to address business issues and build theory.

If the previous two paragraphs have introduced ideas about *how* the content of management theory emerged, the idea of opportunism as a key ingredient of *why* becomes important. Much of the work of early theorists such as Fayol and Taylor can be understood in terms of the emergence of the first modern, large, profit-focused organizations. In turn, much of the reaction to this emergence may be understood in terms of a concern with the impact of such organizations on employees, and the containment of collective organizations that employees developed as protection. If one needs the growth of the firm to understand Taylorism, perhaps one needs the New Deal in the United States (USA) to understand the human relations movement. War was important, and not only in the stimuli that it gave to demand and productivity. Cost accounting emerged during World War I and operations research developed massively during World War II and both were then applied, equally massively, to post-war production, accelerated in the latter case by the increasing availability of computing power. Technological developments initiated for military purpose have often generated new product developments in both consumer and business-to-business markets, but they have also facilitated changes to structures and processes within firms.

From these examples, it should be clear not only that management theory has emerged in reaction to both business developments and external events, but also that such theory may have shaped the world it seeks to explain; for example, a theory about the benefits of multi-divisional structures in firms may lead to their widespread adoption. This tendency has been most noticeable in the development of academic financial economics. The discipline of finance, almost exclusively a post-war and Western phenomenon, can be seen both as the precursor of and the engine for the growth of financial markets and their increasing influence over firm governance and performance. Up to

2008, financial economics exerted powerful pressure on life to imitate art. After 2008, the basics of financial economics, and particularly the efficient markets hypothesis which is rooted in neoclassical economics, have been questioned, much as Taylorism was in the 1920s and Porter's approach to strategy in the 1990s.

This pattern of emergence and decay alone helps focus us on the central issues that will concern this book. The first purpose of the book is to understand how and why management theory emerged from the social sciences in the West in the twentieth century. What problems were academics trying to address, what tools did they use to build their ideas, and what impact did these ideas have on practice? The second purpose is to demonstrate that, in part because they mined shared seams of knowledge, there is common ground at the conceptual level between many apparently unconversant functional disciplines. Common thematic ideas like agency, control, hierarchy, incentives and performance measurement, rent and competition, efficiency and cost, individual and collective action, and—perhaps most pervasively—rationality and irrationality, glue various management disciplines together. The third purpose of the book is to make some assessment of the resilience of this body of thought; the key question is—which elements of it are still useful parts of an attempt to understand and explain business behaviour? We can quite easily point out the ethnic and cultural specificity of the origins of management theory, but it does not follow that its usefulness is similarly constrained. We can, however, expect it to be severely tested.

The approach is critical, but in a specific sense. I look at the origins and development of core management theories and, since we are also concerned with impact, I also discuss the core business practices that emerge from the theories' application. To take an example, I examine the growth of marketing as a process of divorce from economic approaches to price and subject major theories within the marketing field to critical examination. But I also examine the central elements of a marketing plan and what the construction of a plan can achieve. My objective is to convey not simply the strengths and weaknesses of the marketing approach, but also some key elements of the tools of the trade. This is not a 'how-to' book, but it has little focus on purely critical academic work that has no practical correlates.

It is also, to some extent, chronological. Much management theory develops in reaction to the perceived weaknesses of previous theory. Indeed, some theories are entirely reactive. One question we might reasonably ask is to what extent the history of management theory is cumulative or circular. Probably, the processes are more complicated, as some examples may illustrate. Scientific management has limited impact in the field of leadership but is still central to process design and performance management. Portfolio approaches to firm structure are unfashionable in Western business firms but not in Western asset management. Collective action is often seen as in decline among employees, but not among consumers or users of social networks. My conception of the field involves looking at the redeployment of key concepts in different domains.

The Field

Industrialization in Europe, particularly in Britain, prompted an intellectual response. Political economy—the work of Adam Smith and David Ricardo—was concerned with the factory system, technological change (the so-called 'machinery question'), and the growth of an industrial working class (Berg, 1980). Later, in the nineteenth and early twentieth centuries, two founding fathers of sociology—Durkheim and Weber—concerned themselves with the division of labour, the Protestant work ethic, and the problems of bureaucracy. Marx, whose scope challenged any modern conventional disciplinary boundaries, analysed the factory system, the economics of the firm, the alienation of the working class, and the revolution that must ensue.[1] From Smith in the 1770s to Weber in the early twentieth century, intellectuals were wrestling with the major social and economic changes prompted generally by industrialization and specifically by the growth of the large capitalist firm.

However, this remained an intellectual response rather than a guiding theory. When one looks at the development of 'theory' about management and the firm in the early part of the twentieth century, one finds a pragmatism and fragmentation about work on management and the firm. Engineers, particularly military engineers, import ideas about organization and production process. Practitioners summarize their experience into generalizations. The newly emerging discipline of industrial psychology concerns itself with worker productivity. Ideas about organization and management in particular are borrowed from the main set of pre-industrial large organizations—armies, (Christian) religious organizations, and government. Why?

A large part of the answer concerns reactions within economics, arguably the most relevant and certainly the most developed social science at the time. It goes missing. Whereas political economy was concerned with factories and the machinery issue, the neoclassical revolution of the late nineteenth century was concerned with optimization and equilibrium in markets modelled on principles which were increasingly at odds with industrial practice. In Kay's (2004) terms, most economists wanted to be physicists, and so modelled firms as production functions and markets as perfectly competitive. As J. P. Morgan was developing the idea that all industries should be monopolies in the public

---

[1] For a review of the work of Marx, Weber, and Durkheim, see Giddens (1971).

interest, and trying very hard to make it happen in the USA, economists were ignoring the fact that one major effect of industrialization was to take economic activity out of markets and into firms. Nothing like an economic theory of the firm arose until Coase wrote about transaction costs and the boundaries of the firm in 1937. Even then, his work was not developed. In the 1930s, it was more important within economics to be a macro economist like Keynes than a micro economist like Coase.

In sociology, any elective affinity between theories about industrial society and guidelines about how to run one was frustrated by the tendency of the major theorists to deplore what was happening. Durkheim felt that the division of labour would generate a sense of 'normlessness' (anomie), a problematic circumstance in which individuals shorn of the feudal certainties of a society in which position was fixed and expectations certain would experience something close to the more modern idea of existential doubt. Weber, not unreasonably, became very concerned about bureaucratic organizations becoming 'iron cages' for their inhabitants and charismatic leadership degenerating into authoritarianism. For Marx, the problem was more systemic. Capitalism generated a working class alienated from the work process, the work product, each other, and the fundamentals of humanity ('species being'). It contained the seeds of its own destruction, roughly in the sense that it would become increasingly difficult to make a profit, and would naturally fall under the weight of its own contradictions (Giddens, 1971).

There existed a substantial intellectual void. Nonetheless, in the late nineteenth and early twentieth centuries, a managerial curriculum developed to train the growing numbers of those who made capitalism work. First on the east coast of the USA, at Wharton and Harvard, then more generally, universities developed business schools to train managers with a curriculum designed to contain both tools and some theory. I argued above that this curriculum had four main characteristics, some of which are enduring and shape how we study management today. Here they are elaborated.

First, it was *opportunistic*. By this I mean it borrowed or shaped ideas in order to solve some perceived business problem. Early borrowing includes using West Point ideas about production organization and studies of stress on World War I soldiers to frame arguments about working time in factories. Later borrowing involves using heat diffusion equations from engineering to price derivatives in financial markets.

Second, and partly in consequence, it was *eclectic*. Ideas are drawn from just about anywhere—both inside academia and outside. The management field is not a net exporter of intellectual capital to other disciplines. It was, and is, voracious. Ideas come from academic disciplines such as anthropology (organizational culture), economics (competitive advantage, but rent, really), mathematics (portfolio theory), psychology (consumer preference), sociology (social capital), and anywhere else you want (leadership).

Third, since it is very difficult intellectually to reconcile these materials, it was, and is, a *fragmented* field. The modern MBA still resembles a baccalaureate of uncorrelated intellectual material. Optimizing a dependent variable (e.g. worker productivity) will generate different advice depending on whether one addresses it from an organizational behaviour (focus on engagement and the psychological contract) or operations management (maximize the throughput) perspective.

Fourth, it was *derivative*. Put kindly, it generates intellectual capital through second mover advantage. Several ideas that we will discuss below came into the management field to be used and developed. Whatever else the academic study of management may lack, it has money.

Several of the core management theorists we will discuss—Chester Barnard, Elton Mayo, Philip Kotler, Herbert Simon, and Henry Mintzberg, for example— are difficult academically to pigeonhole; they often have interdisciplinary training and their contributions are relevant to several disciplines. Nonetheless, the fragmentation referred to above is not random. There are identifiable and cohesive sub-disciplines within the business field. The most enduring are as follows:

- Accounting
- Operations Research and Management
- Organizational Behaviour
- Marketing
- Strategy
- Finance

These are listed, roughly, in the order in which they emerged in the modern academic literature (or before then). The rudiments of most can be traced back well before industrialization, at least in Europe, mostly in the documentation of practices either in military and religious organizations or of merchants practising trade. Double entry bookkeeping was developed in the Middle Ages; Venetians ran assembly lines to build ships in the *Arsenale* in about the same period. Cistercian monks developed models of decentralization to counter the centralization that characterized the dominant Clunaic tradition. St Paul marketed monotheism and the prospect of everlasting life to gentiles in the first century (often using direct mail). Strategy was documented by military theorists from ancient days. Portfolios and debt exposure were apparently well understood by the Medici.

However, these fields acquired many of their modern characteristics, concerns, and tools in the twentieth century in Western economies as responses to or in some case triggers for developments in business practice. It is thus significant that the twentieth century was quite a peculiar time in the West.

Without assuming too many (I hope) pretensions as a historian, let me offer a few observations on the ways this might have affected the management field.

- There was a lot of war between advanced industrial countries. Hobsbawm (1994) suggests that the 'short' twentieth century from 1914 to 1991 was actually one long war, hot and cold. There were a number of consequences. First, global capital movements shrank massively compared to the nineteenth century (Michie, 2006). If you wanted to invest abroad, putting your money with a domestic firm with substantial international operations (like an oil company) was a sound bet. Second, securities markets traded a lot of government debt (wars cost a lot of money). In the twentieth century, government debt was a risk-averse investment generating secure returns. Third, wars pump massive amounts of money into industries that give governments the means to fight them (e.g. aerospace, which otherwise is not economically a particularly good idea). Fourth, innovations to win a war or not to fight one (computing) subsequently spill out into the private sector. Fifth, and distressingly, principles developed by firms about how to manage operations efficiently are applied to killing people methodically (Mazower, 1998). Dupont delivered the Manhattan Project (Weatherall, 2013).

- In part because the international labour movement of labour also shrank compared to the nineteenth century, and in part because warring governments had to buy off their electorates to keep them fighting, governments either built substantial welfare states that guaranteed labour security and benefits (Western Europe) or made firms simulate welfare states by doing the same (USA; see Davis, 2009). Stability of employment within firms, both as a practice and an objective, developed other practices (such as pensions) that affected both capital and labour markets. In labour markets, best practice on remuneration, motivation, and retention was developed in a specific context. There was a lengthy period of relatively full employment in Western countries, in which the state performed a substantial and specific role.

- The relatively smooth transition between Britain and the USA as the dominant industrial power in the early twentieth century implied that Anglo-Saxon thinking about how to run businesses had some primacy. The apparent success of these two countries in the century's subsequent conflicts arguably reaffirmed this prejudice. After all, major wars were won by productive power (Overy, 1995), and the overwhelming, if temporary, advantage produced after World War II by possession of the atom bomb could be interpreted as a technological lead. Western ideas were adopted elsewhere (Lenin was a fan of F. W. Taylor, the primary exponent of scientific management), Japanese industrial excellence was interpreted as a more fundamental commitment to American principles, and far more people from outside Europe and the USA went to Western business schools than the reverse. A certain imperialism about the primacy of Western management thought emerged. In the 1960s, Clerk Kerr at the University of California developed the idea of convergence theory—the idea that there was one path for industrialized societies such that they would all, with differential lags, converge around one model (guess which one). This emerged with renewed force after the Cold War in theories about the end of history. However, at the time of writing, neither the USA nor the UK has a balance of payments surplus; nor will have by the time you read this.

• After the end of the Cold War in 1989, both capital and labour mobility increased substantially. The liberalization of financial markets in the 1980s was associated with a considerable increase in the financial oversight of corporate governance and practice. Labour movement under free trade arrangements, such as NAFTA in North America and the expansion of the European Union to embrace former socialist countries, similarly liberalized labour markets. Both sets of changes disturbed institutional arrangements, between banks and corporate entities on the one hand and between employers and employees on the other, in a direction characterized as 'financialization', one effect of which has been a shift from building long-term relationships to a more short-term, transactional approach.

Many of these twentieth-century parameters no longer hold. The theories generated to explain or influence business practice may need to be re-examined.

Life and Art

There is one final set of considerations before we begin: it concerns the relationship between academic theory and business practice. The study of management, as we mentioned at the outset, often bears a close relationship to management practice. The early theorists we have discussed above were interested less in academic articles and more in influencing such practice. Later theorists we will discuss below were interested in both academic reputation and generating revenue through influencing practice (Abrahamson, 1996). So there has often been interplay between the study of management and its practice, which takes a variety of forms. Let us pursue one of the medieval religious analogies mentioned earlier. In the academic study of management there are at least the following types:

1. Chroniclers. Those who seek to document the performance of successful practitioners, groups of practitioners (often firms), or national industrial systems as exemplars of 'best practice' to be imitated or, at least, learned from.

2. Preachers. Those who feel in possession of an innovative or at least effective idea that can be sold to a wider audience.

3. Theologians. Those who are interested to develop theories that might guide or change practice.

Each category, in different ways, is interested in the concept of *performativity*; that is, broadly speaking, the idea that theory might influence management practice (Austin, 1962; MacKenzie, 2006: 1–37). There may be another category:

4. Critics. Those who think the whole thing is an exercise in domination or the exploitation of position. After 2008, these views have become more influential.

So, questions then arise about academic work on management:

1. Does the theory or technique design management practice? Is there a model that allows the prescription of managerial best practice? This is the managerial equivalent of **theology**.
2. Does the account, theory, or technique arise from, and in some sense simply summarize, what managers are already doing? This is **chronicle**, and although dissemination might influence practitioners by example, it is performative in the sense of *consolidating* previous insight.
3. Does the theory or technique generalize some definition of best practice? This results from **preaching**, either by academics or by consultancies involved. It may be performative in developing new managerial tools, but it starts from the premise that current tools are defective.
4. Does the account see management as a political or anthropological activity with no appreciable performance consequences? This is primarily a **critical** activity.

Under the first heading, I would list CEO biographies and firm histories, including the work of Chandler; as an influence on practice, they constitute casual empiricism but may have impact if they justify a certain approach or tool. As examples of the second, I would quote academic discussions of the Toyota production system (see Chapter 4) and developments in the balanced scorecard approach to performance measurement (see Theme 5). As examples of the third, in finance theory, the Black–Scholes theorem, the Modigliani–Miller hypothesis, and the capital asset pricing model stand out and, in strategy, the work of Michael Porter on the sources of competitive advantage.

If we are considering the ways in which management writing might influence management practice, then at least two considerations become relevant. First, if any of the categories listed above has an influence, is the performativity *positive* (i.e. it can be seen in some way to have enhanced practice in the way predicted) or *negative* (i.e. it seems to generate outcomes that run contrary to the theory)? This assumes we can think of management writing as having some impact (either positive or negative). Or second, is it simply irrelevant (i.e. it represents fashion, and maybe influences the rhetoric, but makes no difference)? There are complications with this. To give an example, in many large firms in the mid-twentieth century it was seen to be a good idea to give employees occupational pensions in which, in exchange for mutual contributions by employer and employee, employees would be guaranteed a percentage of their final salary indefinitely. This was advocated by many management writers, but you would be fired for suggesting it at the time of writing.

The final idea to introduce at this point is the idea of fashion, or at least herding. Many management practices diffuse across firms and sectors. For example, the multi-divisional organization that I will discuss in Theme 5 became very common in a variety of sectors and countries. In economics, authors such as Williamson would argue that it became common because it was efficient. In economics, any common institutional form must be presumed to have efficiency properties, otherwise one needs a comprehensive market imperfection explanation for its survival. However, there are also arguments that it diffused because of fashion and the influence of certain consultancy firms selling solutions to accountability problems (McKenna, 2006). It may be that, as many sociologists argue, legitimacy—the general acceptance that a business practice is in some sense good—precedes efficiency because the latter follows from the former through the effects that legitimacy has on the cost of various forms of capital. Efficiency is a very under-contested concept (Fligstein, 1990).

The management field shows the circumstances of its birth. One of the many transformations effected by industrialization was the growth of the large firm, which in turn influenced the growth of management as an activity. Developments in political economy and sociology that addressed the large-scale social changes also had implications for the study of organizations, but efficiency concerns often led to the application of engineering principles or simply the adoption of pre-industrial practices from military or religious organizations.

The modern large firm was not, generally, designed and built by academics. It emerged to accommodate rather particular circumstances, in a specific historical context, before anyone thought to develop a theory about it.

The Structure and Content of the Book

Given these considerations, particularly the fragmentation of the field, it is necessary to provide some logic for the presentation of the material in the book. The first structuring device is chronology. We deal with the key elements

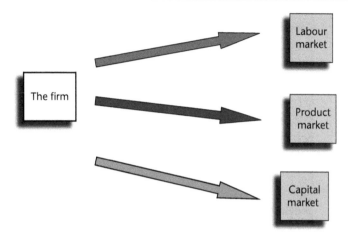

Figure C1.1. Control in hierarchies and markets.

of academic business thought, roughly in birth order. The book is structured into *chapters* that deal with the core elements of an approach or sub-field and offer critique by reviewing the literature they generate.

Figure C1.1 draws loosely on the work of Fligstein (1990). I am suggesting that the body of academic work we call management can be understood in terms of an attempt to solve problems presented initially by the growth of the firm and subsequently by attempts to manage the three main markets in which the firm operates; labour, product, and capital markets respectively. This does some—but I would argue not too much—violence to the history of management thought, and is the core organizing principle for the chapters. We deal with management of hierarchy first, and the field of finance last.

Themes sit between most of the chapters. They deal either with core concepts that are central to a number of disciplines (for example, bounded rationality), or with practices that prompt integrative thinking (for example, performance measurement). The themes are the glue that holds the book together, preventing it replicating fully the patchwork fragmentation of the field, and they are also the location of many of the practical examples on offer. So, to use a term common to the field, the book has a matrix structure.

Unifying both chapters and themes are a set of core concerns. I will argue that there is a set of core concerns common to all of the six disciplines listed on page 8. I offer ten in Figure C1.2. Three characteristics of these concerns are as follows. First, they are topics around which there has been considerable academic theorizing; there are literatures, in several academic disciplines, to address. Second, they each concern several management disciplines. Third, they relate directly to problems faced by practising managers. They thus facilitate the examination of the relationship between theory and practice, which is a core concern of this book.

Concern	Chapter	Theme
Market, hierarchy, and network	2,5,7	3,5,7
Coordination and control	2,5,9	1,6
Contract	3,4	2,3
Individual and collective action	3,6	3,4
Rationality and irrationality	8,9	3,4,8
Incentive and performance	3,4,9	5,8
Price and profit	6,7,8	7,8
Efficiency and cost	2,8	1,9
Agency	2,5	2,5
Competitive advantage	4,6,7	6,8

Figure C1.2. Core concerns of management.

Any list of such a set must, given the nature of the field, be arbitrary, and there may be many more to add, but the list is intended to be a necessary road map to the book rather than a sufficient and exhaustive list of relevant concepts. The figure also relates the concerns to the content of the chapters and themes, indicating where these concerns are primarily addressed within the book.

Conclusion

This chapter has attempted primarily to present the logic for the book which is derived from an examination of the properties of the management field. I have characterized the field as derivative, opportunistic, eclectic, and fragmented but also argued that an understanding of the chronology of its development and the underlying concerns being addressed will help to view it as a whole. A further characteristic—to which we will return in the conclusion—is its stability, which is both a strength and a weakness. However, we begin the journey to that conclusion by trying to understand something of the legacy upon which the field rests.

Theme 1

Accounting for Capitalism

Introduction

The first theme deals with legacies. Here I look at the pre-industrial practices and teaching that influenced modern management practice. There is survivor bias in the account; I focus on the best-documented practices and try to show how they influenced subsequent work. The best-documented case is accounting, which is probably as old as history, but in its recognizably modern form can be dated back to the Italian Renaissance. Indeed, there was a popular argument in the nineteenth century that developments in accounting, particularly double entry bookkeeping, *caused* capitalism to develop (it's not so popular now).

At the core of this is the idea of rational calculation. I am going to suggest loosely that rationality is the sieve through which survivor bias works; by this I mean that nineteenth-century searchers for rational approaches to the management of industrial concerns looked for rational examples from the past. Now this might be a specific version of a very contested engineering notion of rationality (see Shenhav, 1999), but it will serve our purposes for the moment. Selecting the Italian Renaissance is also a contingency, but just as one could hear most of the best music ever written in early nineteenth-century Vienna, you could learn a lot about management in sixteenth-century Venice.

Merchants of Venice[1]

If a nineteenth-century British business owner had left the heart of the Industrial Revolution and pitched up in mid-sixteenth-century Venice, what might he have seen or heard in conversation that would be familiar business practice? The Venice of the time had been effectively a republic for several centuries,

---

[1] This section is indebted to Crowley (2011).

dominated by a few families who selected both the Doge (leader) and who formed the Council; essentially an oligarchy. It had an extensive mercantile empire which required substantial military expenditure to secure it, and it had a strong sense of community identity, defined by its island status. A bit like home, then.

A history of sporadic merchant adventuring, where individuals pooled money into partnerships for long-distance trade, had given way to a more state-sponsored kind of profit making, in which individuals could invest to make money, but on terms defined to give the state a cut and further the Imperial interest. Rather like the British East India Company familiar to our visitor, but more controlling.

Engaging in conversation on the Rialto (no bridge yet), an individual would have heard that business financing could be supplied by banks—in Venice but particularly in Florence. These banks, such as the Medici or Gritti, were trust-based family networks that could finance trade and investment throughout Europe. In fact, they could engage in relatively sophisticated futures contracting in which they would price and fund risky ventures, provided they got their pound of flesh (if Shakespeare is to be believed—see Chapter 8).

These banks also dealt in politics in two ways. First, they ran their little city states, a bit like J. P. Morgan did in the nineteenth century; second, they dealt in sovereign debt. This could be risky. A couple of hundred years before, one bank, the Ricciardi, had gone down in a liquidity crunch when, in 1294, Edward I of England didn't get the loan he wanted and seized everything; but when the Frescobaldi went in afterwards, they made money for years. A bit like the Rothschilds in our businessman's own era.

Looking more closely at business practice, he would have found much to reassure him, in particular in the biggest factory in town, which had been there for hundreds of years. Venice knew about fighting wars at sea to generate and protect trade. In this factory, the *Arsenale*, they built assembly lines.

> [Venice] could standardize designs and build up stores of spare parts, making it possible to complete even major refits in a fraction of the time...the designs themselves, as well as the techniques, could be revolutionized...One of the secrets of Venice's rise to power was that she never saw the twin necessities of defence and commerce as altogether separate...the nobles were merchants and the merchants noble....
>
> (Norwich, 1977: 85).

The Venetians knew how to maximize throughput and reduce production times; standardization of inputs, process, and product was an important component. Alignment of defence and commercial interests was another. You could send out the ships to fight and then use them to carry the spoils home; smart capacity management.

The *Arsenale* was at the centre of a tightly managed multinational operation. It depended on documentation.

> Its principles were continuous oversight and collective responsibility. No officer was to act alone ... All decisions, transactions, commercial agreements, wills, decrees and judgements were set down in literally millions of entries, like an infinite merchant's ledger, which formed the historic memory of the state. Everyone was accountable. Everything was written down.
>
> (Crowley, 2011: 242)

Penalties for failure were severe; terminal, in fact. The terminology would have been different, but for our nineteenth-century visitor, this would look like a bureaucracy with a death penalty. A bit like the British Navy.

The city was also home to innovative international organizations like the recently founded Jesuits (1540), who had chosen Venice as a place to start because of its arm's-length regulation by the Papacy; no Inquisition, relatively free markets in ideas. The Jesuits were developing an interesting approach to global expansion in new markets such as Asia, Canada, and South America, in which a basically geographical structure of organization was overlaid by 'product' areas such as education and conversion. Our nineteenth-century Brit could have called this a matrix if he had known what that was.

Jesuits also knew about accounting. They had resources, international reach, and an objective; saving souls. But:

> A strictly economic analysis of the nature and role of accounting as an instrument for allocating, monitoring, and administering resources within the hierarchical structure of the Society of Jesus would leave undiscovered important aspects of the practices deployed by the Order to manage, organize, and account for its multifaceted activities.
>
> (Quattrone, 2004)

How does one optimize the allocation of resources to maximize the saving of souls? The first thing one needs is a management accounting system to tell you where the resources come from and go to. The second thing, more controversial perhaps, is you have to put a value on a soul. At the margin, one might have to choose which soul to save or to justify the return on investment. Should the resource go to Canada or China; in which location will you get more souls for the unit of investment? As a counter-reformation organization, Jesuits could target Protestants in Europe, or even existing Catholics who might lapse (on the grounds that customer retention is often easier than customer acquisition). Are all souls of the same value? Who is the investor and who is the audience for these accounting statements? All questions with which our nineteenth-century businessman would be familiar, albeit in a slightly different form. In the nineteenth century, railways in the

Americas used similar practices to identify costs and provide balance sheets to absentee creditors in Europe (King, 2006: 8).

And one of the two books on sale that were all the rage was very interesting on these topics. The first, *The Prince*, on leadership and strategy by a Florentine, Niccolò Machiavelli, was interesting, but more about politics than business; our Victorian businessman's grandchildren would become more interested in leadership and strategy. But the second, by Luca Pacioli, describing the Venetian method, was about double entry bookkeeping. Home from home.

If our time traveller had stuck around for fifty years in order to see the bridge at the Rialto, he could have seen something like an audit. From the 1580s onwards, the *Arsenale* was the subject of continuous monitoring and improvement, and clear elements of the modern firm emerge. The trigger was an arms race. Venice had participated in the destruction of the Ottoman navy in 1571, and was shocked when they rebuilt it within 18 months; this had to be matched.

There is a huge debate about the extent of implementation of reform,[2] but the reports discuss:

- The introduction of salaried managers.
- The imposition of labour discipline, including attendance and job descriptions.
- Identification of costs, including standard costs ('man months per ship').
- Measurement of inventory and work in progress with a target of 100 ships in reserve.
- Resistance by employees to these changes.

Two things about this are of huge significance, over and above these specific innovations. First, bookkeeping becomes management accounting; it moves from underpinning inspection and control to a tool for understanding, managing, and changing operations (Zambon and Zan, 2007: 121). Second, this is accounting without economics or markets. The *Arsenale* was a public sector monopoly and the driver for the managerial reforms was war and discipline.

This may seem a bit far-fetched, not least the time travel, but it does serve to remind that many of the problems business owners were trying to solve after the Industrial Revolution had been met and solved before, since they are essentially problems in the management of large organizations. I have no idea whether Venice is the best example, but it is a good one. In the sixteenth century, these large organizations were predominantly state and church, but the *Arsenale* and Jesuit examples show you can have effective business

---

[2] Venice is a history industry since it houses 65 km of records. That the Venetians measured everything and wrote it down tells you something. This section relies on Zan (2004) and Zambon and Zan (2007).

practices in production management and accounting *within* hierarchies and *without* markets. I will elaborate the significance of this in coming chapters.

Note for the moment that the accounts that were being produced in six-teenth-century Venice were as much *legal, juridical* documents as *economic* ones (Power, 2010); they did not seek to make an economic valuation of the organization concerned. They sought to account for transactions and to demonstrate the trustworthiness of the transactor. There is no concern about whether running the *Arsenale* is the best use of the state's assets, only about how to optimize its performance. No consultant is around to suggest diversification into a football club on the basis of increased shareholder value. We will pick this up again. For the moment, let us turn to accounting; it is intrinsically interesting (really), and has some very general implications.

The Balance Sheet that Changed the World

In order to understand why people such as Goethe could get worked up about it, it is important to be clear about what double entry bookkeeping (DEB) is, but more importantly, what it lets you do. It records all transactions, twice. Transactions appear as debits under the account of the seller and credits under the account of a purchaser. It generates a picture of stocks and flows, as shown very simply in Figure T1.1.

From this information one can do a number of things (Carruthers and Espeland, 1991; Robertson and Funnell, 2012).

1. In partnerships, joint ventures, and later in joint stock companies, one can keep track of each investor's share in the capital and revenues of the firm. This enabled the socialization of capital by answering the question: given what I have put in, what is my fair share of the revenues? Investors could collaborate to contribute against a formula on returns.

2. That question works for one-shot ventures, but what about permanent firms where the capital needs to keep working, such as the subsequently

	Credits	**Debits**
Income and expenses[1]	Revenue (sales)	Expenses
Assets and liabilities[2]	Liabilities • Creditors • Loans • Equity	Assets • Fixed • Current

1= Flows; 2= Stocks

Figure T1.1. The balance sheet that changed the world.

19

founded Dutch and English East India companies? For this you need to measure profits in order to pay dividends and DEB allows the distinction between profits and initial capital to be made (Bryer, 2000).

3. For long-term ventures, investors want to make comparisons between different destinations for their investment and DEB allows for a standardized measure of return on capital employed (Bryer, 1993). So DEB enables an answer to the question: is this the best place to put my money? This was important both for Venetian trading ventures and for the railways with which our nineteenth-century time traveller would have been more familiar.

These are so-called 'technical' issues. There are also what are termed, in this literature, 'rhetorical' ones that essentially had to do with legitimacy.

4. Medieval businesses had a respectability problem. In a society where religion dominated many spheres of activity, and where religion disapproved of usury (i.e. lending money at interest), DEB could show that profits from trade were other than interest payments. Pacioli was in part trying to show the legitimacy of mercantile trade (Carruthers and Espeland, 1991).

5. For the *individual* merchant operating in trust-based networks, the record of transactions was a record of trustworthiness. It allowed accountability to trading partners and investors. Once this form of accounting was accepted, if one did not have a complete transaction record, then that said something. 'Showing the books' was a trust issue.

Back to Venice...

Even kings and princes could not have aspired to the trust and credit enjoyed by a good merchant. Reciprocal trust and good faith in their dealings were the ethical elements which distinguished (them).

(Tucci, 1973: 367).

Merchants did not have power in the ways that princes might. They relied on their record of behaviour in what—in the small island nation of Venice—was quite a tight network.

Pacioli almost certainly documented rather than invented DEB; he seems to have been codifying merchant practice, but he was a university 'cleric' and his work certainly prompted its dissemination (Hoskin and Macve, 1994). Of interest to our story is that DEB did not take over the world immediately, or even soon. It seems to have taken a long time to diffuse, and the Dutch and English companies mentioned above, which were operating from the next century, did not seem to use it regularly or systematically (Robertson and Funnell, 2012). Quite why this happened is beyond the scope of this book, but it is of interest to find early social theorists arguing for DEB's influence. It turns out that their arguments are based a little more on styles of thought than direct bookkeeping evidence.

Both Weber and Sombart stress the importance of rational calculation in the rise of capitalism in the seventeenth century. Capitalists needed to calculate income and profit and, for Weber, they did so by using 'the methods of modern bookkeeping and the striking of a balance'.[3] Sombart took this further by arguing that you could not have capitalism without DEB; 'one could not imagine what capitalism would be without DEB; the two phenomena are connected as intimately as form and content.' This is now an unfashionable argument—as indeed are most single-factor explanations of social phenomena—and in the accounting history field it is debunked (Hoskin and Macve, 1994). But it does indicate how important the idea of rational calculation, and the accounting technology in which it was embedded, was to observers of the huge transformation of business taking place in the nineteenth century. In the absence of the voluminous information we now have from accounting historians, Weber and Sombart could not have estimated the limited *use* of DEB, particularly in the Industrial Revolution in Britain that triggered those elsewhere. But for them it was more the idea, or theory, of DEB that mattered. There are deep roots to the problem of the relationship between theory and practice in the management field and I will return to this in my final theme, again using accounting as the example.

Conclusion

The main purpose of this theme has been to flesh out the assertion that large parts of the management armoury were available prior to the Industrial Revolution since they are generic issues to do with managing large organizations. They emerge to deal with common problems such as coordination and control and in turn they raise other problems, such as agency and accountability.

Accounting data in our Venice example is useful for investors looking for a return on capital, for managers looking at efficiency and productivity in the operations they manage, and for governments looking for sources of tax; these remain the main audiences for accounting data. But there is an accountability as well as an accounting issue. Investors can use accounting data to monitor the performance of managers, particularly where the actions of managers are not directly observable. It is probably not an accident that most of our examples of pre-industrial accounting—maritime Venice, Jesuits, the

---

[3] Weber and Sombart both cited in Robertson and Funnell, 2012; by the latter term, Weber means 'creating a balance sheet'.

East India Company, for example—come from operations characterized by action at distance, where investors sink non-transferable assets into ventures controlled by their agents. Exactly the same problem faced subsequent UK investors in American railroads, which were to prove so important in the late nineteenth century to the development of both US business and global finance. By contrast, it seems that owner-managed factories in the British Industrial Revolution, where agents were often directly observable, were slower to use it; there were, after all, substantial set-up and operations costs (see Theme 9).

A secondary purpose of this theme has been to open up discussion of the relationship between theory and practice. Few would support Sombart's argument about theory causing practice, but there is arguably less doubt that the two interact, often in complex ways. To take Pacioli's example, was he an innovator or a chronicler of Italian merchant practice: or maybe just an apologist for the merchant class? And why did his product, DEB, conquer the world 400 years later? Put another way, what held up the diffusion of practice longer than the diffusion of knowledge?

These questions will concern me throughout. I turn initially to the growth of the firm, and to the emergence of modern management thought about it in the nineteenth and early twentieth centuries. Lest you wonder why I am suggesting time travel for the second time in this theme, let me close it with a quote from Hamel, whose main concern is management in the twenty-first century. Addressing a practitioner audience, he argues:

> . . . your company is being managed right now by a coterie of long-departed theorists and practitioners who invented the rules and conventions of 'modern' management back in the early years of the twentieth century. They are the poltergeists who inhabit the musty machinery of management.

> (Hamel, 2007: ix)

But it's much more than a ghost story.

Chapter 2

The Firm

Introduction

The corporate form is a rather late arrival on the scene. Before the nineteenth century, only a handful of corporate-type entities existed and these were largely extensions of state power. Companies such as the Hudson Bay Company or the Dutch East India Company were important agents of empire. They were granted exclusive rights by governments to trade and conduct business in certain markets or products. So, for example, the Hudson Bay Company was established by two French adventurers who were granted exclusive rights to fur trapping in large areas of Canada by the British government in 1670 (having first been turned down by their own government). It was a truly international venture; the Frenchmen gained a Royal Charter in Britain with the encouragement of Boston merchants.

The company built forts, extended the speaking of English, founded cities, and established distribution channels; and it still exists in Canada as a chain of department stores. It had thirty-two investors who shared risks and returns. The Dutch East India Company, founded earlier, in 1602, funded long-distance trading in any items between Europe and the Far East. Investors, primarily in Amsterdam, would pool funds to support risky trips which, if successful, provided huge returns. In the course of this, it prompted the development of the Amsterdam securities market in which spot and future contracts, call and put options, and hedging and short selling were all possible (Michie, 2006: 27). The number of investors was very large indeed. These entities have some important characteristics for the future analysis of the firm. Initial investors control supply-side risk (by securing monopoly) before sharing investor risk, they get government to provide the muscle, and they diversify away some operational risk by embracing a range of uncorrelated activities. These features were all to become important for the development of the twentieth-century divisionalized business. Indeed, there is some evidence that at least one of these monopoly operations, the British East India Company, was divisionalized (see Theme 6).

The Brits

However, it would be too easy to draw a simple line of descent from these seventeenth-century organizations to modern versions. The Industrial Revolution took off in Britain in the early nineteenth century and, as Michie notes, in the period before 1850, 'The British Economy remained mostly untouched by joint stock enterprise' (Michie, 2006: 69). Enterprises were either entrepreneurially owned, as in manufacturing, or owned by local inhabitants, as in utilities and canals, and funded by retained profit or bank loans. Pollard (1965: 250) has argued persuasively that there was neither management (as a salaried, non-owning class) or management 'technology' in the first Industrial Revolution in England. The key developments in both took place in the USA and, as Chandler has famously argued, they rested on the application of military organizational principles—specifically West Point—to production. The Springfield Armoury was the *Arsenale* of its day (Chandler, 1977: 72–5); a military factory which became an example in civilian life.

Railways changed everything, requiring large-scale initial finance but able to set this against the prospect of steady low-risk returns from natural monopoly. This provided investors with an attractive alternative to government debt. The USA itself was different in the nineteenth century, in part because there was no government debt to trade until the civil war in the 1860s and later in the century, when very large organizations were generated by merger waves, the joint stock form became the norm for big business. However, well into the twentieth century, in many large corporations in the USA, such as Ford, Coca-Cola, and Dupont, family ownership and control remained in place.

A crucial early development that did emerge in England occurred in the textile industry: the growth of the factory. As well as the massive impact on output, it is significant for the development of management as an activity. Historically, cloth had been produced domestically (i.e. in the home), usually by workers who had other concerns (farming), using simple equipment and raw materials provided by an entrepreneur, who was also the purchaser of the finished product. This was a flexible and relatively low capital cost operation, but it left the entrepreneur with little control over production volumes. As David Landes, the key historian on the Industrial Revolution, noted:

> ... the domestic weaver or craftsman was a master of his time, starting and stopping when he desired. And while the employer could raise the piece rates with a view to encouraging output, he usually found that this actually reduced output.
>
> (Landes, 1969: 59).

This backward-sloping labour supply curve arose because the workers tended to have a subsistence income target, not a utility maximizing one. Cutting the rates did no good either; it led either to the worker quitting or stealing some of the raw material in compensation (Salaman, 1981: 27). In short, incentives alone did not work. What the entrepreneur needed was control of labour time, and for that, he needed to make sure that workers had work discipline and the absence of alternative income sources. The answer: the factory, in which workers were monitored (or *managed*). This was problematic because it was not, generally, a process workers welcomed. Thompson (1968), refers to the 'making' of the English working class, and he does not characterize it as a voluntary activity.

This development is highly significant. The modern economic theory of the firm relies heavily on the ideas of monitoring, incentives, and hierarchy. Historians have debated the relative importance of these contractual-versus-technological arguments for the growth of the firm; once the factory existed, it became possible to apply steam power and technological innovations in equipment to the raising of output, but the factory came first.

Economic structure aside, there is no doubt that the scale of firms increased. Prais (1976) quotes figures for the USA and UK which indicate that by the late 1920s the 100 largest firms in both countries accounted for approximately a quarter of all output. It was to rise to over one-third by 1960. A vast amount of economic activity was moving from markets into firms. With this, a vast amount of employment came to be located in large, bureaucratic enterprises under formalized employment contracts. Let us look at the story in slightly more detail, and chronologically.

As Cassis (2007: 175) puts it, 'big business in the third quarter of the nineteenth century primarily meant the railroad companies'. They became exemplars in two ways. The first I have noted. They are almost the prototypical joint stock enterprise; they needed lots of investors. The second concerns models of employment and management. They were the first modern organizations to develop 'extensive hierarchies of managerial and white collar staff' (Gospel, 2007: 427). They engaged in systematic recruitment, and set up promotional hierarchies and pay scales. Assuming lifetime, or at least long-term, employment, they introduced welfare arrangements such as housing, health care, and pensions. In the UK at least, they liked to recruit employees with a military or police background, or relatives of those already employed; this led to a readier acceptance of the employment relationship as an authority relationship, necessary for control of a dispersed workforce.

By the start of the next century, as Cassis notes, in a variety of sectors:

'The large enterprise of the turn of the twentieth century . . . appears as a centralized and vertically integrated firm, with its own distribution and purchasing facilities, whose various functions, including marketing, were entrusted to a hierarchy of salaried managers, and which tended to cluster around sectors where economies of scale and scope could be achieved through mass production.'

(Cassis, 2007: 178).

This was more true of the USA than many parts of Europe.

The impact of World War I was crucial. First, these mass production industries—food, chemicals, oil, engineering—became central to the war effort, and expanded considerably; as we show in Theme 9, this had massive consequences for the development of accounting. There was little product market competition. After the war there were further merger waves in these sectors (Chandler, 1962), particularly in Germany (Cassis, 2007: 181). Big business became bigger. Second, there was a massive change to the labour market; labour markets were tight (i.e. labour was scarce) and labour was crucial to the fighting of industrialized war. In Europe, a significant proportion of the male labour force was, first, in the army, then dead. Unions became strong and employers had to bargain. Global securities markets collapsed. There was a mass of government debt to compete with equity investment. Governments wanted to control the securities markets in which this debt was traded and capital markets correspondingly contracted. UK investors sold massive amounts of overseas securities and the London stock market became more localized. US investors had a very good war, and US markets, particularly New York, grew massively. As Michie puts it:

...the global securities market was reduced to a series of compartmentalized marketplaces only loosely linked to each other rather than the fully integrated system that was in full flow before 1914.

(Michie, 2006: 204).

After the war, in the 1920s and 1930s, government involvement in business, particularly in European labour and capital markets, continued. The USA made two clear declarations of its intent to isolate itself from the rest of the world, in both cases defeating its own president. President Woodrow Wilson wanted a League of Nations to help secure peace. He did not want prohibition. He did not get much of the first, but he did get the second: Congress won on both. Arguably, the Wall Street Crash in 1929 cemented introversion.

Readers may at this point wonder why they have been treated to such a selective and potted history. My intent has been to characterize some key historical developments and current circumstances surrounding the period of the birth of modern management theory. As Witzel puts it:

Most of the disciplines of management...developed in their modern codified form during the period from about 1900–1930.

(Witzel, 2002: 179).

He argues that strategy came later. Finance came later still. But he is right about theories of organization, labour management, operations, and marketing. Wharton opened its doors in 1898. Harvard Business School started in 1919. At the risk of being too historically materialist in my interpretation of ideas, let me offer the following observations. I argued in Chapter 1 that management theory opportunistically develops in response to perceived managerial problems; let me now be much more specific. Where labour is scarce and product markets buoyant, labour becomes a critical resource to manage, and one needs theories about both individual and collective labour management, including incentives, control, motivation, and conflict management. Where firms have become very large and centralized and managerial hierarchies elaborate, one needs theories about organizational coordination. Where businesses have become very capital intensive and integrated, one needs theories about production optimization.

On the other hand, where capital markets are inefficient, over-regulated, and compartmentalized, you don't immediately need a discipline of finance based on the idea of an efficient market. And where large firms dominate protected home markets in oligopolistic competition, you don't need strategy to tell you about differentiation. And they did not develop then. They come much later.

Market Failure and Management: The Curious Case of the Dog in the Night

Meanwhile, in 1937, an LSE graduate named Ronald Coase asked why, if markets were efficient, so many people were employed in firms rather than simply contracting with each other in markets (Coase, 1937). It was an interesting question to ask at roughly the same time as two other academics, Berle and Means, were discussing the separation of ownership and control in the large firms that were dominating the USA and most other developed economies, arguing that shareholders in such firms had ownership, but managers had control. Coase spends the first part of the article justifying the mere *asking* of the question in terms of how it relates to the Marshallian (neoclassical) ideas of margin and substitution in economics. It led eventually both to an economic theory of the firm and to the Nobel Prize in Economics in 1991. But, at the time, an interesting thing happened: absolutely nothing.

Coase argued that firms exist because of market—or, more specifically, price mechanism—failure in the presence of transaction costs.

> ... the fact that it costs something to enter into ... transactions means that firms will emerge to organize what would otherwise be market transactions whenever their costs were less than the costs of carrying out the transactions through the market.
> (Coase, 1988: 7).

Certain types of transactions in markets entail considerable costs of price discovery, negotiation, and enforcement. For such transactions, Coase argued, it may be more efficient for what he terms an 'entrepreneur' to use 'authority' to direct resources to their most efficient ends. The boundary of the firm is set where the costs of organizing a transaction within the firm equal the costs of carrying it out through the market. Within this boundary, the firm makes products or services; beyond it, it buys or sells them.

The revolutionary idea was the notion of a transaction cost. Much later, Coase argued that without transaction costs firms would not exist, but nor would markets (1988: 6–8). Economists were primarily interested in markets, but they focused mainly on prices, and when they discussed market *structure*, they referred to the number of firms, and products, rather than the 'social institutions that facilitate exchange' (Coase, 1988: 8) and thus defined transaction costs.

In economics, indifference spread like wildfire in response. Recently Morrison and Wilhelm noted (apparently without irony) that 'Coase was ahead of his time. His work spawned a related literature from the late 1960s' (Morrison and Wilhelm, 2007: 51—my emphasis).

This is only a sensible remark if applied solely to mainstream academic economics. In the 1930s, huge enterprises such as US Steel, Dupont, Standard Oil, General Electric, and AT&T dominated industrial sectors. They also straddled sectors, developing multi-divisional structures to manage diversified product ranges. Vertical integration was also extremely advanced. As Davis notes about a single Ford factory:

> The (River) Rouge was an entire industrial economy in two square miles, bringing iron ore, coal, rubber, and sand in one end and sending cars out the other. In the 1930s over 100,000 people worked at the Rouge in the most vertically integrated factory the world had ever seen, with its own fire department, police force and hospital.
>
> (Davis, 2009: ix).

The reason why Berle and Means (1932) were concerned about ownership and control was that some of these very large firms (like Ford) were controlled by their owners but, in many others where shareholding was more dispersed, the many managers who were employed to run the businesses had substantial freedom of action; the modern corporation was a threat to property rights, and the specific threat lay in the behaviour of managers. I have much more to say about this in the next theme.

Coase had pointed the way to an explanation of why so much economic activity took place outside markets, but it was many years before this insight was pursued: I will explain how below. But what the market failure approach did *not* do was to offer a route to the study of the firm's internal operations. The stylized 'entrepreneur' allocates resources using 'authority' to maximize 'efficiency' and sets the boundary of the firm where market and hierarchy transaction costs equate; none of these concepts is defined, and they really do not tell you much about what went on in River Rouge. Coase was not really concerned with why some 'entrepreneurs' might be better than others. As a result, Coase made little impact—at the time—on the study of management either. However, in the longer term, the impact was substantial.

Several features of the Coase argument are replicated in much economic theorizing about organizations down to the present day. First, in the pursuit of a theory of the firm, organizations are considered simple alternatives to markets; that is the pursuit of efficiency by other means. There are two problems with this; first, firms may pursue multiple objectives of which efficiency is one, and since these objectives may be in conflict, efficiency may not be the prime objective in the short term. Moreover, there is no obvious reason why markets could not emerge from organizational failure, rather than vice versa. In fact, much later—with the growth of outsourcing—they did, and one needed to explain why a 'make' decision turned into a 'buy' decision, with the corollary that firm size tended to shrink (Pfeffer, 1997). Transaction cost arguments can provide a perfectly reasonable explanation for this shrinkage, but Coase did not pursue it.

Second, as Penrose (1959) was to note many years later, markets do not make anything; they exchange but do not produce—firms do both, and are thus much more than merely alternatives to markets. She makes the perceptive observation that there is a difference between a theory of the firm and the economics of the firm. Much later, Bromiley (2005: 13) makes a parallel point about the difference between explaining why firms exist versus explaining what they do. For business strategy,

> The existence of firms stands more as a constraint on theorizing than an interesting problem; a theory that predicts firms should not exist is clearly deficient.

To use a metaphor; on the one hand, economists tended to see the world as a sea of markets with the occasional island (the firm). Those who have studied management tend to see the world as a desert of firms with the occasional market oasis. In the early twentieth century, if one is to believe Coase, there must have been an *awful* lot of market failure in the USA, given the dominance of large firms.

The second feature which has endured in economics is the representation of the firm in terms of one or more stylized actors; for Coase it is the 'entrepreneur', for later economists it is the 'principal' and 'agent'. This simplification enables formal modelling but is not receptive to ideas about organizational diversity or complexity; firms are timeless and geographically unembedded. The third feature is that intra-organization relationships are treated in a very unproblematic way. Coase's 'entrepreneur' exercises authority and those she hires obey. For Jensen and Meckling (1976), who were to codify 'agency theory' much later, monitoring ensures compliance and incentives provide motivation; other approaches to the study of management treat monitoring and incentives as costly and problematic, but in economics they are simply causal. Fourth, and related, rationality is an assumption not a variable. Actors within firms are built the same way as actors within markets, so that if one replicates the competitive conditions of markets within firms, the same behaviours will emerge. By extension, if an organizational feature is empirically common, logically it must be efficient, since inefficient organizations will disappear over time. Organizational diversity should disappear too.

This has had consequences for the relationship between economic theories of the firm and empirical studies of what managers do, such as those discussed in Chapter 9. Specifically, as both Pfeffer (1997: 46) and Donaldson (1995) note, the economic approach sees hierarchy design in terms of the prime need to control managers with self-interested goals and employees who are effort-averse. These assumptions about individuals within firms lead to the argument that hierarchies have control and coordination costs, rather than focusing on the positive impact managers might have on firm performance. In fact, as we shall see, were one to design an organization according to economic principles, it would probably be inoperable, primarily because of the reaction of employees to such organizational controls. However, before I turn to this, we need to look at the development of economic ideas about hierarchy. Coase looked at market failure, but what about the dynamics of hierarchy?

Transaction Cost Economics

Oliver Williamson's early work concerned managerial decision-making; he found that managerial discretion often undermined efficiency (Williamson, 1963). Much later, he would articulate the problems of the 'propensity to manage' in two forms. It exists:

1. *instrumentally*—managers pretend they can manage complexity, when they cannot, and;
2. *strategically*—managers pursue their own sub-goals (Williamson, 1985).

However, rather than turning to markets as the answer, he focused on the internal operations of the firm. The two aspects of 'propensity' rest on two assumptions about individual behaviour that are core to the entire project. Individuals are boundedly rational; that is they have limited capabilities to deal with information complexity and information uncertainty. Specifically, and crucially, they cannot write complete contracts. Second, individuals are opportunistic, in that they pursue 'self-interest-seeking with guile' (Williamson, 1985: 47); this is an extension of the conventional economic assumption about the pursuit of self-interest, which may roughly be summarized as the idea that, since one cannot discover in advance who is trustworthy, organizations need to be designed to cope with a pandemic of dishonesty.

The third leg of this structure is the idea of asset specificity. The central issue is the existence of human or physical assets which are locked into a particular exchange relationship, that is they have lower values elsewhere. This might be *ex ante*; for example, in the oil industry, you have to build a pipeline from a market to an existing oilfield and you are creating (in effect) bilateral monopoly. Or it might be *ex post*; for example, you have worked in the same firm for many years developing firm-specific skills; you cannot find a ready market for such skills and the firm may find it difficult to replace you. The three legs come together, as Bromiley notes: '...efficient operation may require investments that have little value outside that operation, but the parties cannot trust one another, nor can they write the perfect contract... bringing both parties to the transaction into the same company (internalisation) may be more efficient than doing the transaction in the market' (Bromiley, 2005: 97).

Put another way, firms arise where boundedly rational individuals exchange very specific assets with counter-parties who need to be watched. As with Coase, transaction costs in markets and hierarchies are important and Williamson borrows Arrow's (1974) definition as follows:

- *Ex ante* costs: the costs of drafting, negotiating, and safeguarding an agreement.
- *Ex post* costs: misalignment, haggling costs, the costs of running and referring to governance structures, 'bonding' costs.

But contractual governance costs can be optimized in either markets or hierarchies: 'transactions, which differ in their attributes, are aligned with governance structures, which differ in their costs and competences' (Williamson, 1995: 27), so that transaction costs are minimized.

The influence of transaction costs economics has been substantial perhaps because of its scope, but also because of the nature of its assumptions. Asset specificity alone does not give you the firm; opportunism is key. Since opportunism is a very strong form of the self-interest assumption, it has attracted substantial criticism; it is a very negative view of human propensities (Ghoshal and Moran, 1996), it may well be ethnocentric (Dore, 1983), and it is not empirically grounded (Simon, 1991). However, it gives you not only a theory of firm formation—firms arise from the original sin[1] of opportunism—

---

[1] I owe this expression to Arthur Francis (1983).

but also an approach to the optimization of firm structure; for example, Williamson explains the growth of the multi-divisional firm in terms of efficiency—it economizes on the transaction costs of capital markets and minimizes the managerial activity that detracts from shareholder value (1985: 288).

I will discuss multi-divisional structures in depth in Theme 6. Here, however, the focus is on the approach to hierarchy. Williamson develops an approach to the employment contract which is of generic interest to the relationships between owners, managers, and labour I discussed at the outset.

Employment contracts are often characterized in economics as incomplete. They also have asymmetric authority (the employer issues instruction), asymmetric information (sometimes in favour of the employee), asset specificity (the skills and equipment used are often not transferable), and they are often of long duration. They are, empirically, the building blocks of hierarchy, since monitoring and incentives are central to them. Williamson's approach can be illustrated by reference to Figure C2.1.

Williamson (1975: 69) discusses three contractual possibilities for employment contracts. Under spot contracting the parties contract at time 1 (T1) that when event 1 (E1) occurs, the exchange of money for effort (X1) will occur. If this occurs once, the spot contract form is efficient. However, if the game is repeated, two problems emerge. First, the transaction costs are high, both *ex ante* and *ex post*; you have to bargain with the same counter-party each time. Second, opportunism—by both parties—is likely. Under contingent claims contracting, the parties at T1 try to write a comprehensive contract covering all events and their related effort bargains. This fails the bounded rationality

```
Spot contracts
T1............ E1......... X1

T2............ E2......... X2

T3............ E3......... X3

Contingent claims
T1............ E1......... X1

              E2......... X2

              E3......... X3

Authority relation
T1...........

E1........... ............. E3

X1..................
```

Figure C2.1. Alternative contractual forms.
(*Source*: Derived from Williamson, 1975)

test in many circumstances, particularly where the number of discrete events is high; it becomes very difficult to imagine and cover all future contingencies. The third option is adapted from Simon (who was Williamson's PhD supervisor). In this approach the parties agree to an authority relationship. The employee, in exchange for a single comprehensive effort bargain, agrees to allow the employer the authority to make state-of-the-world definitions across a range of events (Willman, 1982). The problem here is how to define the acceptable range of events. However, an authority relationship economizes on transaction costs and does allow some form of monitoring.

Let me make this concrete with examples. A casually employed gardener or window cleaner has a series of spot contracts with the households that employ him or her. A contingent contract to cover repairs to a domestic appliance says what will and will not be covered by the engineer under a specified set of circumstances. My employment contract is an authority relationship because it says I will do whatever is asked of me by my head of department within a mutually understood (?) range of academic activities. These contracts have very different transaction cost properties and fit different contingencies. Where the future is highly unpredictable and the task can be specified, spot contracts may be the easiest option for both parties. Where we can effectively make a list of tasks and embed them in a job description, that is where the future is predictable, a contingent claims contract might work well, but unclassifiable events may be ignored. An authority relation is, in Williamson's view, more robust in the face of uncertainty.

The great step forward from Coase to Williamson is that the latter is theorizing the dynamics of the operation of hierarchy rather than simply explaining how market failure might bring it about. Hierarchies arise because of transaction costs in markets, but hierarchies themselves may differ in terms of their transaction costs' properties depending on the choice and mix of contractual forms. Williamson does not, however, use this insight as a platform for analysing differences between firms. Since he is concerned primarily with the efficiency properties of hierarchies, and inefficient hierarchies must disappear in the face of competition from more efficient forms, he is concerned to identify the most efficient hierarchical form.

What Williamson came up with as the optimal form relies very heavily on Doeringer and Piore's (1971) idea of an 'enterprise market'; this is essentially an authority relationship with a set of clear rules. He emphasizes several elements; internal promotion ladders to encourage on-the-job training and cooperation, pay rates attached to jobs within these ladders—rather than individual performance—ascending with position on the hierarchy, moderate rather than intensive metering, and job security bolstered by a grievance or arbitration procedure to resolve disputes. This might be regarded as a hybrid form—an authority relationship with many contingencies spelt out. It was widespread in the USA at the time Williamson wrote (1975), and as we saw it has a history going back at least as far as the nineteenth-century practices of rail firms.

Williamson is in effect describing the institutional structure of managerial capitalism—what Davis has referred to as 'corporate feudalism'—in which long-term attachments between firms and employees, bolstered by firm-specific benefits and privileges such as pensions, profit sharing, and long-term employment, characterized not only the fabric of managerial work but, increasingly with the advent of labour unions and particularly in the USA, that of all permanent employees. This was widespread practice (in the USA, if not elsewhere) so it must, if you are an economist, have efficiency properties to be unearthed. Unfortunately, it was disappearing almost as Williamson wrote (Davis, 2009: 195–200); I shall have much more to say about this in Theme 8.

For Williamson, a key part of the efficiency gains that come from this considerable investment in hierarchy comes from its impact on the behaviours of those in the hierarchy. His distinction between 'consummate' and 'perfunctory' cooperation outlines, but does not perform, a theory of value creation by managers.

> Consummate cooperation is an affirmative job attitude—to include the use of judgment, filling gaps, and taking initiative... Perfunctory cooperation, by contrast, involves job performance of a minimally acceptable sort... where... incumbents... need merely to maintain a slight margin over the best-available inexperienced candidate.
>
> (Williamson 1975: 27)

All other things equal, a firm in which managers generate consummate cooperation will out-compete one in which they do not. Understanding this difference has provided the motivation for the development of theories about both management and labour performance based on findings from different disciplines, which I examine in the next two chapters. They all challenge Williamson's assumption that such cooperation stems from contractual design alone.

Let us pursue this by looking at the idea that the different parties might have, in the short term at least, different preferences for the form of contract. Figure C2.2 illustrates the issues using a simple game theoretic framework of the sort that we will explore in more depth in Chapter 6. Two parties—employer and employee—are seeking to agree which contract to use under two conditions: offensive and defensive. Both parties adopt offensive strategies when they feel their bargaining power is high and defensive when they feel it is not. Offensively, the employer will wish to establish an authority relationship to throw contractual risk on to the employee and the employee will wish for spot contracting to maximize the opportunities for opportunism.

SPOT/AUTHORITY

	Offensive	Defensive
Offensive	Authority Spot contracts	Contingent Spot contracts
Defensive	Authority Contingent	Contingent Contingent

EMPLOYEE STRATEGY

Figure C2.2. Employer and employee contract strategies.
(*Source*: Willman, 1986: 97)

Defensively, both parties will wish to control counter-party risk with a complex contingent claims contract.

The simple example shows that contractual consensus is only unproblematic when both are on the defensive. Offensive strategies lead the employer to seek to impose authority and the employee to seek to bargain. It also indicates why contractual choice may not be homogeneous or stable and why consummate cooperation might be elusive.

Conclusion

In this short chapter, I have tried, first, to describe in brief the emergence of the large firm and, second, to outline the first main attempt to develop a theory of it. This theory has a number of features that are significant for the chapters that follow.

First, it emerges as essentially a negative explanation about market failure; firms are implicitly second-best structures that arise when markets fail. A hierarchy is essentially a set of incomplete contracts bound together in an authority structure, but the existence of authority is an assumption not a finding. Logically, one optimizes the performance of a firm hierarchy by making sure it runs as close to being a market as possible. Within firms, managers potentially engage in problematic behaviours because the structures bring out the worst in them—opportunism. Coase is the precursor of a range of *anti-managerial* theories of organization.

Second, the theory is not empirically based. Not only is it surprising that economics developed a theory of the firm long after firms came to dominate industries (and then ignored it), it is surprising that the theory was not informed by any extensive observation of industry structure or firm behaviour.

Empirical examination of the internal operation of the firm has remained unfashionable within economics and, as we shall see, it does not infect the modern field of organizational economics very much either.

Third, because the transaction costs approach remained marginal to economics for thirty years, and economics remained relatively uninterested in the firm, a space was created into which business disciplines such as marketing, organizational behaviour, and strategy moved. Academic economics becomes much more involved with the study of managerial behaviour with the growth of the economics of strategy and organization and, less directly, of financial economics from the 1960s. One interesting consequence of this is that we can look at the central themes of the management field from the varieties of perspective available from different disciplines.

I turn to the first. Our railway example is a useful way in. Investors in railways wanted clear accounting measures to ensure that managers whom they could not directly monitor were acting on their behalf. Managers of railways wanted institutional arrangements to secure a labour force they could not see most of the time who would keep the trains running. They both faced agency problems.

Theme 2

The Agency Problem

Introduction: Pins and Managers

The following might be one of the most famous quotes about the division of labour. It is from Adam Smith and concerns pin making.

> A workman not educated to this business, nor acquainted with the use of the machinery employed in it, could scarce, perhaps, with his utmost industry, make one pin in a day, and certainly could not make twenty.
>
> One man draws out the wire, another straights it, a third cuts it, a fourth points it, a fifth grinds it at the top for receiving the head; to make the head requires two or three distinct operations; to put it on is a peculiar business, to whiten the pins is another; it is even a trade by itself to put them into the paper; and the important business of making a pin is, in this manner, divided into about eighteen distinct operations, which, in some factories, are all performed by distinct hands, though in others the same man will sometimes perform two or three of them.
>
> I have seen a small manufactory of this kind where ten men only were employed, and where some of them consequently performed two or three distinct operations ... they could, when they exerted themselves, make among them about twelve pounds of pins in a day. There are in a pound upwards of four thousand pins of a middling size. Those ten persons, therefore, could make among them upwards of forty-eight thousand pins in a day.
>
> (Smith, 1776, *Wealth of Nations*: Book 1)

Smith goes on to remark that working this way might not be in the best interests of the individuals involved; specialization might make them 'stupid and ignorant'. He foresees (or maybe observes) a central problem about the management of factory labour that would concern many practitioners later on, particularly after task fragmentation was raised to an art form by F. W. Taylor and his followers: how do you ensure they 'exert' themselves? But there is a very interesting omission from this example ...

Who manages this? Do the non-educated workmen come together in the generation of spontaneous order similar to that characteristic of the invisible hand of the market mechanism? Or does there need to be a coordinating mechanism that manages production speed and quality at each work station, buffer stocks between each activity, and the job design choices that determine whether men do 'two or three distinct operations'? Does this coordinating mechanism operate by authority or consent? Does it impart the expertise needed by the uneducated? If production moves from one pin per day to 48,000, who gets the benefit? When the unit cost of pin production falls, who sets the internal transfer prices of part-finished goods and final product price? How are individual workers rewarded when there is such interdependency of tasks? Why should workmen as the 'small manufactory' he saw 'exert themselves'?

These are only some of the basic questions about the management of a production process. Although much more interested in the practicalities of production than many subsequent economists, Smith assumed that efficient organization emerges in both hierarchies and markets. He assumed that resources would be naturally allocated to their most profitable use, and that less-efficient divisions of labour would yield to more efficient ones. As I will demonstrate below, the originator of the term 'invisible hand'—about the operations of the market—had no theory of what much later Chandler would term the 'visible hand' of management in the generation of value and profit. In fact, like many subsequent economists, Smith had ideas about the problematic nature of managerial agency.

Adam Smith, again, on the firm.

> The directors of...companies, however, being the managers rather of other people's money than of their own, it cannot well be expected that they should watch over it with the same anxious vigilance with which the partners in a private company frequently watch over their own. Like the stewards of a rich man, they are apt to consider attention to small matters as not for their master's honour, and very easily give themselves a dispensation from having it. Negligence and profusion, therefore, must always prevail, more or less, in the management of the affairs of such a company.
>
> (Smith, 1776).

This is one of the earlier statements of what much later came to be known as the agency problem (Jensen and Meckling, 1976). It goes to the heart of what management is about: how to delegate and coordinate tasks in an efficient and effective manner. Once large industrial organizations emerged in which the number of activities and of employees was so great that they could not be monitored directly by a proprietor or even a family of proprietors, hierarchies of delegated authority emerged in which salaried managers managed (mostly) wage-earning employees. In these hierarchies, two major problems emerged in the following historical order, concerning coordination and control.

The first, which was evident in Smith's lifetime but peaked in the nineteenth and early twentieth centuries, concerned the need to create, manage, and develop an industrial labour force compliant enough to operate an efficient division of labour in the large manufacturing or service organization. There is much debate amongst economic historians about whether and when the Industrial Revolution improved the living standards of wage-earning employees in the West, but there is ample historical evidence that issues of compliance, attendance, productivity, and collective withdrawal of effort affected a number of industries in a number of countries. Thus, one finds that many early management writers concern themselves with the 'labour problem' and with the practices firms should adopt to resolve it.

The second, which is the one Smith directly addresses above, stems from something first characterized by Berle and Means in the USA (1932) as the separation of ownership and control. They argued that the development of large firms had led to the emergence of a class of professional managers whose independence of action and practical control of large businesses was supported by limited effective property rights for shareholders, particularly small ones, and limited oversight by capital markets. So, those who owned businesses in a property rights sense did not control what happened within them. Aims might be pursued that served the interests of salaried managers, preserving their job security and bolstering their earnings.

These can be presented fairly simply, but in practice the issues involved and the implications for theories about management are a bit more tricky. In the early twentieth century, international mobility of both labour and capital was more limited than in periods before or since (Gospel, 2007; Michie, 2006). Firms in many Western countries could not easily find substitute skilled workforces if their current ones sought more share in corporate rents, nor could they easily relocate productive activities to low-wage economies; and investors did not have an operative global market for capital and money, particularly after the Wall Street Crash. Constellations of corporate stakeholders in the USA at the time when Berle and Means were writing embraced organized labour and government in ways they do less today, and excluded consumer and investor interests more. So the context of the first set of agency issues was the employment contract, and that of the second was the financial market. I shall look at each in turn, stressing the conceptual similarity but not continuity.

Optimizing Production?

The nineteenth and early twentieth centuries in Europe and the USA were, arguably, characterized by two features relevant to the design and conduct of business. The first was a belief in technological progress (and its benefits). The second was an inclination towards optimization; put differently, if one thought systematically and rationally about a business problem, one could improve the chosen dependent variable—efficiency, productivity, profits, and so on. In the void I have outlined above—that is the absence of a theory of the firm—many analysts and practitioners felt the appliance of science to the factory could yield substantial benefits. Many had an engineering background (Witzel, 2002) and, again arguably, saw the optimization problem as an engineering problem.

The problem to be optimized was how to run the most efficient business. Intellectual furniture existed; there were not many examples of large-scale manufacturing businesses but there was a history of large-scale organization in two fields: government (particularly military) and religion (particularly international religious orders). In these organizations, many 'managerial' techniques had been developed. Earlier I offered the example of Venetian navies (military) and Jesuit bookkeeping (religious).

How are these examples relevant to the operation of the industrial firm centuries later? First, they indicate that techniques for resource allocation and mass production had a long history in ostensibly non-commercial operations that could be adapted: there was something to work on for engineers to optimize. Second, they hint at the source of the agency problem in business. Military operations (which are a matter of life and death) and religious organizations (which are a matter of afterlife and eternal death) can generally exert more forces for cooperation or compliance on organizational participants than organizations that rely primarily on shared financial interests; in the latter, the sharing can easily decompose, and that is the agency problem. Borrowing the techniques from such organizations did not borrow the underlying cooperation.

In much of the West, for much of the early period of industrialization, it was not entirely clear why a pre-industrial workforce would wish to become an industrial one (Marglin, 1974; Thompson, 1968). I have noted the living standard debate above, but there were also issues about workload. If one invested in a factory in, for example, the cotton industry in England (which was important for the first Industrial Revolution), the capital investment required in steam production and productive equipment required high rates of utilization which in turn required long hours of work. Control of absenteeism, of turnover, and of simple inactivity ('downtime') was required to generate a rate of return. What incentives could be used to exact this? Money is one obvious answer, but we saw also the problems with simple incentives in the last chapter. Moreover, what would one buy with it? Consumer markets were poorly developed. Penalties are another answer; throughout the nineteenth century in England, employment in factories was governed by the 'master and servant' acts. It did what it said on the tin: the presumption of obedience was central. A third was the removal of other opportunities. Prior to factories, farmers and their families used to spin cotton as an activity supplemental to their central activities. With the advent of expensive machinery, such an approach became hazardous to profit, and the need for a workforce with no other means of support became paramount.

Many management 'theorists' emerged in the late nineteenth and early twentieth centuries, convinced that applying scientific principles to the management of firms would result in improvements in efficiency and productivity and, for the more messianic, a better world. The term 'scientific management' has often been applied to the ideas they promoted. I will look at just the most influential, F. W. Taylor. However, several characteristics of the set are relevant. First, they were obsessed with efficiency as an outcome variable; many of their works display a strong tendency to sample on this dependent variable, often with erroneous results. Second, they believed in general rather than specific solutions; their recipes were in principle universally applicable and promoted one best way of doing things. Third, they inclined, like Emerson and Fayol, to sets of points or principles which summarized their approach; 12 principles of efficiency for Emerson, 14 points of administration for Fayol. Fourth, since they were often engineers, they saw agency problems in engineering terms. Employees were important appendages to machines 'and in the interests of plant efficiency should be treated at least as well as we treat machines' (Emerson, cited in Witzel, 2002: 227). Some were even military engineers who saw the exercise of authority as unproblematic.

An enormous amount has been written about Taylor (e.g. Braverman, 1974). He tends to be better thought of by those in operations management and research who are interested in the optimization of processes than by those in organizational behaviour who are interested in the human response to this. He has two points of significance here. First, he was the first modern agency theorist. Second, his work shows greater awareness of the limitations of agency theory than some more recent offerings, and is still used to design many mass production and service delivery operations in the twenty-first century.

Frederick Taylor (1923) argued that 'scientific management' consisted in devising the one best way to complete a task and then ensuring the worker closely followed the rules, using supervision and monetary incentives. Five principles were central:

- The separation of conception from execution: managers analysed and designed work tasks, employees performed them.
- Simplification of tasks: each task was broken down into simple components which were then aggregated to exclude unnecessary efforts (as in the pin example above).

41

- Close supervision: employees were closely monitored to ensure adherence to best practice.
- Strict obedience to 'one best way': employee innovations in work design were excluded.
- Monetary performance incentives were applied to output generated in this way.

After initial successes, Taylorism was adopted by large firms such as Du Pont and Ford. It was seen at the time as industrial science, not capitalist ideology—Lenin, in the Soviet Union, was a fan. As we shall see, elements of it were adapted much later. It provided one basis for the modernization of Japanese industry in the post-World War II period. Its utilization in service businesses grew as scale economies were pursued; most call centres use Taylorist principles, writing 'scripts' for employees to answer calls efficiently, setting target numbers of responses per hour, and monitoring intensively.

However, it generated some of the characteristic problems of later versions of agency theory. The model 'first class' workman in Taylor is a passive and obedient agent, indeed selected on those characteristics. Two problems emerge. First, recalcitrance: agent resistance to this managerial process raises costs all round. Second, information loss: agents who perform precisely specified tasks are not sources of task improvement.

Let's put the above Taylor list together again, in a negative way.

- Separation of conception from execution—the operator has no incentive to learn or share learning. If the operator does learn a better way, he is likely to appropriate the benefits.
- Simplification of tasks—skills are not worth developing, neither for the firm nor the employee. Indeed 'de-skilling' and thus loss of market power by employees is seen as one major consequence of the application of Taylorism (Braverman, 1974).
- Close supervision—many supervisors are needed and overhead rises. Taylorist firms develop high supervisory ratios and efficiency losses.
- Strict obedience to 'one best way'—attracts the intrinsically obedient who are unlikely to innovate.
- Monetary performance incentives—given that people respond to symbolic rewards, this is expensive and likely to generate a simply calculative approach by the employee.

In fact, Taylorism depends on what in a different context Granovetter (1985) has referred to as both an oversocialized and undersocialized idea about the employee; oversocialized into obedience and undersocialized in being entirely motivated by monetary, and not intrinsic, rewards. Moreover,

Taylor's optimal employee is individually selected, not collectively organized; in the early nineteenth-century USA, this emerged as a problem.

Let us look at the model of organization and of management. Organizations are seen as machines. Some of the machines are people but they can be managed the same way; managers think, workers do. Standardization of (labour) input, work process, and product output are the sources of efficiency; this is a mass-production model. The market does not send in shocks that disturb the organization of work on a regular basis. Employee recalcitrance is endemic and monitoring is permanent. Task or peer-based intrinsic rewards do not operate and the employee is *homo oeconomicus*. How well has Taylor understood the employee as economic man?

I would argue that in at least two respects the Taylor approach anticipates later developments by academic economists, albeit that Taylor's ideas are not formally mathematically presented.

- In the emphasis on the importance of selection and fit, there is understanding of both moral hazard and adverse selection.
- In the rigid adherence to the separation of conception from execution, there is a grasp of the problems of information asymmetry.

Let us move forward. In 1976, Jensen and Meckling focused on agency, property rights, and finance theory to discuss the issue of firm governance.

> The growth in the use of the corporate form as well as the growth in market value of established corporations suggests that, at least up to the present, creditors and investors have by and large not been disappointed with the results, despite the agency costs inherent in the corporate form.
>
> (Jensen and Meckling, 1976: 360)

Agency costs in this formulation are the sum of:

1. the monitoring expenditures by the principal;
2. the bonding expenditures by the agent;
3. the residual loss.

> Since the relationship between the stockholders and the managers of a corporation fits the definition of a pure agency relationship, it should come as no surprise to discover that the issues associated with the "separation of ownership and control" in the modern diffuse ownership corporation are intimately associated with the general problem of agency.
>
> (Jensen and Meckling, 1976: 308).

The domain of relevance for the modern version of agency theory was not management control of labour, but investor control of management. Operating with a negative view of the behaviour of managers (the provenance of which we will discuss), the modern version concerned itself primarily with how risk-averse managers, acting in a self-interested way, and benefiting from a greater understanding of the operation of the firm than investors (information asymmetry), might pursue goals such as the growth of the firm or security of tenure that differed from those of investors, who were primarily interested in return on investment. Particularly where shareholdings were dispersed among multiple investors, where monitoring costs were high, and where investor exit costs were low, economists felt that a situation could emerge where managers could secure rents at the expense of investors.

Economists soon found evidence of agency problems. For example, Amihud and Lev (1981) found that what they defined as management-controlled firms engaged in more conglomerate acquisitions and were more diversified than owner-controlled firms. Their view was, roughly, that managers were engaged in generating their own investment portfolios through the firm, rather than focusing on returns to investors who could develop portfolios for themselves. Walking and Long (1984) found that managers who did not own equity in the firms in which they worked were more likely to resist takeovers because they would not benefit from any increase in the stock price (which is common) during the takeover.

The resolution of this problem was seen to exist first in aligning investor and manager interests; one obvious way to do this was to reward managers for improvements in firm performance by rewarding them either directly with stock or by proxies for stock price movements. The second thing was to encourage monitoring, which in this instance meant closer investor oversight of firm operations. So, increasingly in the latter half of the twentieth century, senior managers had remuneration structures, particularly in UK- and USA-based organizations, which were leveraged on some proxy for firm performance, often the use of stock options.

Now, *if* you believe that senior management performance has an impact on firm performance distinct from the rest of those who work in the organization, and *if* you believe that you can devise an operationally effective performance measure, and *if* you believe that there is a functioning market for senior managers such that the best leveraged reward package will attract the best managers, and *if* you believe that monitoring can be sufficiently effective that the managers cannot manipulate changes in the chosen performance measures, and *if* you believe that you can get rid of managers who default in any serious way without excessive costs, then you will probably buy this approach. A surprising number of otherwise intelligent people did believe all of these things.

A number of things happened once this approach began to be implemented. First, executives became rich; internal (to the firm) inequality expanded massively as those who benefited from stock price changes moved away from those who did not. Second, those parts of firms associated with telling a good story to investors (investor relations) expanded massively. Third, firms set up remuneration committees filled with other stock-owning managers from different companies to decide remuneration; remuneration consultants became the elite of the HR profession. Whatever else the large Western corporation produced at the end of the twentieth century, it was a massive generator of income inequality (see Theme 8).

Taylor would never have bought this as good practice, since two items critical to his earlier version of agency theory were missing. First, if you fragment labour and separate conception from execution, you go a long way to solving the information asymmetry problem. Power moves from employees to managers. Second, if you rigidly control the selection process, you have a chance of controlling adverse selection and moral hazard (i.e. that you will pick as senior managers those who just want to get rich quick and are good at convincing you they can perform). With senior managers who appropriate significant informational advantages, manage the design and implementation of performance measures, and can make enough money in the short term when they do so to retire, the control problems are intractable.

On agency theory, the *Economist* remarked in the early twenty-first century:

> When Mr Jensen first pondered agency issues, the big problem was under-utilisation of company assets, and their consequent under valuation. In the 1990s, the most salient corporate-finance problem was overvaluation—an eventuality seemingly so unlikely that few economists had ever given it much thought.
>
> Once a firm's shares became overvalued, it was in managers' interests to keep them that way, or to encourage even more overvaluation, in the hope of cashing out before the bubble burst.
>
> It also encouraged behaviour that actually reduced the value of some firms to their shareholders—such as making an acquisition or spending a fortune on an Internet venture simply to satisfy the whims of an irrational market.
>
> (14 November 2002).

The emergence of major frauds such as Enron, and the events surrounding the financial crash in 2008, raise doubts about whether the 'agency problem' is under control (see Theme 8).

What, taken together, are the implications of our consideration of scientific management and agency theory?

1. Both approaches assume an endemic problem of divergent objectives within industrial organizations. In the first instance the conflict is manager–employee, in the second it is investor–manager. In both cases the offered solution is monitoring plus incentives that align the otherwise divergent interests of the latter to the former. There is a faith, first, that this combination can work towards, respectively, efficiency

and shareholder value and, second, that the agent is an economically rational actor who will respond.

2. In consequence, issues of value-creation are not considered; why do firms, all of which involve agents, perform differentially well?

3. In this resolution of divergent objectives, both approaches seek to imitate the operation of markets within organizations. In the conventional approach to perfect markets, there are rules (Coase) and rewards. It is assumed that hierarchies work to the extent that they imitate markets in embedding monitored rules and financial rewards.

4. The individual is the unit of analysis. Where collectives are conceptualized (e.g. investors), they are assumed to be aggregates of individual interests.

5. The parallel offers our first example of the circularity endemic in the study of management. The fundamental assumptions about human nature and motivation do not differ substantially between Taylorism and modern agency theory. There are two problems with both. The first is that they are not parsimonious; as Eisenhardt (1989) shows, agency theory requires stronger and more restrictive assumptions about human nature than many alternative approaches in organizational behaviour. The second is that they do not work. Study of Taylorism might have informed agency theory but the fragmentation of the management field is a formidable barrier.

In fact, there is substantial evidence, which I will review in Chapter 4, that the idea that one can generate any consistent change in a significant dependent variable (such as productivity or efficiency) by a simple combination of monitoring and incentives is not only wrong but, in many cases, generates net loss. Put briefly, individuals subject to a combination of both monitoring and incentives often react rationally by gaming (they manipulate the monitoring performance measures in order to generate better rewards) and, apparently, irrationally (they generate non-monetary benefits by cheating the system).

Conclusion

In this theme I have looked at agency theory both because it is central to the understanding of the firm and because it illustrates generic issues about studying management. Firms are hierarchies, not markets. They operate under conditions that imperfectly mirror market mechanisms. They account for a very large proportion of economic activity. We need to understand how they work.

Within firms, there is a problem about agency. By this I mean specifically that it is not clear from any theory about firms how managers and employees come to act in the interests of investors, who are the owners of firms, nor, by extension, any set of otherwise interested stakeholders. This cooperation is at the centre of most theories about management. There are serious issues involved in explaining how hierarchies in firms work.

Agency has concerned management theorists throughout the twentieth century. They have revisited simple models about monitoring and incentives in a non-cumulative way. Few theorists would argue in the modern era that a society can function on the basis of calculative self-interest. Large firms are arguably the most powerful economic and cultural influences within modern Western society. Yet many economists argue nonetheless that firms can be treated as solely economic entities which are networks of contracts (see Theme 8).

There is a very different view within the study of management, that organizational members—management and employees—can be assets rather than agency problems. I will turn to this in subsequent chapters. First, we need to understand more about the firm and how the agency problems discussed above initially became a concern.

Chapter 3

Workers of the World . . .

Introduction

Although circumstances in the nineteenth century differed between Western countries, particularly between nation states in Europe and the then immigrant society of the USA, it is fair to say that industrialization in both cases required the creation of an industrial labour force. The rhythms, seasonality, and control structures of a pre-industrial and agrarian society were very different from those needed by factory systems in the nineteenth century. This was the transition that obsessed Marx and Durkheim. Although their analyses were very different, they were both concerned with the disappearance of one labour pattern and its replacement by another. In practice, it was a process that was both political and economic, full of conflict, and lasting in its impact on both industrial practice and academic theory.

This chapter is by no means a history of this process. It is structured around several propositions. First, industrialization in general and the factory system in particular required a labour force substantially different both in its social structure and its labour practices from what preceded it. Second, this was neither a comfortable nor welcome process for many members of that labour force, and their resistance to it took the form both of unionization and political action. Third, the performance attributes of that labour force were sufficiently central to the success of specific firms that strategies for the management of workforces needed to move beyond compulsion to cooperation; capital-intensive operations required both skills and continuity, and both gave employees bargaining power. Fourth, the generation of labour compliance generated a specific set of managerial activities that began as labour welfare and continued as human resource management. Fifth, it emerged as the subject of both academic and practical concern that consummate cooperation, in Williamson's terms, be an outcome of management practice. Sixth, that the filling in of the 'silences' in incomplete employment contracts has from the outset of modern management theory been a central component of what management is. The silences can be filled by leadership, commitment, and engagement, to use modern language, or they can be filled by resistance, gaming, and obstruction.

Hobsbawm's (1994), 'short twentieth century' from 1914 to 1991 covers the period from the start of World War I to the collapse of the USSR. It was, in his interpretation, one long set of wars conducted by different means but involving, particularly for Europe, a central paradox for labour and labour markets. Millions of employees put on uniforms and were killed. Millions did not, and were killed anyway, since civilian casualties were very high. Immigration to the USA aside, international labour mobility shrank massively. But production and labour compliance became central to the fighting of wars won increasingly by industrial production of food, energy, and fighting machinery. In the later part of the period, the central conflict was between a capitalist system and an ostensibly socialist, worker-owned, one. The paradox for both was that labour had to be controlled, but it also had to be bought. In this climate, we see the elaboration of the institutional machineries of labour performance and cooperation. In order to set the stage for this, let us turn to the nineteenth-century background.

Farmers and Workers

In the first industrial revolution in England, factory owners installed machinery, attracted labour, and exerted control over it (Marglin, 1974). Advocates and critics alike were under no illusions about the dominant forms of managerial control. Contemporary commentators, such as Ure, spoke of the 'bloodless strife' of trade and used military analogies to describe hierarchy and authority (Berg, 1980: 201). Critics such as Marx spoke of male employees as 'sergeants' and women and children as 'soldiers of the line' (Braverman, 1974: 64). Machinery fragmented work, controlled workers, and shifted power to owners; machinery was broken in riots, rioters were imprisoned and transported. Unionization emerged, but—significantly—among the 'sergeants' who possessed scarce skills and bargaining power, not among the soldiers. Textile unions consisting of male workers became among the largest in Britain. Similar patterns of labour force development, but not necessarily unionization, developed in the USA and Japan (Gospel, 2007: 425).

As I noted above, railway companies came to dominate both the industrial landscape and the capital markets but, although military analogies were explicitly used in employment relations, the direct control approach to labour management was not. Railway operation does not generate huge concentrations of employment; employment is dispersed across the network and direct supervision is very expensive, but the potential for disruption of service by a discontented workforce enormous. The solution was largely the same in both the UK and USA; railways developed elaborate internal labour market structures with equally elaborate employment-dependent benefit systems to retain and pacify labour.

Subsequently, as we have seen, large firms came to dominate Western economies. There are a number of ways to measure firm size; we could use volume or value of output, financial resources, market value, or market share. For the present purposes, employment is the appropriate measure and Gospel has summarized the broad historical sweep of labour concentration. Referring to the UK, USA, Italy, and Germany, but also to Japan, he observes:

> With slight differences between countries, the typical large employer in the early to mid-nineteenth century was a textile company; by the mid- to late nineteenth century, the biggest single group of major firms in most economies were railway companies; by the mid-twentieth century, the main groupings were manufacturers (steel, chemicals, automobiles, electrical) and by the end of the twentieth century, the biggest single group of large firms was to be found in retailing and financial services.
>
> (Gospel, 2007: 424)

Throughout the 'short' twentieth century in Western economies, which also roughly coincides with Davis's (2009) period of 'corporate feudalism' characterized by managerial autonomy, these large firms had to come to terms with the 'labour problem'. As we will see, organizational size is a potent variable that explains many features of organizational structure and performance; labour conflict is no exception. Unionization spread in Western countries throughout the large manufacturing and service companies listed above. It also spread throughout government employment. The trends for the USA and UK are shown in Figure C3.1.

Band of Brothers

In both countries, the 'short twentieth century' was a better period for union membership than that before or since. However, the Great Depression was a bad hiccup. The initial turning point was World War I; the recovery from the depressionary dip roughly coincided with World War II. As I have noted above, tight labour market and product market conditions were very important, but governmental action to incorporate an organized labour movement into the war effort was also key. This was particularly important in Europe; for example, in 1914 it was by no means clear to contemporary politicians that trade unions loosely coordinated by the international socialist movement would support a call to arms that would have union members from different countries fighting each other (Tuchman, 1962). High levels of unionization

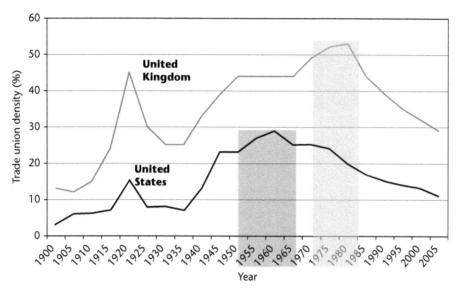

Figure C3.1. Long-term unionization trends; USA and UK.
(*Source*: Gomez et al., 2010)

were sustained in many Western economies throughout the post-war period of corporate feudalism, but as the figure shows, decline set in from the late 1950s in the USA, and the 1970s in the UK. There are very few Western countries (mostly in Scandinavia) that have not seen sustained decline in union membership, particularly in the private sector, since the mid-1970s.

Three questions concern us here. First, why did unionization become widespread in the short twentieth century? I decompose this into two subsidiary questions: why do workers join and why do managers in firms choose to deal with them? Second, what changed to cause union decline in the late, short twentieth century? Third, what is the impact of this phenomenon on theorizing about management? These questions will concern the remainder of this chapter.

I will start with union membership. Unions provide their members with three kinds of service (Pencavel, 1971). First, they represent them collectively in wage and benefit bargaining; second, they represent them individually in collectively agreed grievance and disciplinary procedures; and third, they offer personal insurance against misadventure such as unemployment or ill health and provide financial support. There is widespread evidence from Western countries in the modern era that unions can generate benefits for workers who are members. These benefits may be monetary; there is a union wage differential (i.e. a premium that union members are paid compared to similar non-union workers) in many Western countries and particularly for the USA for

Table C3.1. The union wage differential in selected countries.

Country	Years	Union % increase
Australia	1994, 8 & 9	12
Brazil	1999	34
Canada	1997–9	8
Denmark	1997–8	16
France	1996–8	3
Germany	1994–9	4
Italy	1994, & 8	0
Japan	1994–6, 8, 9	26
Netherlands	1994 & 5	0
New Zealand	1994–9	10
Norway	1994–9	7
Portugal	1998–9	18
Spain	1995, 7–9	7
Sweden	1994–9	0
UK	1993–2002	10
USA	1973–2002	17

(*Source*: Blanchflower and Bryson, 2004)

much of the twentieth century, although it declines as union density declines in the latter half (Blanchflower and Bryson, 2004). Table C3.1 indicates that the amounts in some countries may be substantial; there are also sectoral and skill-based differences within countries.

There is, equally, substantial evidence that employees want to be represented in their dealings with employers (Freeman and Rogers, 1999). I mentioned in Chapter 2 that employment contracts are incomplete; they contain many 'silences' that must be filled by discussion or negotiation and individual employees often want to be represented in this process. There is some evidence from the UK that this is increasing in importance compared to collective action. Figure C3.2 shows how in the UK strikes (collective withdrawal of labour) have declined in volume as individual appeals to employment tribunals have risen.

We read this modern evidence back into the argument for the early twentieth-century growth of unions at our peril and with some conditions. Strike activity in the early twentieth century was—to generalize—much higher than in the last quarter of it in most countries, but it is probably the case that most employees who joined unions did so for instrumental—that is benefit-related—reasons, so it was in the union interest to confine those benefits to members and prevent spillover to non-union members. This is relevant to the third category of services—individual insurance. Early unions operating in the absence of a welfare state were often as much benefit societies as bargaining agents—having funds to provide sickness benefit, unemployment benefit, and funeral benefits (Willman et al., 1993). Over time, and with the growth of corporate feudalism and government-provided welfare, these benefits

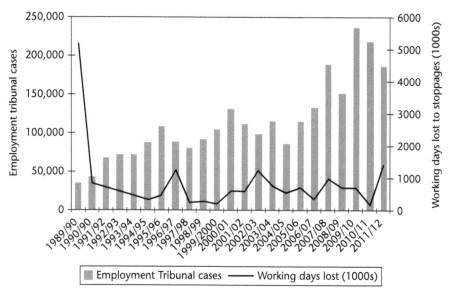

Figure C3.2. Disputes: the national picture.

dwindled. In late twentieth-century Western Europe, employees were likely to rely on the state for many benefits. In the USA it was the firm. As Davis notes:

> . . . some American multinationals look more like European welfare states than does the US government.

(Davis, 2009: 59)

Either way, whether the state or the employer provided benefit, since the wage differentials of union membership were often generalized to all employees, unions in the late twentieth century had a harder and harder time justifying the instrumental rewards of union membership. There is very good social psychological evidence to show some people join unions for ideological, or at least non-monetary, reasons, but none to show this can be the basis of mass membership. As Crouch notes;

> A mass organisation has to develop a range of services which are secondary, possibly even unrelated, to its central public purpose, but which meet some individual need of potential members and which are available only to members.

(Crouch, 1982: 55).

If employees could see some benefits in union membership, why would firms agree to deal with unions? There are at least three ingredients to the answer. First, because the economic benefits often outweighed the costs; this is essentially a bargaining power argument. In a railroad or steel mill, for example, labour costs tend to be a small proportion of total costs, but withdrawal of labour can lead to enormous cost; the union wage differential might seem cheap at the price. Second (and implied by the first), there *are* economic rents that managers, autonomous of owners, can share to make their job easier, as Figure C3.3 implies. The agency argument may be relevant here; what if management concede wage increases to make the managerial job easier? But, third, what if unions could be managed to provide benefits to the firm?

Often, in labour markets, switching costs are high. Both employer and employee may lose where an employment contract ends; exit of employees through dissatisfaction probably often works to the disadvantage of both parties. If a mechanism exists to provide employee voice—which Hirschman (1970) defines as a contribution to improvement of organizational performance—it may be worth engaging with even if it has costs in the form of a wage premium. This is the argument for why firms deal with unions put forward by Freeman and Medoff and it is presented in Figure C3.3.

Their dependent variable is labour productivity; the outcome is indeterminate dependent on the three effects, the reasoning is purely economic, and the identification of 'voice' solely with labour unions is an assumption. But the argument is that, since higher-priced labour (monopoly wage gains) should either get you better labour or make it easier to automate, and 'voice' should both lower exit and improve the quality of management, these two effects could generate net benefits if management controls are sufficiently strong to prevent the establishment of unproductive work rules (featherbedding).

The data they use to justify their argument is from the USA. There is some data from elsewhere that points the same way. To repeat, this is an argument about why firms need voice, not why they need unions, although Freeman and Medoff assume they are the same. But it also indicates why unionization might have become so prevalent in Western private sectors where

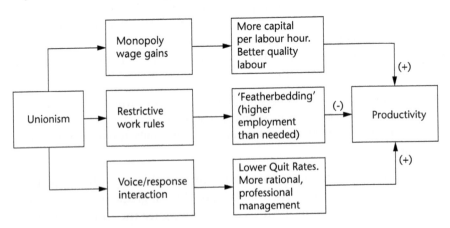

Figure C3.3. The net effect of union activity.
(*Source*: Freeman and Medoff, 1984)

oligopolistic competition existed, since it defines the set of firms in which the costs of unions to employers might be less than the benefits (Farber and Western, 2002). It may also point the way to the answer to the third question about union decline.

However, first we need to identify some properties of the set in which the net impact of unions is negative. Under what circumstances is the positive 'Freeman and Medoff' outcome unlikely, and the costs of union activity likely to outweigh the benefits to employers? A caution: such circumstances still exist. I identify four; they are not mutually exclusive.

• **Perishable products and spot contracting**. Perishable products are those that need to be produced, sold, or moved before their market value disappears. Where their production, sale, or movement depends on labour, collectively organized labour develops substantial bargaining power. In many such markets, there is volume volatility or uncertainty. Let me offer two historical examples (Willman, 1986). Newspapers used to be produced by typesetting methods that required substantial, skilled labour. But nobody knows how much news there will be tomorrow and nobody needs yesterday's paper. Labour power is substantial. Labour demand is variable. Dock (longshore) work is similar. Ships arrive at uncertain times and, because ships are charged to be in dock and because many products need to be unloaded fast, similar uncertainties existed. The central question is who bears the volatility risk. In both industries, in many countries, the employer solution was to generate a hiring hall; each day, employers would hire from a much larger pool of workers the labour they needed, so the potential employee bore all of the risk. This is, in Williamson's terms, a spot contract. Recall from Chapter 2 that the employee response is to try for a spot contract in the labour market. The union response was uniform, which was to shift the volatility risk; shrink the available labour pool by limiting it to union membership and exact compensatory payments equivalent to wages for those not hired, so the employer has limited hiring options and no incentive not to do so. In the two industries mentioned, it meant that union members became amongst the highest-paid manual workers in their respective economies, the USA and UK. In the short term, the management control problem is intractable. In the longer term, both industries completely automated the problem away.

• **Natural monopoly**. Whether public or private sector, unions maintain substantial powers in situations where monopoly enables them to inflict considerable damage on the consumer. Examples would be power supply and transport in the private sector, or education and health, often in the public. Bargaining power for unions is enhanced where skill levels are high, and thus substitution of current employees is difficult in the event of conflict. This natural monopoly may be local. By this I mean that it may be internal to the firm in the form of a production bottleneck. For example, in a large-scale retailing operation, unions find it difficult to organize a high turnover and dispersed group of employees in stores, but much easier to organize drivers who distribute saleable and perhaps perishable products, who are concentrated and smaller in number. (See also the example given in Box C3.1.)

- **Occupational communities.** Some industries have historically been more conflict-prone internationally than others. They are often characterized by a strong overlap between community networks and employment networks. Examples would be mining, dockwork (as above), rail employment, prison officers, and lumberjacks. Where a community depends on a single industry or employer, disputes with the employer often become disputes between the employer and community. Unions become representatives of the community and union membership becomes socially compulsory. This is known as the Kerr–Siegel hypothesis. Again it can operate at a micro level; even in large metropolitan areas, organizations that recruit serially from the same families can experience the same effects (police, fire services).

- **State ownership.** Public sector union membership is much higher than private in many economies. Several factors are at work. First, disruptive potential is considerable. Second, government often wishes to maintain employment standards as exemplar to the private sector. Third, organizational size is often very large. Fourth, political decisions, rather than product market conditions, often define employment terms and levels. Fifth, organizational aims are essentially contestable; performance measures in public sector organizations are often set with organizational objectives in mind that are not fully shared by the employees subject to them. Put another way, the employer benefit might not equate to a definition of the welfare benefit of such organizations.

So I turn to the question of union decline; and, implicitly, its permanence or otherwise. At the heart of the issue is voice. Employees want voice. But the key property they want is that the employer will listen and respond, improving their relationship with the firm. Employers may want voice, but they do not necessarily want the wage premium or the joint decision-making involved in negotiating with unions. So it could become rational for employers to reject union voice and invest in their own. Consider Figure C3.4. This contains data from the UK.

Firms do want voice. They want mechanisms for feedback to managers from employees. It leaves open what kinds of feedback occur, and whether the firm uses it to respond to employee concerns, but it is wholly inconsistent with the separation of conception from execution at the heart of Taylorism, and quite difficult to reconcile with the idea that firms are OK with perfunctory cooperation. There is substantial evidence from other Western economies that employers find the need to engage with, learn from, and explain to, those

Box C3.1 GRAVY TRAIN

In the UK, train drivers are very highly unionized, well paid, and scarce. There are a number of train companies in different regions (the union is national) and they poach each others' staff. Few spend much money on training new drivers. The union uses health and safety legislation to try to make training a driver as lengthy as possible.

They are employed by companies who do not own the track but operate the rolling stock on franchises that last 4–6 years. They bid for these franchises on promises of revenue over the franchise lifetime, which the government shares. Brief strikes can damage revenue; longer ones can eliminate the profits of an entire franchise. Action short of a strike which makes the trains late can lead to fines of the companies by the government.

There is little incentive for any individual franchise operator to engage in a battle with the union. The companies compete with each other for new franchises so find it difficult to operate collectively.

Demand for train travel is rising substantially, even though it is expensive. It is estimated that costs in the UK are 40% higher than those for publicly owned rail systems elsewhere in Europe.

(*Source*: *Economist*, 24 November 2012)

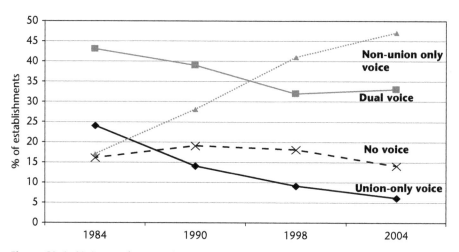

Figure C3.4. Union and non-union voice.
(*Source*: Gomez et al., 2010)

who work for them under conditions of incomplete contracting such as those we describe above, and that they will expend resources to do so. The next chapter examines this more closely.

This figure is based on very comprehensive survey data and it covers private sector employers (Kersley et al., 2006). It is interesting data not only for the UK, but as a test case on employer choice, since for the period covered there was no legislation requiring employers to deal or not to deal with unions. There was also very little legislation requiring them to have any mechanisms within the firm supporting voice, so employer choices represent demand for voice. Three categories decrease. Two are related to unions. Union-only voice, where the firm relies for voice entirely on unions as in the Freeman and Medoff model, goes down most. Dual voice, where managers use both union and non-union voice, declines, but less rapidly. But, if we focus on the other two curves, we see that voice mechanisms that the employer sponsors (non-union voice) expand, and the sector where there is no voice contracts.

Figure C3.4 shows that many *employers* want voice, independent of the presence of unions, and they are, by implication, prepared to pay for it. If they are acting rationally, this must be because the benefits of voice exceed the costs. This may be considered as a specific case of the 'make or buy' decision considered by Williamson (1975). Just as firms may decide to make or to buy a component in their products, they may also decide to buy voice from unions, the price for which would be the wage premium discussed above, or they may spend their own resources to make it by embedding voice mechanisms in the management process. In the UK, at least, they predominantly now make it. The corollary is also significant. Very few firms try to manage without voice. I discuss this further in the next theme; first let's look at a particular case of the demand for voice.

Gaming the Games

There is a tide in the affairs of academics, in which disciplines or sub-disciplines achieve high status, and then maybe lose it. In the early days of academic study of management, many of the problems related to the management of labour, particularly organized labour. At the end of the twentieth century, the sub-discipline of 'industrial relations' had disappeared from the curricula of most MBA schools. Labour market deregulation, the growth of migration, and the outsourcing of many activities to relatively cheap labour economies diminished the perceived importance of labour management and control.

This section presents a particular example of a set of circumstances where the management of collectively organized labour becomes a primary necessary condition for the success of a project. The project is the Olympic Games. What are the generic issues?

1. Cities bid for the games competitively, presenting a plan of how they would do it that itemizes facilities that often need to be built, organizational processes that are not in place, and sponsors that may not be fully committed. The International Olympic Committee (IOC) makes the decision; it appraises the costs of the bid, but it does not bear any of them. Its risk is purely reputational.

2. Once you win the bid, the clock is ticking on the construction. You do not move the timing of the Games. Labour supply becomes important in construction and security. Contracts need to be constructed to deliver on time (for the IOC) and somewhere near predicted cost (for everyone else). Delay is more critical than price, so bargaining power for employees or subcontractors is high, particularly if there are few substitutes. Generally, there is no back-up site, so if delay takes place (as it did in Athens in 2004) pressure from the IOC and sponsors increases.

3. Getting it built is no predictor of running it successfully. Two sets of labour-management issues arise in *running* the Games. First, creating a labour force for the Games. There is a massive spike in labour demand, but it leads to few long-term jobs (except in security). However, the spike involves uncertainty in that it is very difficult to predict the precise nature of labour demand between, for example, catering, audience management, and transport. Generally, volunteers are used together with full-time employees and so people who get paid are working next to those who don't. Second, the infrastructural labour force in, for example, airlines, railways, and immigration experiences a higher than normal workload and is in a powerful bargaining position in the short term. But, again, the bodies who employ these people are not direct beneficiaries of the Games.

4. Once the Games start, they can't stop. Any labour disruption must be bought off or otherwise pacified. This can happen by spot contracting (i.e. dealing with it as it happens) or by contingent claims contracting (i.e. designing a conflict resolution process that at the least puts the problem on hold until after the Games). After the Games, the bargaining power between employer and employee shifts completely, and both sides know this.

A dilemma, then, for the organizers is: what mechanisms should we put in place to manage this labour force? Politics play a part. If you can completely direct labour, and prevent conflict coercively, many problems don't arise. But in relatively free labour markets, a key issue is whether you pursue an individualistic or collective solution.

- In an individualistic approach, one excludes labour organizations, hires employees and volunteers freely, and substitutes any unsatisfactory employee at will.

- In a collective approach, one signs agreements with union confederations about labour supply, labour management, and dispute resolution. One defers any conflicts to be dealt with after the Games by agreed procedure.

The Atlanta Games in the USA in 1996 took the first approach. In that legislative regime, it would have been difficult to take any other. In any event, within one hour's drive of Atlanta there appeared to be easily enough spare labour supply (including volunteers) to cover the Games. But problems emerged. Employees, both voluntary and paid, went through screening, picked up their free uniforms, and disappeared. Security became problematic; there was a bomb incident. Turnover was very high. Some employees just stayed for the events they were interested in, then left. Employees and volunteers who worked outside the stadia—and so could not see any of the events— had particularly high turnover.

Sydney 2000, regarded as a very successful Games, took a very different approach, under different conditions.

1. Labour shortage. Australia had tight labour markets and low ability to allow immigrant labour.

2. Strong unions. Particularly in transport, unionization was high. The legislative framework supported union rights.

3. Massive investment in the Games, both in the construction of sites and the preparation of athletes.

In this circumstance, the incorporation of labour unions into the organization of the Games was imperative. The main ingredients were:

1. A framework agreement with the central union confederations that secured labour supply, terms of employment, and dispute resolution. In particular, centralized labour supply allowed some deployment across the set of activities where demand for labour was unpredictable.

2. Delayed bonus payments conditional on completion of tasks and the absence of disputes. So, for most paid employees, they were paid most of their salary at the end. If they left or went on strike, they lost it.

3. For infrastructural workers, for example in transport, a similar set of deferred bonuses was put in place.

Labour turnover was low, and there was no disruption. Labour costs rose through the bonuses, but labour costs were a very small proportion of total revenues for the Games.

This Olympic example may seem like an extreme one but it shares characteristics with many major projects in which the disruptive potential of conflict is out of proportion to the costs of resolving it. Employers who in these circumstances face enormous disruption costs may see the only effective way to manage this risk as to engage in negotiation with a collective labour organization that controls its members and bears liability for their default on contracts. Any event that requires substantial sunk costs, generates very high revenues and reputational benefits when delivered and massive equivalent losses when not, and in which labour costs are a small proportion of total costs, falls into this category.

Conclusion

Two key points from this chapter are:

- Engagement of employees with the firms for which they work is intrinsically problematic. An employment contract is initiated by a firm in order to generate an outcome, which may be measured in a variety of ways—as I will demonstrate—but will involve measures of productivity, customer satisfaction, contribution to profit, or a variety of preferred measures. It may be accepted by an employee for many reasons, but these reasons are likely to be both economic and non-economic; I mean by this here only that there is overwhelming evidence that employees want more from work than just pay.

- This employment contract is incomplete, and in most Western economies in the twentieth century the employer would fill the 'silences' unless constrained by the state or by collective organization of employees in a union. However, filling the silences involves a 'command and control' approach in only a minority of cases and managerial practices to generate employee voice predominate even in the absence of any compulsion for their use.

For much of the short twentieth century, large firms engaged with collective organizations of employees in bargaining and consultation. By the end of the short twentieth century this was much less likely to be the case in the private sector. This happened in part because, from both the employer and employee perspective, there were potential benefits in excess of the costs (see the next theme). Employers could use voice to reduce internal transaction costs and improve firm performance. Employees could share in the rents so generated to increase earnings. Note that a necessary condition for this arrangement is that there exist rents that can be shared.

Roughly from the end of World War I in Europe and from the New Deal in the USA, governments put their weight behind labour market institutions that would support improvements in productivity and reduce industrial conflict; this was particularly true in wartime, including Cold War time. However, by the end of the short twentieth century, these institutions were becoming, in many countries, less influential, and collective action by employees was on the wane. Employers still wished to secure the consummate cooperation of their employees, including voice, but they chose other mechanisms to do so. I will begin analysis of these other mechanisms in the next chapter, but first, I will go on a short tour of the dynamics of collective action.

Theme 3

A Short History of Collective Action

Introduction

In the last chapter I looked at labour, and in particular at the rise of labour organizations. Most Western countries in the twentieth century saw their rise—and labour unions were powerful influences on early management practice—and their decline—and arguably certain management practices themselves played a role in that. I also argued that the peculiarities of employment contracts—which are both hierarchical and incomplete documents with the 'silences' continuously negotiable—encouraged collective action by employees as a way of increasing bargaining power.

But I did not look at collective action as a generic issue. It pervades business life. In Germany, and to a lesser extent in the UK, when labour organized into unions, employers responded by forming employer organizations, primarily to take labour costs out of competition. Professional groups, such as lawyers and doctors, form collective-action organizations, both to set standards and control prices. Victims, sufferers, and sympathizers form collective-action organizations to combat disease, protect the environment, and pursue other political causes. Sportsmen in nineteenth-century Europe and the twentieth-century USA formed clubs that populate such bodies as La Liga and the Premier League, the NFL and NBA; several (though by no means all) of these entities have evolved into publicly quoted companies. Consumers unhappy with their experience of product or service markets also combine into various forms of consumer association. They may be generic protest groups (like the UK Consumers' Association), or specific geekfests like the Apple consumers group (of which more below).

These are all examples of collective-action organizations emerging *after* the Industrial Revolution. But the decline of such organizations—then, they were churches and guilds—*during* the Industrial Revolution caused much concern about the decline of social integration and the emergence of 'dysfunctional' behaviours; one of Durkheim's key publications, for example, was called

'Suicide' (Durkheim, 1951) and he argued it increased where social cohesion declined. He wanted to see 'corporative organisations' emerge, in which individuals who have common interests associate in order to lead the same 'moral' life together (Durkheim, 1933: 15). Given his time and location, he was much concerned with the imbalance between an overpowering state and an 'atomised' individual. Writing later, when firms were very much on the scene, Parsons, one of Durkheim's intellectual heirs and the writer of arguably the most turgid prose in modern social science, looked to 'democratic associations' to fill an important social void left by markets and bureaucracies (Parsons, 1969: 51–5). This remains a concern for modern social theorists (Putnam, 2000).

I would suggest it would be very unwise for a student or practitioner in management to ignore collective-action organizations. If you are working for an energy, drug, or agricultural firm, they will be a central consideration in decision-making. If you are working for a government or quasi-governmental organization, they will be organizing the lobbying. If you are working in a country where membership of the right political group defines career advancement, you will probably join. If the development or enhancement of your skills cannot safely be left to your firm, it will probably be enhanced by a professional association. And if your occupation requires a licence to practice, you have to be in. So what are they, and how do they work?

A Piece of the Action?

Here is David Knoke's definition (Knoke, 1990: 5–7). Collective-action organizations:

1. **Seek non-market solutions to particular individual or group problems.** Individuals join to enjoy 'benefits and satisfactions' that can only be achieved by collective action. As we shall see, the distinction between benefit (rational choice) and satisfaction (affect) can become very important. Can you build a rational model of the development of collective-action organizations? In associated fashion, delivery of solutions to individual and group problems often involves a trade-off between public and private goods.

2. **Maintain formal criteria for membership on a voluntary basis.** Again, two big issues emerge here. The first is about who gets in: is it a good idea to widen or restrict access? A small group may be easier to manage and have more common interests; it may also generate scarcity in supply of whatever it produces. A larger group, however, may have more power. Commons (1909), probably the original institutional economist, noted of labour unions that if, as Smith claimed, the division of labour was defined by the extent of

the market, then labour unions had to expand as markets expanded. The second question is what does 'voluntary' mean? Specifically, what is the balance of incentives and punishments involved? I might join the American Medical Association because it offers me pecuniary and non-pecuniary benefits or because I cannot effectively practice if I do not. If I am running a collective-action organization, I may lobby governments to put positive or negative inducements in place to control membership.

3. May employ persons under the authority of organizational leaders. A German sociologist, Michels (1915 [1962]), argued about political parties that, 'who says organisation says oligarchy'. He was pointing to a trend for collective-action organizations to develop hierarchy. Membership becomes, in an Orwellian sense, unequal; that is, all animals are equal, but some are more equal than others. The key issue here is the balance of power between membership and management. At one extreme, without some form of hierarchy, it may be difficult for a collective-action organization to make decisions and take action. At the other extreme, a centralized organization may not adequately represent the (diverse) wishes of the membership. This may be characterized in more or less positive terms. There may be political parties that become dominated by some power-mad leader. But there may be other collective-action organizations where there are serious issues about objectives. Hudson (1999) notes the example of cancer charities. One may start out as a voluntary organization focusing on care for victims of a particular form of cancer, maybe reliant on relatives of victims for voluntary support, then move 'upstream' to first fund treatment, then do research on the underlying causes of the disease which tends to emphasize the commonality with other forms of cancer cause. The net effect is to move concern and resources from a small and specific set of individuals to a wide variety of concerns and activities. Is this sensible or just mission drift?

4. Provide formally democratic procedures to involve members in policy decisions. Now this more than anything introduces the core collective-action problem. Some members just want the benefit; I might join a price club to get a discount; if it does not work, I want out, not a vote. Similarly with a labour union; if the wage hike it gets me exceeds the subscription, I stay in. If not, I may leave. But, as we will see, collective-action organizations cannot work without activists. In Hirschman's terms, these are people for whom the benefits of collective action are not *net* of involvement costs. They are the *sum* of the two, since involvement is not a set of opportunity costs but an intrinsic benefit in its own right. This requires, at the very least, an approach to collective organizations that recognizes different utility functions and, at the most, a theory of collective action.

The Free Lunch

Probably the most influential modern theory of collective action treats it as deeply problematic (Olson, 1971). This is counter-intuitive, since the approach needs to explain why something which has existed widely in certain circumstances is not inherently likely. The key elements are the distinction between public and private goods, and the notion of calculative rationality. We need to define these ideas and their relevance.[1] A private good is one whose benefits can be restricted to those who have paid or contributed to its creation; so, for example, if we combine into a sports club, we can restrict access to those who buy membership. A public good is one whose benefits are available to all, whether they have contributed or not. Periodically, in my neighbourhood, there are attempts to expand the nearby airport, Heathrow, which arouse local protest. When this protest is successful, all local residents, not just activist protesters, benefit from noise and pollution control. However, it is the activists who spend all of the time and effort. Olson's key insight is to show that public goods may not be provided even if everyone would be better off through their provision. Let us use the labour union example here, although this is more a general theory than one of union organization (see Box T3.1).

Since a theory that shows unions cannot exist is not much use, Olson needs to have some conditions under which collective action can occur. One resides within the logic above; in small number conditions, where the impact of individual membership on positive outcomes has a high probability, collective

---

Box T3.1

We all work for Firm X. If we form a union, we could get a £10-per-week pay increase. We have calculated that to fund the union organization will cost each individual membership fees of £1 per week. So everyone who joins will make a net gain of £9 per week. Olson is able to show why it might nevertheless be rational for no one to contribute and no union to form. The logic of collective action here is as follows. Each worker will think of what else, aside from membership, she could spend the £1 on. If everyone gets the wage increase in question, it is sensible not to join the union and free ride (net benefit: £10 v £9). The rational worker will also ask; what difference will *my* membership make? Let us assume there are 100 workers. My additional membership will raise the probability of the pay rise by 0.01; assuming utility is a linear function of money, then the expected utility of a £1 contribution is 10p. If everyone reasons this way, no one will contribute, no union will form, and no wage increase will emerge. So this argument overthrows the conventional wisdom that like-minded individuals will always combine to pursue common interests.

---

[1] I am indebted in this section to Heath's excellently clear exposition (1976: 29–32).

action is more likely. Elsewhere, he needs to rely on *selective incentives* and *special conditions*. A selective incentive is a private good dependent on membership; in the union case, examples would be unemployment insurance or representation in disciplinary matters. A special condition is a form of coercion or constraint; so some unions have enforced 'closed shop' conditions—that is the requirement to be a union member in order to start or remain employed. Olson puts particular emphasis on this punishment-centred approach, arguing that the major growth spurts in US unionization from 1897 to 1904 and during World War II were based on compulsion (1971: 88).

As Elster (1989: 26–42), among others, has noted, there is a serious problem with the simple form of the selective incentive argument. In order to offer incentives or threaten punishment, one needs an existing organization with some central authority. Put another way, one needs to solve the first-order collective-action problem of founding a union before you can solve the second-order collective-action problem of enforcing discipline within it. Moreover, one would need second-order selective incentives, since punishment is costly to the punisher, which raises a third-order free rider problem; 'we must not only penalize shirkers, but people who fail to penalize shirkers' (Kay, 2003: 244). And we might also need to penalize the people who fail to penalize the people who fail to penalize... and so on. We would then construct organizations in which mercy droppeth not like the gentle rain. Such organizations have been termed 'punishment-centred bureaucracies' by organizational sociologists (Gouldner, 1954).

Olson's main response is to argue the small group size point; unions began as small organizations (for a rejoinder, see Kelly, 1998: 78). It could also be argued (at least for the UK) that many unions began primarily as mutual benefit societies (i.e. providing private goods; Willman et al., 1993). But these are essentially empirical points and much of the literature describing collective action, particularly unions, takes issue with the more fundamental point of the usefulness of treating collective action as an *n-* person non-cooperative game.[2]

Olson's other empirical point—that compulsion matters—has been heavily contested by writers in the industrial relations tradition (see Crouch, 1982; Kelly, 1998). The argument is, essentially, that it is difficult to correlate union growth spurts with compulsion, that in many Western societies, compulsion has been limited, and that union density by sector is highly variable when compulsion is not (Kelly, 1998). A highly influential study of a major growth spurt in the UK, namely rapidly increasing unionization of white-collar workers in the 1960s, found compulsion less important than two other effects; a

---

[2] For more of the language of game theory in the context of business strategy, see Chapter 6.

threat effect, namely that such workers felt living standards were threatened by rising inflation, and a *credit effect*, namely that existing union organizations were credited with an ability to protect living standards in the face of inflation by bargaining for higher pay (Bain, 1970). Within this framework, unionization becomes a rational, if imitative, response to the existence of unions elsewhere.

Exit or Loyalty?

A more generalized framework for understanding collective action, not only in labour markets but also in product markets, is provided by Hirschman (1970). It is essentially a transaction costs approach; Hirschman extends his scope to look not only at firms and markets, but politics too. Since he introduces the idea in consumer markets, so will we here.

Assume a firm produces a product for customers. Assume further that there is a small deterioration in product quality; one large enough to be noticed by consumers, but not so big that it could not be remedied by managers in the firm. What do consumers do? For Hirschman, there are two options (1970: 4):

1. *Exit*. This is the standard economic response, in which consumers in a competitive context switch to another firm's product. The initial firm sees consumer churn, revenue decline, and possibly reduced profitability. Managers then need to find out what the fault is, correct it, and then try to get the consumers back.

2. *Voice*. Alternatively, the customers complain to management directly, and the fault gets rectified by managers who appreciate the costs of mass exit.

Hirschman's central concern is; 'under what conditions will the exit option prevail over the voice option and vice versa?' Let's take an example. If you are having problems with your iPhone and you go to your local Apple Store you may find they are busy, so you wait, and then you can't get your problem solved when you talk to the staff. Do you switch to another product? This would be, in Hirschman's terms *exit*. Most readers who are Apple users will probably say no. There are substantial switching costs; it has all your stuff on it, and you probably spent a lot of time with it. You do not know whether another product will be any better, and anyway the iPhone was your first choice. You have what Hirschman terms,

3. *Loyalty*. This does not necessarily mean you need to love and obey Apple (although you may). It means you have high switching costs; you like the product, you know how it works, it interacts with your other products. You may have an iPad and buy lots of apps and spend lots on iTunes, and so on. Loyalty promotes voice.

But you want the problem solved. So you may escalate your complaint and indicate the impact your exit will have on Apple. This voice takes more time, so there are limits to the amount of voice you will engage in. If you have some form of mechanism, ideally collective, to complain or pressure Apple to solve it, this will be the better option; for you *and* for Apple so that they do not lose a customer.

If collective voice in the form of a consumers' association exists, you may refer to them. But we encounter the Olson problem. Setting up collective organizations is costly. Hirschman gets round this in three ways. First, he delineates certain situations in which the sunk costs are so big for the customer that setting up a collective organization is worth it; for example, a few large customers of a declining firm may form an industry association. Second, as we have seen, he argues that some would not regard the voice decision in simple cost–benefit terms; there are some who would see collective action as having intrinsic utility such that their returns from voice are not the returns to voice minus its costs but rather the *sum of returns and costs*. Put slightly more technically, he solves the second-order collective-action problem by varying the utility function. Third, he argues that benefits from voice can accrue to both firms and consumers, since excessive exit may be costly for both.

What then, in our example, are the benefits to Apple of having a users' group?

- Exit is informationally inefficient, in that one does not have a mechanism for establishing cause, and it may be costly to find out why consumers are leaving.
- Customer acquisition and re-acquisition may be more costly than retention (it normally is).
- Voice allows for more effective feedback to remedy defects.
- Voice may allow the firm to *raise* switching costs for consumers by product bundling, or targeting discounts.

For Hirschman, there is an optimal balance of exit and voice. But from the above example one can see that there may be negative outcomes of excessive voice for both parties. An organization that speaks only to its retained enthusiasts is unlikely to be effective in marketing to a broader base, but nonetheless has elements of monopolistic control over that base. To stick with Apple for the moment; at the time of writing it is one of the most successful companies in the world, but it was not always so. In the 1990s it was a declining niche producer of computers that protected its operating system and allowed Microsoft to develop the imitative Windows system as the industry standard. It spoke to and focused on its existing customer base of MacAddicts.

But we know excessive exit can be costly too, in both labour and product markets. In the former context, the dominant retailer in the UK, Tesco, works with its main trade union, USDAW, to reduce labour turnover in its stores. The rate of turnover is very high in the first six months among store staff and this is enormously expensive to Tesco in selection and training costs and USDAW in membership loss. The mobile phone companies that sell you the iPhone will offer it cheaply in return for your signing a long-term contract for phone and data services, because customer churn is a problem in the industry where the service is, largely, undifferentiated.

Let us return to Hirschman's point about the utility function and collective action. He argues that in labour, consumer, and political markets, there is activism that sustains organizations and interest groups, and that this is due to the presence of individuals who derive intrinsic utility from collective action. There are large literatures on activism that would support this individual difference argument. However, there may be instrumental returns also to collective action, or at least membership of a collective-action organization. As I noted above, instrumental returns (money) from union representation seem to be the major reason behind the decision to join a union (Charlwood, 2003). Involvement in voluntary or charitable organizations is a key element in the CV-building activities of applicants to elite universities. It signals attributes to universities and to employers about candidates. And there is evidence also that social capital—the involvement in networks of exchange and influence—is associated with career success.

Howdy

One form of collective organization we have not touched on so far has great significance; the partnership. The early merchant organizations were all partnerships, often small ones (Hancock, 1995). In such partnerships, liability was unlimited, and the partners were incentivized to take a long-term view of a business from which they could not easily extricate themselves. What Morrison and Wilhelm refer to as the 'technological requirement of trust' (Morrison and Wilhelm, 2007: 107) is central; managers in partnerships were owners of the business, so that straightforward agency problems were avoided, but mutual monitoring was essential where both financial and reputational exposure to one's partners were extreme. Two features were important: first, the willingness of all to accept liability for all contracts made by any individual on behalf of the partnership and, second, the sharing of profits.[3]

---

[3] Though not necessarily equally.

Such organizational forms were inappropriate to the raising of external capital, so, with the introduction of limited liability for joint stock companies, partnerships were at a disadvantage in those industries where capital requirements were large. However, in several business and business-related areas, such as investment banking, management consultancy, accounting, and law, partnership became in the twentieth century the dominant organizational form. Moreover, whereas the early merchant partnerships were small, partnerships in some of these other sectors became very large.

These sectors have in common a reliance on human capital to generate revenue; they sell their members' information and expertise, and that expertise is not easily codified or transferred. In such informationally intense industries, reputation is very important, since the purchaser of the partnership's services tends to have high switching costs if they are unsatisfactory. Reputation is important in the choice of partnership firm, but it may also be important for the collective form as a whole. For example, McKenna (2006) argues that management consulting firms—which were a fairly late arrival—adopted partnership structures in part to emulate the status of lawyers and investment bankers who already had them.

How do partnerships solve the collective-action problem? The answer is twofold: first the technology of trust, and second the activity of monitoring. Sako (1992) makes a useful distinction between forms of trust which assists analysis here. She distinguishes:

1. Contractual trust; this is close to the informal understanding of honesty—that is, does someone do what they say they will do?
2. Competence-based trust; does the other party have the skills, information, and experience necessary to complete an allocated task?
3. Relationship trust; is the person committed to sustaining the long-term relationship and to foregoing short-term advantage to do so?

Partnerships adopt mechanisms to solve these trust questions in several ways. The first is selection. Morrison and Wilhelm (2007) note that the early investment banking partnerships tended to select family members, or members of particular ethnic and social groups. Modern hedge funds tend to be partnerships of individuals who have long experience of working together. Scale frustrates these simple solutions, but many large partnerships rely on the attainment of a professional qualification to minimize the competence-based risk; many also recruit from specific elite universities.

After selection, aspirants to partnership are often subjected to lengthy periods of monitoring and mentoring in competitive 'up or out' career tournaments. This may be seen as a form of long-term exchange, in which existing partners lend reputation and share expertise with juniors, who generate revenues for the partnership in excess of their remuneration; during the exchange, monitoring of the trust attributes of aspirants takes place (Maister, 2003). Once partnership is achieved, partners may be forbidden to take all of their remuneration until retirement. This was the practice at Goldman Sachs while it was a partnership and, as Morrison and Wilhelm note, no partner left to join a competitor between 1955 and 1973. However, retirement rules are often rigidly enforced to preserve the supply of partnerships!

Conclusion

All forms of organization solve the collective-action problem to survive, but here we have focused on those that do so without use of simple hierarchy. Monitoring and incentives remain central even in the absence of agency issues. Membership rules—both those that exclude and those that enforce membership—are important.

However, collective action remains problematic and both of the forms we have focused on declined in the late twentieth century. Unionization rates fell in most Western countries. Partnerships disappeared in investment banking and parts of management consulting; where they remained, they modified into 'limited liability' partnerships. We will return to look at this again in Theme 8.

Chapter 4

The Search for Consummate Cooperation

Alien to Captain Kirk; 'Why are there so many carbon-based units on this ship?'
(*Star Trek: The Movie I*)

Introduction

Readers will recall from Chapter 2 that 'consummate cooperation' is Williamson's term to describe cooperative and productive job performance by employees. This chapter will argue that securing such cooperation is an endemic and enduring problem for business organizations and that, as a consequence, they are prepared to expend resources to get it. However, the chapter differs in a fundamental way from what has gone before. I have been using the language of transaction cost economics to describe features of the firm and of collective action. The sections that follow introduce ideas from sociology and, in particular, psychology, since these are the disciplines that have had the most substantial effects on the design of techniques for the management of labour. I will argue eventually that the different disciplines are examining roughly the same things, but not only does their terminology differ; many of their conclusions do also.

I look first at scientific management and its relationship to operations management; then I will turn to the 'human relations' school and the development of the discipline of organizational behaviour.

Scientific Management: the Apogee

Scientific management in general, and Taylor's version in particular, left a substantial legacy. The engineering efficiency approach to the design of operations generated huge returns to scale, and many large businesses in chemicals, engineering, and car manufacture adopted it (Nelson, 1980). Fligstein

(1990: 75–115) goes so far as to argue that there developed a 'manufacturing conception of control' in large US firms, characterized by an engineering-based approach to maximizing the flow of goods through tightly integrated production processes in order both to lower costs and raise competitive barriers to entry. In such a conception, interruptions to production flow caused by labour problems were to be avoided.

Much of the thinking was to become incorporated in the academic disciplines of operations research and operations management, which in turn found a central place in the MBA curriculum. For many, the ultimate expression of the engineering approach to production management came in the car industry, and in particular the operations of Ford, the most successful of the early car manufacturers.[1]

Ford dominated the early history of the car industry, both in success and failure. The Model T, introduced in the 1920s, was based on a strategy of low price and simple design; this generated huge growth in car ownership and thus market size. The production approach underpinning this was standardized design, assembly line technology, and mass production. This had a number of implications. For Ford, the most serious was inflexibility; his early factories could only produce Model T cars, and retooling for product innovation required long-term plant closure that led to the lengthy loss of market leadership to General Motors (Lewchuk, 1983).

In assembly line car production, capacity utilization is vital. Mass production degenerates into batch production whenever the line is stopped or product rectification is required; fixed capital costs are high, and the gap between capacity and output needs to be small. These concerns are exacerbated by vertical integration; car assembly—the final operation before distribution and sale—has lower minimum efficient scale than upstream operations such as engine manufacture and body production, so interruptions to assembly within an integrated car manufacturing operation generate costs throughout the firm. Assembly is also the most labour-intensive phase of production.

Figure C4.1 identifies the cost components of car assembly. There are three sets. First, capital equipment in the form of plant layout; this defines capacity and is fixed. The next two concern labour. The second component is the hourly cost of labour. If the system is optimized at 100% operation, these are the only costs. The third component represents lost capacity; the source of most lost capacity is labour behaviour, and control of this is at the centre of the derivative of Taylorism that some commentators call 'Fordism' (Jurgens et al., 1993). The key dependent variable is 'man hours per car', that is the labour input to each unit produced. Absenteeism, errors in work, stoppages

---

[1] This section relies on Abernathy (1978) and Willman (1986).

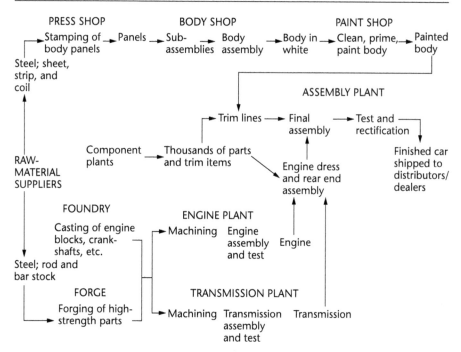

Figure C4.1. The manufacturing process in car production.
(*Source*: Willman, 1986; 146)

due to disputes, and the need for direct supervision inflate this denominator. Abernathy et al. (1983) explain the productivity differential (man hours per car) between the largest automobile firms in their sample in terms of the following factors.

- Product design   7%
- Automation   10%
- Equipment utilization   40%
- Worker deployment   18%
- Quality control system   9%
- Work intensity   4%
- Lower absenteeism   12%

It can be seen that 83% of total variance is dependent wholly or in part on the behaviour of assembly labour.

The key elements of the labour strategy that support optimization were as follows:

- The simplification of tasks and high assembly line speeds; automation of simple tasks where possible. Automation tends to turn a variable cost

75

(labour) into a fixed cost (equipment) and raises the stakes on equipment utilization.

- Use of high levels of hourly pay and the avoidance of bonuses. Ford introduced the '$5 day'[2] to attract and retain the labour required, and to reduce absenteeism. If you have 5% daily absenteeism, you need a workforce just over 105% of that necessary.
- Close supervision of employees and strict discipline, both inside the factory and outside.
- Avoidance of labour unions. In the terms of the last chapter, Ford made his own voice.

In order to do this, Ford favoured company towns and company housing. Most significantly the firm invested in a 'personnel department' that not only provided welfare but acted as a labour police force monitoring absence, sickness, agitation, and dissent. Optimizing workforce performance was the key to optimizing capacity utilization. The main Taylorist absentees from this labour-management formula were incentives and heavy supervision; assembly line speeds substituted for both (Guillen, 1994: 56).

Many of these considerations still apply to the modern car industry, as we shall see from the analysis of Toyota later. By extension, they apply to many capital-intensive mass-production operations. Labour costs may be a small proportion of total costs, but labour control becomes vital. As Braverman has put it:

> Taylorism dominates the world of production; the practitioners of human relations and industrial psychology are the maintenance crew for the human machinery.
>
> (Braverman, 1974: 87)

How did psychology intervene, and what is 'human relations' in this context?

Engineering and Psychology

There were parallel but discrete origins in the USA and the UK. In the USA, Munsterberg at Harvard—an admirer of Taylor—became concerned with fatigue, monotony, and learning in industrial work; he advocated selection testing and motivational tools (Wren, 2005: 193–4). In the UK, the influence of wartime research on soldiers was deployed in the 1920s by Myers, among others, to study stress and fatigue and to develop recommendations on the optimal working day and rest periods and the avoidance of accidents and

---

[2] This was a lot of money at the time.

absenteeism (Rose, 1988). The unit of analysis tended to be the individual worker (and by extension individual differences), but the concern was less directly with individual well-being and more with those variables also of concern to scientific management. As Wren puts it:

> While the engineer studied mechanical efficiency, the industrial psychologist studied human efficiency with the same goal in mind of improved overall greater productivity. Acceptance by industry of the heretofore ivory tower psychologist was facilitated by the psychologist's interest in efficiency.
>
> (Wren, 2005: 193)

There is quite a big point in here. Academic psychology and sociology (which we turn to later) were not primarily disciplines that focused on efficiency or indeed any business performance measure. Sampling from these disciplines in order to develop industrial applications of academic knowledge was quite selective. There were schools of thought within both disciplines that were ill at ease with the entire process of capitalist industrialization because of the effects it was deemed to have on the individual or society respectively. Applying knowledge developed in these disciplines to the cause of efficiency and profit created tensions within such disciplines between those preferring analytical approaches and those who felt OK about getting their hands dirty. As we saw above, economics went missing at this point; but other social sciences got worried about the terms of engagement.

Rise of the Groupies

A paradox of early theorizing about employee behaviour was that both scientific management and the early psychologists focused on the individual as the unit of analysis but the employee response to both frequently involved collective action, which in turn generated the high levels of labour conflict that were of so much concern. An alternative approach relied on late nineteenth-century sociology and focused on the group.

Durkheim focused on the bonds that held societies together to generate solidarity (Giddens, 1971). Traditional societies were bound together by kinship, religion, and similarity; this generated 'mechanical solidarity'. The division of labour, the growth in differentiation of status, and the scale of modern societies broke down these bonds and generated *anomie*; this was an individual state of confusion, normlessness, and anxiety, but it was generated by the absence of any groups or institutions that could provide a set of norms and values appropriate to a highly differentiated society—'organic solidarity'. Durkheim's work contains far more analysis of societies with mechanical solidarity than those with organic and he is a little short on detail about how the latter might be achieved. The enduring legacy for the management field was his concept of the individual as plastic, shaped and shapeable by membership of norm-generating groups.

To get from this to a set of management techniques one needed something approaching an optimization model—and it came from economics. Pareto, a nineteenth-century polymath who was engineer, economist, sociologist, and producer of many *bon mots*,[3] referred to the idea of a 'social system'—characterized by interdependent and varied components with self-equilibrating tendencies. This went into Harvard University as a broad idea and came out as a major influence on academic sociologists such as Parsons and Homans on the one hand and, on the other, as a central plank of what became the 'human relations' school—the idea of the factory as a social system that could achieve equilibrium. In order to explore this approach and its effect on modern management theory, let us look at its most famous piece of research—the Hawthorne studies.

The Hawthorne studies took place in the Mid-West of America in the eponymous plant of Western Electric from 1924–33.[4] It was a massive factory; by 1929, 40,000 men and women worked there. Western Electric was one of the forerunners in applying scientific management to its production units and it was regarded as a well-run plant. Numerous researchers using a variety of methods performed a series of behavioural experiments and deployed interviewing and observation techniques in ways that would get modern researchers fired and, given that the experiments involved some behavioural manipulations and physical deprivations, maybe sued (Wren, 2005: 370–3). In fact, the most widely quoted finding is simply a method flaw. Over time, researchers realized that every time they paid attention to a group of workers (subjected them to a 'treatment') output rose temporarily, then fell back—the 'Hawthorne Effect'.

The studies began with a concern for physical environment. The illumination tests, 1924–7, subjected groups to lighting variations and, broadly, found no correlations between lighting and productivity. Subsequently, the 'relay' tests, 1927–9, involved experimental alteration of bonus arrangements, rest periods, and hours of work, with mixed results. A third set of studies, in the 'Bank Wiring Room', probably had the greatest impact. Researchers discovered output restriction under incentive schemes which was enforced by informal groups. Workers felt that if they produced too much output, management would cut the rates, and if too little, they would be disciplined. Informal work groups emerged, enforcing output norms lower than those management wanted, using emotional and physical sanctions. Further studies analysed informal group structure in depth, finding that supervisory behaviour with respect to informal groups was important. Managers who listened and communicated well were likely to be more integrated into work groups.

---

[3] 'History is the graveyard of aristocracies' is my favourite.
[4] This section relies on Rose, 1988. The original is Roethlisberger and Dickson, 1939.

The results had potentially radical implications. Workers would apparently act against self-interest (i.e. maximizing earnings) by obeying group output restriction norms. Managers who integrated with informal groups, using what would later be called a management 'style', gained much better understanding of group structure and how to manipulate it. Such groups could be used to improve output. In these studies we see the seeds of the organizational behaviour discipline—in its concern with intrinsic (non-economic) motivators, teams, and team building and leadership. We can also see a logic which leads to the development of the modern human resource function; individual and collective affect (emotional states) may have an impact on firm performance, and it is thus worth investing to control these variables. More immediately, it allowed one of the key researchers, Elton Mayo, to identify worker discontent as 'anomie' remediable by intervention designed to restore Pareto equilibrium to the social system of the factory. The intervention points were selection of workers, allocation and organization of tasks, leadership style, and the construction of teams (Guillen, 1994). The hallmark of human relation theories was to see organizations as 'human cooperative systems' rather than 'mechanical contraptions' (Mayo, 1933). Since cooperation was the objective, unions were peripheral to the analysis.

Hawthorne in particular and the human relations school in general have been subject to a number of criticisms (Landsberger, 1958). One academic commentator has even argued that Hawthorne was part of a plot by Harvard Business School (where Mayo worked) to achieve industrial legitimacy (O'Connor, 1999). However, the impact of human relations thought on subsequent academic research agendas is considerable, and the notion that the 'mechanical' and the 'social' systems of industrial enterprises must be jointly maximized was exported from the USA, most particularly in the work of the Tavistock Institute in the UK.

In an influential study, Guillen (1994) has analysed the theoretical development of both scientific management and human relations thought, and their impact on business practice in four Western countries. He argues that:

> The development of engineering as a profession was the direct cause of scientific management, much as the development of social-psychological science accounted for the appearance of the human relations paradigm.
>
> (Guillen, 1994: 26)

Scientific management adoption always precedes human relations adoption, and indeed in Germany he finds, for various reasons, human relations thinking has little effect on practice. The more consistent impact of scientific management on production is associated with the simultaneous development of cost accounting, production and inventory controls, and incentive schemes (also developed by engineers) (Guillen, 1994: 41).

If, as in the USA, human relations thinking emerges as a solution to problems of labour unrest generated by the application of scientific management, its ideological component becomes important. Several eminent sociologists in the 1950s, such as Daniel Bell, C. Wright Mills, and W. H. Whyte, saw human relations as a manipulative technique promoting solely managerial ends. Later Marxist sociologists, such as Braverman quoted earlier, saw it as 'manufacturing consent' (see also Buroway, 1979 and Sabel, 1982). In Britain, however, it gave rise to a set of concerns about humanizing the workplace through the reorganization of work.[5]

One key question emerging here is the relative primacy of engineering and social considerations. Does one, as Braverman implies above, (a) optimize on process efficiency and productivity, and mould social concerns around that (as the human relations approach implies); or (b) is it worthwhile to choose a sub-optimal production technique because it has compensatory effects on the workplace as social system which, in turn, positively affects some performance measure? Framing it this way reveals that it is almost certainly an empirical question. Analysing the literature on job design reveals at a more abstract level why the answer is more commonly (a) than (b) and, by extension, why many modern industries—including many service businesses—have Taylorist job design (but not always Taylorist management styles; Batt and Moynihan, 2002). To pursue this we need to cross the Atlantic and go underground.

Mines and Machines

Historically, coal mines produced much conflict between managers and workers and strong unions. They displayed many of the features, discussed above as supporting unions, that are difficult to manage; spot contracting, strong occupational communities, elements of monopoly (you can't move the coal to another workforce), and product market power (it's a major source of energy). But mines were late to automate. In the immediate post-World War II period, in the face of high demand for coal, automation came in the form of long-wall coal mining.

The process was studied by the Tavistock Institute, which had developed a variant of the human relations approach. A key concept was that of the 'socio-technical system', stressing the inter-relatedness of technical and social elements of an organization and the objective of *joint* optimization—optimal technical performance and quality of working life. The change to long-wall

---

[5] Guillen puts this 'peculiarly British' (274) phenomenon down to the simultaneous application of scientific management and human relations thinking; he, however, also argues that structural contingency theory began in the USA, not Britain. He is probably wrong.

mining is straightforward to describe. The manual system involved autonomous self-selecting groups of six miners, working in pairs across three shifts, and paid according to output; three main activities were involved—preparing the coal face for digging, 'getting' or digging the coal, and moving the supports and transport forward to the new coal face exposed by getting. Each group was responsible for a particular piece of the coal face, could adapt work methods to the face, and could decide how to split the rewards. The 'long-wall' method dissolved the groups and created three large groups, by shift, with specialization by shift into preparation, getting, and advancing activities. Payment systems also changed. The new system was safer and cleaner than the old, and involved less volatility in earnings.

Chaos followed. Each shift, involving less cohesive groups, had no direct interest in the activities of the next shift. Work was often incomplete, leading to poor levels of equipment utilization, and output was much lower than potential. Other measures deteriorated; there was increased sickness and absenteeism, increased conflict, and workforce dissatisfaction. The researchers, Trist and Bamforth (1951), argued:

> A qualitative change will have to be effected in the general character of the method so that a social as well as technological whole can come into existence.

(Cited in Rose, 1988: 191)

In the socio-technical systems approach, the division of labour itself appears as a variable, subject to managerial choice. Certain principles emerge. A focus on whole tasks and minimum specification of the rules of task completion, granting responsible autonomy to cohesive groups, understanding the interdependence between tasks, and a focus on making the task meaningful for the employee are the four key ones. Out of this developed both theories and practices.

The most influential theory about the motivational impact of job design, that of Hackman and Oldham (1976) depicted in Figure C4.2, shows a clear debt to Tavistock work. In this approach, core job design dimensions such as skill variety, autonomy, and feedback ultimately generate both psychological states, such as satisfaction and motivation, and behavioural outcomes, such as retention and performance; crucially, there is an individual difference variable mediating the model—the worker's 'growth needs strength'—which means selection of the appropriate individual is a necessary condition for the model to operate. Crucially also, there are no economic (can one find capable workers with growth needs in this labour market?) or engineering (does this organization of work outperform scientific management?) parameters built into the model.

The evidence of subsequent attempts at improving productivity and performance through job redesign are mixed. Wall et al. (1987) and Kelly (1992) argue that the performance improvements resulting from job redesign and

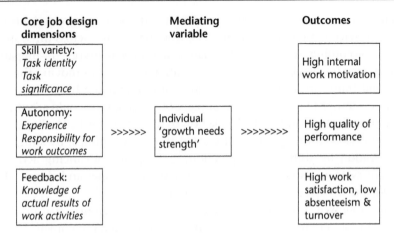

Figure C4.2. The Hackman–Oldham model.

enrichment are more elusive than its impact on the positive psychological states specified in the model. Empirical examples of job redesign exercises, notably in Scandinavia and particularly in the automobile industry, were ultimately abandoned (Jurgens et al., 1993). In fact, the influence of scientific management has spread from its manufacturing 'home' to large bureaucratic organizations in the service sector. Call centres in a variety of sectors appear to be organized on Taylorist lines, with customer service representatives working with low skill levels and pay, simplified tasks embedded in 'scripts', call monitoring with set call targets, and no job rotation.

This ought not to be interpreted necessarily as a triumph of scientific management. First, human relations thinking and the adoption of its techniques was often associated with the creation of personnel departments. Guillen (1994: 73–4) notes the rapid spread of personnel departments in manufacturing in the USA in the second quarter of the twentieth century. Significant organizational changes followed from the ideas of human relations; personnel departments became the modern human resources departments whose toolkit is the human relations legacy.

Second, there is an academic legacy. As Rose notes:

> Technology supplanted the human relations climate as the favourite variable for explaining human behaviour...increasingly, investigators took the title of "organisation theorists". Combined with applied psychology, the sociology of organisations formed the core of a newly popular and heavily promoted academic area, organisational behaviour.

(Rose, 1988).

We shall look at both the practice of human resource management and theories of organizational behaviour later.

However, the third part of the legacy lies in the particular blend of scientific management and human relations insights which is the Toyota production system. Originating in the car industry in Japan, it rests on principles that have been exported and copied in other countries and industries.

Lean, but not Mean

In the 1980s and 1990s, a wave of Asian competition worried Western business people. Japanese firms, in particular, appeared to out-compete Western firms in a variety of manufacturing sectors, notably cars and consumer electronics, and a rash of management texts appeared arguing this was 'cultural'— to do with specifically Japanese ethics, norms, and practices (Ouchi, 1981; Pascale and Athos, 1981; see also Chapter 9). Pretty soon, it became clear that rather more concrete and less idiosyncratic practices of lean production were at the core of success (Cusumano, 1985; Hayes et al., 1988).

Lean manufacturing is an optimizing approach employing many scientific management principles; it minimizes production costs, inventories, and job cycle times. However, it is focused on demand rather than supply in two ways: customer orders trigger production, rather than the other way round, and any activity or resource in the production process which does not provide customer value is eliminated (Holweg, 2007). Monetary incentives are downplayed, and teams are important for motivation, control, and continuous improvement. If we compare this with Taylor's principles above, we can see that the main survivor is standardization and optimization of tasks. Crucially, conception is not separated from execution in process improvement, and close and expensive supervision is deemed unnecessary.

In Toyota, there are four basic rules underpinning the production system.

1. All work is highly specified in terms of content, sequence, timing, and outcome.
2. Every customer–supplier connection must be direct, and there must be unambiguous ('yes or no') two-way communication.
3. The pathway for every product and service must be as simple and direct as possible.
4. Any improvement must be made scientifically, under the guidance of a teacher, at the lowest level possible in the organization.

(Spear and Bowen, 1999: 4)

Any workforce operating to this system must display consummate cooperation. Jurgens et al. (1993) have laid out the key aspects of the 'social dimension' at Toyota:

1. Job security supporting both employee commitment and return on training investment.
2. Job flexibility—vertical and horizontal.
3. High entry qualifications and on-the-job training.
4. High status of direct production—inclusive of quality control and maintenance.
5. Primacy of groups for performance, improvement, and social identity, but...
6. Strong individual performance rating.
7. Strict production targets and time flexibility.

It is by now something of a cliché to observe that this system involved the adoption and systematization of Western ideas about scientific management and human relations into an improved manufacturing strategy with which to beat Western firms. As Guillen notes (1994: 292–3), Western authors responded enthusiastically, if not always with full understanding. Interesting questions arise about why lean production emerged in Japan. Cusumano argues that contingencies such as protectionism and union busting in the post-war period are important (1985: 72–182). The reverse question—why did it not also develop from its twin roots in the West?—is equally interesting. It may have something to do with the changing nature of the Western managerial firm (Davis, 2009).

However, two developments from human relations did occur in the West after 1945. The first is an issue of practice; the rise of human resource management (henceforward HRM). The second is the development of the business discipline of organizational behaviour; I will look at each in turn.

Managing HRM; and What it Tells us About Managing

In this section, we trace the lineage of the human relations approach down to the twenty-first century. In fact, there are several descendants to consider. In practical terms, we need to look at the evolution of the human resource function within the firm. There are, of course, enormous variations in human resource practice, but one may generalize to say that the concerns of the human relations movement with the management of people have been generalized into a set of practices employed by firms concerning recruitment, retention, rewards, motivation, and commitment of employees. In many firms, there is a key departure from the spirit of the human relations approach in that HRM is a staff function separate from line management; arguably this is a central issue in how HRM works and we will discuss it both specifically, in terms of the effectiveness of HRM, and generally, in terms of line-staff arrangements within the firm. There is also an academic discipline called HRM, which tends to focus on the design and effectiveness of individual HRM practices and the firm performance implications of combinations or bundles of practices; it involves serious measurement problems.

The second descendant is the very sizeable academic field of organizational behaviour (OB). Its theoretical agenda is (somewhat distressingly) similar to that of human relations, but it is methodologically far more sophisticated, in part because it has developed as a branch of applied psychology. It is not primarily concerned with rationality—compared with economics rationality it is treated as a variable not an assumption—and not always concerned to measure business outcomes such as efficiency or productivity. This chapter seeks to illustrate rather than summarize this field and its contribution, and it will do so by looking at how OB deals with two concepts which have been central so far: hierarchy and contract. These emerge prominently in the OB literature as studies of leadership and the psychological contract respectively. I turn first to HRM.

The Emergence of HRM

One of the most influential modern models of the practice of the HRM function has been developed by Ulrich (1997, 2005). He argues for the organization of the function to be framed around three types of activity, all of which support the activities of line managers in the management of people in different ways.

- **Shared services** is the set of basic administrative tasks in the management of a workforce through which economies of scale may be achieved by the concentration of activity on an enterprise-wide basis. These activities include management of payroll, absence control, and employee databases more generally. The measures of performance of such units are essentially the quality and timeliness of data provision and cost. There are clear outsourcing possibilities, since inter-firm scale economies can be exploited subject to confidentiality concerns about employee data.

- **Centres of expertise** focus on areas of knowledge where there may also be economies of scale but where the complexity of information required is such that line managers require support and advice where relevant issues arise. Examples would be selection of employees, designing and applying reward systems (including pensions), employee relations (including dealing with unions), training, and termination of employees' contracts. Compliance with relevant law is often an issue in all such areas. Performance measures here are more complicated, but would include, in addition to those for shared services, some line management evaluation of quality of advice.

- **Business partnership** involves small HRM teams working with high-level line management to improve firm performance. Examples would be issues such as strategy implementation, organizational design, and change management. HRM is central to the business of the firm, assisting it to maximize its use of human assets. Measurement problems here are intractable.

This is a simplifying, prescriptive, and aspirational model which summarizes both the activities a firm may require from its HRM function and also the variance in relationships between line and staff. The shared service and expertise activities essentially deal with, first, the rise in bureaucratic employment issues within large firms and, second, the regulatory burden on employment. The assumptions underlying business partnership are qualitatively very different and are tied to a resource-based view of the firm (see Chapter 7); they include the idea that the management of human assets may be a source of competitive advantage. Pfeffer (1995) argued that there was a substantial body of evidence demonstrating the connection between how firms manage their people and the economic results achieved. The relevance of this model here is twofold. First, using this threefold division is a useful heuristic for describing the development of HRM practice historically. Second, as we shall see, it outlines the core tensions within HRM practice. Let us look at each in turn.

Two early and uncorrelated developments are noteworthy. First, in some large nineteenth-century firms, 'welfare' departments were established concerned with the provision of canteens, medical services, housing, and in some cases social work. This was particularly strong in Germany. In the UK it was associated with philanthropy by owners whose concerns were religious or social, rather than economic, for example Cadbury, the confectionery firm, and Wedgwood in ceramics. The earliest recorded such department in the USA was the National Cash Register Company in 1897 (Wren, 2005: 186). Retrospective cynicism might see in these ventures the pursuit of business objectives—for example, seeing the company doctor might be seen as a form of absence control—but there is probably also a genuinely altruistic interpretation, and there is no systematic evidence of cost–benefit analysis in the well-documented examples such as Cadbury (Smith et al., 1990).

More focused activities were driven slightly later by the workforce quality needs of scientific management; selective hiring, incentive pay, and absence control were all central to the pursuit of efficiency. If this pursuit generated recourse to trade unions by employees, a set of bargaining and consultation arrangements needed to be designed and monitored. In addition, as Gospel notes:

> Over time, in most countries, there has been a gradual build up in (government) intervention in terms of rights off the job (state welfare and pension systems) rights on the job (workmen's compensation, health and safety, racial, and sexual equality legislation) and regulation of collective employment matters (the law on trade unions, collective bargaining and information and consultation at work).
>
> (Gospel, 2007: 423).

These tendencies came together in the post-World War I period in many firms and countries through the formation of a 'Personnel Department', which was essentially a lubricant to the bureaucratic employment relationship providing shared service and expertise type functions to line management. As such, it tended towards reactive response and problem solving according to a line management agenda or in order to ensure compliance with external rules. This should not lead to a view of the personnel department as marginal. For example, Dobbin et al. (1993) argue that a combination of equal opportunity law and the power of the personnel function is a better explanation for the spread of internal labour market structures in the USA than is the efficiency argument on which Williamson relies. But, significantly, the role did not include the strategic elements Ulrich identifies.

The major change to what we now characterize as HRM came in the 1970s and 1980s, first in the USA. It required several intellectual developments elsewhere and, as is frequently the case, a sharp shock and an opportunity. First, if HRM were to influence strategy, somebody had to be doing strategy explicitly. As I show below, the academic study of business strategy was a relatively late arrival, and even early versions such as strategic planning post-date the emergence of personnel departments. But, second, the role of the management of people as an element in strategy needed to be articulated in a particular form. Once this intellectual toolkit was in place, and employees could be seen as a source of competitive advantage, the stage was clear for HRM to make a bid to be strategic.

The sharp shock was provided by the emergence of Japanese competition described above, and in particular the use of what became described as high-performance work practices within systems such as Toyotaism. Consummate cooperation required HRM technique. The opportunity was provided by the removal of a constraint; the decline of trade unionism. The language of personnel management changed. An influential text was Beer's *Managing*

Human Assets, embedding the idea that 'people are an asset not a cost' and thus the HR function needs to be 'fully aware of and involved in all strategic and business decisions' (Beer et al., 1984: 292). HRM became strategic—defined as the 'pattern of planned human resource deployments and activities intended to enable an organisation to achieve its goals' (Wright and McMahan, 1992: 298). And the idea resonated among popular strategy authors such as Prahalad and Hamel (1990: 1994), who argued that the way firms organize and leverage our intangible assets, primarily vested in people, was one of the most fundamental and sustainable sources of competitive advantage.

Three central issues emerged to beset this literature. First, what *were* these HRM practices that one deployed in order to generate competitive advantage and how did one deploy them? Second, were these practices the same everywhere; if firm strategies were different, were different bundles of HRM practices required to deliver them? Third, how could one measure the impact of HRM practices on competitive advantage? I will look at each in turn.

Pfeffer (1994) offers seven *generic* (i.e. universally applicable) practices for building profits by 'putting people first'. They are:

1. employment security
2. selective hiring
3. self-managed teams or team working
4. high pay contingent on company performance
5. extensive training
6. reduction of status differences
7. sharing information[6]

This is an influential list but it is not the only list in play. Meta-analysis of the field (Wall and Wood, 2005) shows a variety of different items listed as HRM practices across a variety of studies. There is no widespread agreement on what should be included or excluded. So there is not a 'theory' of HRM and performance here. It is not clear whether the effects of these practices on performance would simply be additive or whether in particular combinations the whole would be greater than the sum of the parts. Some empirical studies around the relationship between these kinds of practices and performance variables generate very specific numbers; Huselid (1995), for example, argued that a dollar value of firm benefit could be identified for unit value increases in HRM use. However, the path by which these practices generate outputs remains obscure. The proposition that any firm adopting any HRM practice

---

[6] The reader may note the similarity between this set and those listed as characteristic of Toyota on pages 83–4.

or set thereof will generate a performance improvement is weak. As Macduffie has remarked:

> Innovative human resource practices are likely to contribute to improved economic performance only when three conditions are met: when employees possess knowledge and skills that managers lack, when employees are motivated to apply this skill and knowledge through discretionary effort; and when the firm's business or production strategy can only be achieved when employees contribute such discretionary effort.
>
> (Macduffie, 1995: 199).

However socially unattractive the Taylorist model of the excellent worker might be, it contains a model of the relationship between labour input, production process, output, and reward that studies of the HRM performance link have so far failed to generate. This is of course partly because the unit of analysis for Taylor is the individual, while that for HRM studies is variable.

The second issue concerns inter-firm variation; if strategies are different, maybe HRM practices need to be. Wall and Wood (2005: 431) identify three types of 'fit' between HRM practices and the firm.

- *Internal fit* 'posits synergy among the practices, meaning that their collective effect will be greater than the sum of their individual parts'.
- *Organizational fit* 'concerns the role of HRM in enhancing the effectiveness of other organizational practices or technologies, and vice versa'.
- *Strategic fit* 'assumes that HRM practices need to be aligned with the organization's strategy to have their full effect on performance'.

The first concept of fit suggests that some combinations of HRM practice may be better than others. The second implies that some combinations may optimize the performance of certain technologies. But the third reaches to the heart of Ulrich's idea about the organization of the HRM department and its relationship to line management. For Ulrich, the essence of competitive advantage from HRM is the HRM–line relationship, rather than a bundle of practices. The bundle of practices is a dependent variable. Let us look at the line-staff relationship.

Witzel (2002: 51–4) offers an interesting set of observations. First, he notes that the line–staff division that became common practice and parlance in the business world originated in military organization; he uses the Prussian army in the nineteenth century as an example. Second, he noted that the line units had to be Taylorist and the staff units should coordinate, integrate, and be goal focused. Third, he offers a specific example—the Franco-Prussian War of 1870—as an example; less well armed and less experienced Prussian troops defeated an apparently superior French army by virtue of the line–staff relationship that generated flexibility and rapid response. Fourth, he notes that a prominent early management theorist, the American Harrington Emerson, observed this conflict directly and incorporated his views of it in his writings. The core issue that links nineteenth-century military operations and twenty-first-century management of people in organizations is the observation that an organizational attribute, rather than a capital or resource asset, can be the source of competitive advantage and, moreover, that organizations that are asset-poor can outcompete those that are asset-rich. The idea that the smart can outperform the rich is one of the most seductive, and dangerous, ideas in modern management theory, and we will return to it later.

The third problem is of a rather different nature. Whatever the claimed impact of HRM practices on a dependent variable such as performance, it is still unclear whether any competitive advantage is being generated. If, as many authors have implied, effective management of human assets leads to competitive success, it is necessary to show that these 'bundles' of practices can be implemented better by some firms than others. There has been little analysis of this. In the car industry example used above, the key performance variable 'man hours per car' has fallen across the industry, in part as a consequence of the adoption of high-performance work practices, but this can simply generate a price war rather than a competitive advantage (Jurgens et al., 1993; Willman and Winch, 1985).

De Menezes et al. (2010) have used data on both operations management practice and the use of HRM in a longitudinal study that indicates the way forward in this field. They show that firms that innovate early and integrate HRM with production practices generate sustained performance improvement, arguing:

> An integrated managerial philosophy is potentially a source of competitive advantage, highlighting the importance of continuous improvement and learning that is often allied to the lean production concept.
>
> (De Menezes et al., 2010: 1065).

This integration is part of the Toyota story I discussed earlier.

So, in the HRM field, it does not seem that simply adopting a practice or set of practices employed by a successful competitor offers a high chance of replicating their success. Many firms in many sectors do so for both practices and for targets, in processes known as 'benchmarking'. As we have seen, we may improve an aspect of our own firm's performance by adopting 'best practice' but it may not improve *relative* performance. However, there are other issues to consider. The anthropology literature on 'cargo cults' describes indigenous people in the Pacific Islands building piers and even airstrips in the mistaken belief that doing so would lure the ships and aeroplanes filled with manufactured goods that arrived when Europeans did the same building. It is a simple mistake of cause and effect which arises from not possessing full information on the causal chain, or modelling causality according to some mistaken model. Methodologically, it involves sampling on the dependent variable and can give rise to unexpected, often disappointing, results. In the HRM field, many studies even use cross-sectional data to study allegedly causal HRM performance relationships; these methods cannot discriminate effectively between firms that might be improving performance using HRM and firms that have improved performance and so can afford the investment in HRM.

So, why do firms, in this area as in others, copy practices so much? In the absence of legal constraint, it may be that professional standards in a management field, such as those noted by Dobbin et al. above in the spread of internal labour markets, cause convergence. It may be more simply that copying is the safe thing to do; herding is a risk-averse survival strategy for animals, and it may be for firms. In this case the reduction of uncertainty in environments where signals of competitive success are drowned by noise may be served by copying. We shall pursue these considerations about *bounded rationality* in the next theme.

Organizational Behaviour

This has recently been influentially defined as:

> A field of study devoted to understanding, explaining, and ultimately improving the **attitudes** and **behaviours** of individuals and groups in organizations.
>
> (Colquitt, LePine, and Wesson, 2009: 7).

Let us deal with the omissions from this definition first. Organizational behaviour (OB) academics are not primarily concerned with firms, or with firm performance. And they seldom study markets. The disciplines on which OB draws—psychology and social psychology—are deployed in markets by others (looking at consumer behaviour—see below) but these literatures have emerged separately. The field looks at affective states as worthy of study in themselves, and generates sophisticated models to relate affective states to each other and, sometimes, to behaviours. It is highly fragmented, with no core body of theory delineating a model of human behaviour comparable to economic man, and it is arguably held together by rather looser assumptions and a commonality of method (Pfeffer, 1997).

Two sub-fields illustrate how this field differs from one making assumptions about rationality and self-interest. Economic approaches use principal–agent theory to describe hierarchy, OB talks about leadership. Economists describe employment contracts as incomplete, OB academics study how these silences

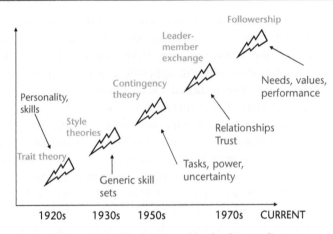

Figure C4.3. The history of leadership studies.

are filled. We look at each in turn, as illustrations of the difference between rational choice and psychological approaches to organization.

Concern with leadership precedes the business literature on the matter by centuries, with much of the literature concerned with military leadership. The academic business literature emerges in the 1920s and the unit of analysis is the individual; leadership is about traits possessed by individuals, which may be innate (dispositional) or acquired (through experience). Trait theory is fundamentally depressing for the business literature because it implies that efforts to improve the quality of leadership in an organization must be limited to appropriate selection. The development historically of the literature away from this (Figure C4.3) may be viewed as an attempt to embrace an increasing array of organizational variables in order to understand how leadership might be developed or enhanced within particular contexts.

Sensitivity both to the idea of leadership as an attribute of a finite set of persons and more generally to any notion of innate advantage was high in the West between the rise of the Third Reich and the decoding of DNA (which was to provide a language for discussion of genetics). Leadership became about behaviours that individuals could practise, although it was acknowledged that different individuals might practise them to different degrees. The approach was developed in the Midwest of the USA. The Ohio State University studies identified two categories of leadership behaviour:

- **Consideration**: develop relationships of mutual trust, respect for followers' ideas, regard for their feelings.

- **Initiating structure**: define and structure one's own role and those of one's followers.

These behaviours could score either high or low and were independent of each other, but it was claimed that the most effective leaders were high on both. The research was based on questionnaires to leaders and subordinates. The Michigan Leadership Studies began in the 1950s and indicated that leaders could be classified as either 'employee centered' or 'job centered'. Twin categories of 'task' and 'relationship' behaviours—similar to the Ohio studies— were identified which were theoretically independent but empirically associated in being 'high' in the most effective behavioural pattern.

These two categories have, in modified form, very wide currency in the management literature, being used in the analysis of teams and teamwork at the micro level, and organizational culture at the macro level. They have deep roots in anthropology (see Chapter 9). They replicate in this literature the broad engineering concern for efficiency and the human relations concern for work relations respectively. It is thus worth mentioning that in these large-scale sets of studies direct measures of efficiency were not taken.

Although these studies used questionnaires from subordinates, they were still generic in arguing for leadership behaviours independent of either context or audience. The next two developments in leadership research addressed each in turn. Contingency theories suggested sources of variation in leadership effectiveness based in the power of the leader, the nature of the task to be completed, and the level of uncertainty in the work situation; this mirrored an almost contemporary development of contingency theory in organizational design at the macro level (see Chapter 5).

Subsequent theories placed more emphasis on the leader–follower relationship as the unit of analysis; leader–follower relationships were variable, but patterned, and follower reactions to leadership became increasingly the most significant dependent variable. For Yukl (2006: 23):

> leadership is the process of influencing others to understand and agree about what needs to be done and how to do it.

Increasingly, the desired outcomes of leadership were seen to be follower emotional states and behaviours associated with them. Increasingly, too, the leadership behaviours seen to be associated with such states and behaviours were distanced from monitoring and incentives. A simple interpretation of what an effective economic 'principal' should do would be 'bad leadership' in the OB literature. A corollary of this is that many writers on organizations treat the combination of monitoring, incentives, and discipline as counter-performative; that is, likely to generate precisely the outcome it was intended to avoid (Ghoshal and Moran, 1996). Leadership is a set of behaviours performed *independent of* hierarchical position.

A pervasive theme in the literature contrasts ostensibly rational activities around monitoring and exchange relationships with those focused more on affect. For example, Bass (1985) distinguishes transactional leaders who motivate employees through an exchange process involving rewarding and correcting, from transformational leaders who motivate employees by activating their higher-order needs, offering inspiration, intellectual stimulation, and individualized consideration. Using different language but basically the same dichotomy, Kotter (1990) distinguishes managerial activities such as planning, budgeting, and controlling—the business of 'coping with large organisations'—from leadership activities such as setting direction, providing vision and inspiration, and building teams. In more modern versions, ideas such as 'authenticity' and 'charisma' are used to describe effective leadership.

Now this literature is a bit difficult to evaluate, not least because the definition of leadership is elusive. The prime concern is with its impact on followers and any influences that generate positive affect can fall into the definition; indeed some authors argue it is difficult to define but easy to observe, which scarcely makes it the subject of academic activity. Moreover, it is not always clear whether the unit of analysis is the individual, a dyadic relationship, a set of behaviours, or an outcome. But it is generally premised on the idea that a hierarchy based on monitoring and transaction will underperform one in which members are experiencing shared objectives and positive affect. Or to put it another way, non-rational behaviour is important.

A Psychological Contract?

'A verbal agreement is not worth the paper it's written on.'

(attrib. Samuel Goldwin)[7]

Sociologists have long been interested in exchange. But these *social* exchange theorists tended to take a broader view than simple economic exchange. Resources, both tangible and intangible, are included, and there needs to be some notion of balance (Homans, 1961: 13). Social exchange is voluntary and continuing but it entails unspecified obligations about the exact nature of reciprocity (Blau, 1964). Where social exchange continues, norms of reciprocity are established, such that people both help and avoid injuring those who have helped them. Continuing reciprocity generates trust between exchangers, which may provide the basis for enduring and profitable network linkages. Trust relations have dynamics, such that trustworthiness is rewarded and its loss can lead to a cycle of mistrust (Fox, 1974).

One important strand of OB develops this line of thought to analyse employment relationships: psychological contract research. Again, the Human

---

[7] I think he meant oral.

Relations movement is in the lineage. Argyris (1960) used the term 'psychological work contract' to describe a Hawthorne-type relationship between informal work groups and managers involving a trade between stable wages and employment security for the former and higher productivity and fewer grievances for the latter. The cognitive elements in this approach were refined by Schein (1970) in a focus on the matching of expectations and exchange performance where each party might have a different set of both preferences and perspectives.

But the defining approach that has generated the bulk of research on the matter is from Rousseau. She defines a psychological contract as:

> Individual beliefs, shaped by the organisation, regarding terms of an exchange agreement between individuals and their organisation.
>
> (Rousseau, 1995: 9).

The content of the contract involves both tangible and intangible elements; a considerable segment may be 'promise-based obligations' made by one party concerning long-term commitments to the other, and these promises themselves may be both implicit and explicit. While there is much debate and critique about the definition of constructs (see Conway and Briner, 2005), it is clear what the objective is here; to capture the sum of the relationship between employee and employer where that relationship involves, for the employee at least, a massively significant social exchange where both economic interests and psychological concerns are embraced. The former is captured by the notion of a transactional contract; typically short-term economic exchanges with limited emotional investment. The latter is captured by a second dimension, the relational contract, where both parties make considerable idiosyncratic investments (Taylor and Tekleab, 2005: 263–4). The underlying ideas are familiar from Williamson's work.

Psychological contract breach—termed rather emotively 'violation'—is both significant and common; employees, at least, perceive violation, in terms of broken promises, quite frequently, and studies have indicated consequences, depending on the seriousness of the breach (or its perception) in terms of lowered satisfaction or commitment or even absence and exit (Turnley and Feldman, 1999). Breach appears to have a bigger downside impact than contract fulfilment has as an upside, and Rousseau herself (2005) appears to see them both as independent constructs rather than a dichotomy or continuum; employees report both fulfilment and breach coexisting within the same contract. Repeated breach generates a shift from a relational to a more transactional contract.

The approach has been criticized. Rousseau appears to focus primarily on the *employee*, a tendency reinforced by over-reliance on her graduating MBA students as research subjects (Guest, 1998). However, even if it is only a theory of employee behaviour, it has substantial scope. It is not particularly helpful to management practice, since the circumstances under which an individual generates a psychological contract involve individual difference variables and are quite idiographic. But it does quite clearly allow one to fill in the silences in the employment contract noted by Williamson. Moreover, it stresses the social and psychological factors that allow for the effective operation of highly incomplete contracts in ways that help to understand the impact of affect on contract performance.

There are clear links to institutional economics, not least the distinction between relational and transactional contract dimensions. Rousseau herself explicitly uses Hirschman's exit-voice model in explaining responses to violation (1995: 134). And many violations develop out of what are fundamentally agency problems; promises are made by recruiters or line managers who then leave the organization, which subsequently neither recognizes nor honours the perceived promise. However, at the most fundamental level, similarity is assured by the fact that the psychological contract approach is a bounded rationality model.

This can be elaborated by looking at how individuals construct contracts. Rousseau suggests individuals have contract schema; prototypical mental models about how contracts work. These are rooted in 'predispositions' then based on work history, and develop by accumulation of information about contract obligations in work settings. Typically, new entrants have incomplete information about the organization, and Williamsonian problems about the construction of complicated contingent claims contracts covering future contribution and reward. Information cues originate with co-workers or managers, and information search and processing is discontinuous—higher where there may be contract violation. Once formed, they have heuristic characteristics (see Theme 4); they frame information search and are resistant to change (Rousseau, 1995: 27–36; 2001).

Conclusion

This chapter has tried to trace the human relations legacy down to more modern theories (OB) and practices (HRM). At the most fundamental level, both are concerned to explore or manage the non-rational side of organizations, or at least the interactions between rational and non-rational. OB is based on the premise that it is intrinsically worthwhile to study attitudes and behaviours in organizations independent of any concerns with measures of performance. Now, as a manager, one might study leadership with a view to improving personal performance or career prospects, but this raises rather different issues.

HRM is based on the premise that one can apply this knowledge to how people are managed in organizations in order to improve performance.

The contrast between studying principals operating in hierarchies versus leaders operating in teams, or between studying economic versus psychological contracts, is considerable and basically turns on the rationality issue. Good economic principalship involves monitoring and incentive practices that in many circumstances identified in OB would constitute bad leadership by ignoring such irrationalities as vision and inspiration (and vice versa). If we want to understand further the differences between these two approaches, we need to look in the next theme at how rationality has been dealt with in the management field; it is quite a good story.

Theme 4

A Short History of Bounded Rationality

'Good reasons must, of force, give place to better.'

(Shakespeare, *Julius Caesar*, Act iv, scene iii, l. 202)

Introduction

In the last chapter, I spent some time talking about the study of affect. I also tried to show why affect matters to business performance. If the pursuit of the apparently rational (improved performance) can be attained by the achievement of the non-rational (positive employee affect) we have clearly come to the point where we need to concern ourselves with the study of rationality in the context of management. This might seem like an unpromising field; what ideas about rationality can management theorists have that philosophers, or even economists, have not already elaborated?

In fact, the answer is more positive. Two economists, Coase and Williamson, won the Nobel Prize for thinking about firms rather than markets. Bounded rationality is clearly implicit in Coase, and very explicit in Williamson, for whom, without bounded rationality, there are no firms. Two non-economists, Simon and Kahneman, won it for thinking about decision-making behaviour; not how decisions ought to be made or could be modelled, but how they were made in practice. They found that individual decision-making is not perfectly rational. No surprises there. Adam Smith had long before used the idea of 'common sense' to address the limitations of individual decision-making. The surprise came in discovering patterns of non-rationality in decision-making, by empirical study.

In this theme, I look at the development of theories around bounded and impaired rationality. The theorizing involves some psychology and sociology. Concerns with bounded rationality prompted economists to discover the concept of information asymmetry so that they could hang on to the optimization and the maths. And studies of the limitations on cognition led to the vast literature on decision biases which has not only changed the study of decision-making but in doing so affected disciplines such as finance and strategy. However, the idea of bounded rationality is problematic because it is loosely used, often without definition. Herbert Simon, who arguably originated the modern debate, had argued against a hyper-rational conception of the economic agent, saying that it assumed people know things they do not know and can perform calculations that they cannot do; unfortunately this confounds at least two sources of deviation from economic optimizing behaviour. If one adds to this the idea of the existence of systematic decision biases, then one has at least three senses in which the term bounded rationality is used:

1. The human brain is a slow computer and it has severe information processing limitations; this is close to Simon's original idea.

2. The human brain is a very fast and optimizing computer that sometimes lacks information and is aware of information search costs; this is often how economists use the term.

3. The brain computes slowly and also the software has serious design problems; it is really just a series of apps. This is essentially the behavioural decision-making perspective.

We will look at each in turn. Note that the unit of analysis for 1 is the decision itself, particularly its complexity. For 2, the prime unit is the information environment. For 3, the prime unit of analysis is the individual.

Simon Says

We begin with the Carnegie Mellon school of empirical decision analysis; it is one of the most significant contributions of management theory to social science. Simon's original concern was as follows:

> Social sciences suffer from acute schizophrenia in their treatment of rationality. At one extreme, economists attribute to economic man a preposterously omniscient rationality... At the other extreme are those tendencies in social psychology... that try to reduce all cognition to affect.
>
> (Simon, 1947/1997: 87)[1]

He follows this with the famous remark that 'human behaviour is *intendedly* rational, but only *boundedly* so' (1997: 88). So, part of this was a protest about

---

[1] The reference is to the 4th edition of *Administrative Behaviour*. The first was in 1947.

extremes, but in order to move from protest to concept, Simon needed not simply to offer a criticism of economic man but also a theory of decision-making. Let us look at each in turn; both the critique and the subsequent theory were empirically based.

The model of economic man causing Simon so much concern had the following characteristics:

> An actor will choose an action rationally, based on a hierarchy of preferences (values, utilities) that promises to maximize benefits and minimize costs, or more precisely that promises a net gain of benefits minus costs or, still more precisely, that promises the highest net benefit to the actor and the highest probability of its occurrence.

> (Zey, 1998: 2)

Now it is worth saying, first, that this conception is not exclusive to economics since it underpins social exchange theory and rational choice theory in sociology, and, second, that not all modern economists, particularly behavioural economists, use it any more. Second, it has been subjected to rigorous, if not brutal, criticism by social theorists and philosophers (e.g., Elster, 1989; Sen 1977; for a review, Zey, 1998) and, third, Simon was concerned primarily with how it applied to administrative decisions, rather than its intellectual content; for him, people simply did not do it (Simon, 1997: 92–118).

So what we might term the Carnegie Mellon project developed as an empirically based critique of this hyper-rational decision model. Over subsequent years, Simon and his colleagues, particularly Cyert and March, studied decisions and built a theory of the firm based on decision analysis. Among their key findings were that economic models appear to describe approaches to repetitive and well-defined problems with pre-established options, but that long-term or strategic decisions of a non-repetitive sort appear to generate highly unstructured search and decision processes. Economics provided a valid descriptive model for a category of decisions but:

> We should be sceptical in postulating for humans...elaborate mechanisms for choosing among diverse needs.

> (Simon 1955: 137)

Empirical study of specific organizational processes by Feldman and March revealed:

- Much information that is gathered and communicated has little decision relevance.
- Much information used to justify a decision is collected after the event.
- Much information requested is collected then not used.

- Regardless of information availability, more information is requested.
- Complaints about lack of information coincide with relevant information being ignored.

(Feldman and March, 1981).

Out of these studies, a distinctive concept of bounded rationality emerged (Cyert and March, 1963; Bromiley, 2005: 8–31) and in turn a behavioural theory of the firm based on information processing. The bounded rationality model has individuals making decisions according to sets of rules, and *satisficing*; that is finding solutions that are 'good enough'. Simon's own illustration is of finding a needle in a haystack; satisficing means you stop when you find a needle and economic optimizing means you carry on until you find the sharpest one (but it's not that easy, see below).

When you apply this way of thinking to organizations, what comes out is the following:[2]

- Organizations are bundles of routines for making decisions. The routines allow coordination and increase reliability; they break down the world into manageable parts and economize on cognition. They can be conscious or unconscious (see the discussion on organizational culture in Chapter 9), and they may facilitate change not least because you can have routines about routines (as in quality management in the Toyota system in Chapter 4).

- Non-routine decisions are dealt with by satisficing. Organizations develop aspiration levels exceeding current performance. Aspirations are set by past performance and competitor performance. They have dimensions (content) and levels.

- When there is a gap between aspiration and performance, organizations engage in search; that is, ways of solving the problem. Search can end either when a satisfactory solution is found or by dropping the aspiration level.

- Organizations have slack; this builds up in excess staffing or budgets when times are good. When search kicks in, slack is removed. Removing slack involves negotiation between interest groups. Slack is a necessary concept since it is central to the bounded rationality and satisficing argument in two ways; first that sub-optimal behaviour is endemic and, second, that, as Bromiley nicely puts it, 'No optimal firms lurk in the bushes to attack sub-optimal firms' (2005: 32).

---

[2] This section relies heavily on Phil Bromiley's excellent summary (2005: 18–34). The key original studies are March and Simon (1958) and Cyert, et al. (1956).

The approach attracted its criticism, and not just from believers in optimization. It is hardly a full theory of the firm and it presents the firm as reactive, situated in an environment composed of other reactive firms, but not of institutions, employees, or customers. But the idea of bounded rationality has been hugely influential, and it is not possible to envisage certain subsequent developments in strategy, such as the resource-based view of the firm, without ideas such as organizational routines.

The Power of Sunk Costs: the Reaction in Economics

One of the most direct and easily observable legacies of Carnegie Mellon comes through Oliver Williamson who did his doctorate there, sang the university's praises in a review of his own contribution (Williamson, 2005), and made the concept of bounded rationality a building block of transaction cost economics. Whether it was Simon's concept that Williamson ended up using has been debated (see Dietrich, 1994, for a discussion).

There are two elements here: information complexity and information uncertainty. Information complexity is an attribute of a problem or problem set. An information processing approach like Simon's puts heavy emphasis on it, and the Carnegie Mellon approach to organizational decision-making stressed intra-organizational collaborative routines to solve it. The Williamson approach tends to stress information uncertainty; a strategy for self-interest seeking with guile raises questions about the veracity of information and another Williamson concept—'information impactedness'—refers to the stickiness or difficulty of discovery of information; information impactedness is not a property of individuals but of the contractual circumstance. Another issue concerns *where* in the transactions framework you get bounded rationality and, as Bromiley notes, there is an inconsistency in the use of bounded rationality in Williamson; it exists in the writing of contracts, but not in the design of the governance arrangements; that is, there are endemic problems in contracts, but you can optimize the governance arrangements for contractual forms.

> To assume managers who never learned TCE[3] knew how to structure governance relations according to TCE principles **even before Williamson discovered those principles** conflicts with a bounded rationality assumption.
>
> (Bromiley, 2005: 98).

Now this is a bit more than simply an irritatingly good observation about TCE. The reactions to bounded rationality approaches within economics

---

[3] TCE is transaction cost economics.

varied. To Simon's arguments that the assumptions of optimizing behaviour were implausible, Friedman's response (1953: 14) was simply to say that verisimilitude was irrelevant; 'the more significant the theory, the more unrealistic the assumptions'. Since the theory Friedman was advocating at the time he wrote this made explaining the existence of firms impossible, this was going some. More commonly, the approach was to treat bounded rationality as an information problem of two possible types. First, you could assume lack of knowledge; as an example, in principal agent theory discussed above the principal knows everything except what the agent is doing (and the agent knows everything, so why is he not rich enough to be the principal?). Second, you could argue that acquisition of information has costs and make the cost endogenous to the choice. So, if traditional economic man looks for the sharpest needle in the haystack, and bounded rationality man satisfices with the first needle found, 'information cost' man searches the haystack until the expected returns to further search (finding an even sharper needle) match the expected cost of further search (time). But how could one know enough to do the cost–benefit calculation without knowing where the sharpest needle was?

As Simon (1997: 121–2) and economists themselves (Arrow, 2004: 52) note, this rational expectations approach requires computational powers of the economic agent not only inconsistent with any idea of bounded or limited rationality, but greater than the neoclassical economic concept of rational man we started with. The own goal of incorporating bounded rationality as information cost into economic theory has been to suggest economic actors possess hyper-rationality. If this hyper-rationality extended to economic practitioners themselves, several features of the world in which this author writes in late 2013 become very difficult to explain.

Gigerenzer summarizes this type of bounded rationality simply; the bounds in bounded rationality are merely constraints, under which optimization takes place.

> The idea of optimization under constraints is to propose one or a few constraints (too many would make the mathematics too hard or even intractable) while retaining the idea of optimisation … Introducing real constraints makes the approach more realistic, but maintaining the ideal of optimization, that is, calculating an optimal stopping point, does not.
>
> (Gigerenzer, 2008: 81).

Where the constraint is information cost, one also experiences the 'infinite regress' problem; how much information do you need to have in order to know you should not collect any more information?

Less difficult to explain is why this reaction happened, and it is a unit of analysis issue. If you assume first that bounded rationality is an information problem and second that information problems are functions of contractual situations or broader market circumstances, you can retain models built on optimization and study circumstances in which information issues are a constraint on optimization. This is essentially the approach of modern academic finance (see Chapter 8). If you assert that bounded rationality is an issue about human cognition, then one encounters intractable modelling problems in the absence of theory that predicts precisely to what extent rationality is bounded, whether boundedness is patterned, when it is most likely to kick in, and the extent of interpersonal differences. I turn to literature that worries about these issues.

Recipes for Action

'Thinking is very hard and the mind tries to avoid it whenever possible.'
(Danny Kahneman).

I have discussed a notion of perfect rationality and a couple of ideas about bounded rationality. Simonian bounded rationality implies that it's OK within the boundary. What if we had an idea about rationality which is in some sense systematically impaired? The literature I now turn to on heuristics and decision biases discusses the idea that there may be deviations from rationality which are not about complexity of problems or lack of information but about the idea that we use decision-making tools in which rationality is a variable, not an assumption.

In the 1970s, Danny Kahneman and Amos Tversky started worrying about how people make decisions (Kahneman and Tversky, 1979). In an early study, they presented identical propositions to subjects in an experiment. The two propositions were identical in terms of outcome. If subjects were rational optimizers, the results would have been neutral. They were not. Framing of results mattered. People preferred things that were positively framed (focusing on good outcomes) to those that were negatively framed (showing the same figures, but mentioning the bad). To take a very simple example, if you tell someone a meal has 20% fat content, they react very differently from how they do to the statement that it is 80% fat free.

Figure T4.1 shows diagrammatically what is involved here. The y axis is utility (subjective) and the x axis is value (objective); so we are contrasting subjective and objective evaluation of outcomes. In the top-right quadrant, the curve is an expected utility function, with diminishing marginal returns such that, if gambling, we would not take an even bet because the disutility of a loss outweighs the utility of a similar gain.

By contrast, and this was the novelty, in the lower-left quadrant, the disutility of a loss is greater than its 'objective' value and, if gambling, we

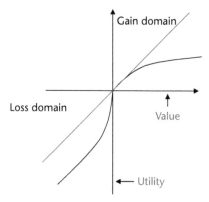

Figure T4.1. Prospect theory.
(*Source*: Kahneman and Tversky, 1979)

chase our losses. Put another way, in the gain domain we are risk-averse, and in the loss domain risk-seeking (Kahneman and Tversky, 1979). This insight, which they term 'prospect theory', was an early successful venture—published by psychologists but in an economics journal—into the discovery of similar sets of patterned deviations from rationality.

There are many identified decision biases and heuristics, indeed this is one problem with this literature. Let us look at an additional, widely cited, one. In another experiment (Kahneman and Tversky, 1983), subjects (undergraduate students) were presented with the 'Linda problem'.

Linda is 31 years old, single, outspoken and very bright. She majored in philosophy. As a student, she was deeply concerned with issues of discrimination and social justice and also participated in anti-nuclear demonstrations.

Which of two alternatives is more probable:

1. Linda is a bank teller.
2. Linda is a bank teller and is active in the feminist movement.

85% of subjects chose no. 2. Logically, this is a set inclusion problem since set 2 must be included in set 1. For Kahneman and Tversky this is an error, and they term it the 'conjunction fallacy' arguing that it is inconsistent with adherence to more complicated principles of judgement such as 'Bayesian updating, external calibration and the maximisation of expected utility' (1983: 313).

This intellectual agenda has two broad goals; first, to understand the cognitive processes underpinning judgements and, second, to map systematic deviations from rationality which are 'cognitive illusions' (Gigerenzer, 2008: 6). It also has two key conceptual components. First, the idea of a heuristic. Heuristics are mental shortcuts used in judgement. They are, in a very different and socio-logical language, like 'recipes for action' (Schutz, 1972); they give guidance on action that ignores some information (as in bounded rationality), is mostly intuitive, and works most of the time. The second idea is a bias; biases are systematic deviations from rationality. They are not simply error, which is random. So an example of a bias is that we tend to overestimate the frequency of high-impact events, such as plane crashes, and underestimate the frequency of low-impact events (unless you are involved) like car crashes; we estimate frequency by consequence.

This is an experimental agenda, both in method and maturity. There is no alternative to the elegance of perfect rationality here. The idea is to explore decision-making descriptively, making no assumptions about human deci-sion-making other than economizing on thinking. We have so much to think about that we need to compress thought into heuristics; and they work most of the time. For example, if we overestimate the frequency of high-impact events, it may cause us to avoid circumstances in which we may be exposed to a high-impact event. There are those who see evolutionary implications here; the heuristics and biases are about survival and reproduc-tion (Nicholson, 2000).

As an agenda, it has been subject to a number of criticisms. First, not all social scientists are comfortable making broad generalizations about human cognition based on data from experiments with student subjects. Second, it generates no overarching theory of decision-making; it identifies heuristics. It is not easy to generate testable propositions about decision-making. Since it has been very influential, its main output (apart from a Nobel Prize) has been a growing list of cognitive illusions produced by both behavioural economists and psychologists. Most fundamentally, as Gigerenzer (2004) has noted, in naming patterned deviations from rationality as illusions or errors, the agenda implicitly endorses the optimization agenda against which Simon initially protested. As the quote in the Linda example above indicates, the deviations are from a standard of rationality which is itself not subject to empirical test. The Linda example shows error because people make mistakes about sets. But being able to make the link between the description of Linda and her social preferences may be a useful social decision heuristic; for example, if you were trying to engage her in conversation. Gigerenzer describes the research venture rather unkindly as a 'repair program' for eco-nomic rationality and prospect theory specifically as 'tinkering' with utility functions. One is unlucky to get critics this eloquent.

Figures T4.2 (a–d) elaborate this point. They present a simplified four-stage optimizing approach to decision-making and indicate those cognitive biases

(a)

Cognitive bias	Consequence of bias
Influences on information gathering	
Retrievability and availability bias	*Selective attention given to what stands out, or springs easily to mind*
Base-rate insensitivity	*Focus is on objective not relative frequency*
Failure to apply sampling theory to small numbers	*True likelihoods are miscalculated*
Conjunction fallacy	*Unconnected information is falsely assumed to be linked*
Framing and order effects	*Different weights are assigned to first versus last in a sequence*
Subjective frequency estimates	*Infrequent events are overestimated, frequent events underestimated*
Confirmation bias	*Search is biased towards confirming rather than disconfirming evidence*

(b)

Cognitive bias	Consequence of bias
Influences on information processing	
Loss aversion not risk aversion	*Lottery behaviour occurs—gambling on long odds*
Miscalculated probabilities	*Only hits not misses are scrutinized, or vice-versa*
Gamblers' fallacy	*Connections are mistakenly perceived between unconnected events*
Over-confidence and self-esteem	*Optimism is greater than objective chances merit*
Ego-involvement	*Too little or too much emotional attachment is given to events or outcomes*
Stress	*Load, uncertainty, and conflict affect ability to think and act clearly*
Framing of targets	*Behaviour changes according to whether a target is conceived of as 'avoid worst case' or 'achieve goal'*
Insufficient anchoring adjustment	*Re-adjustment to target after feedback is insufficient*
Representativeness bias	*Isolated events or information are assumed to be representative*

Figure T4.2. A catalogue of decision biases (a–d).

(c)

Cognitive bias	Consequence of bias
Influences on decision taking	
Asymmetries of loss and gain	*Losses are chased more than gains*
Endowment effects	*What you have to sell is undervalued relative to what you buy*
Social norms	*The risk or decision profiles of the local culture are followed*
Groupthink	*Intragroup momentum governs a decision, and censors dissent*
Herding	*Instead of making rational choices, we watch what others do*
Incentives	*Risk–reward outcomes are distorted by personal pay-off system*
Impression management	*More important to look good than do good*
Competitive pressures	*It becomes more important to win than to achieve*

(d)

Cognitive bias	Consequence of bias
Influences on reactions to decision outcomes	
Hindsight bias	*History is rewritten; 'I knew this would happen'*
Regression to the mean	*Random variations are perceived as systemically caused*
Rationalization of outcomes	*Failures are re-evaluated as benefits*
Illusions of control	*It is believed uncontrollable outcomes can be controlled*
Escalating commitment	*Good money is thrown after bad; motivated by sunk costs*
Failure reactions	*Learning is for future avoidance rather than analytical or constructive insight*
Attribution errors	*Errors are over-attributed to will and personality, and too little to situation and chance*

Figure T4.2. Continued.

which might affect the steps in the process of information gathering, processing, decision-making, and post-decision review. The list is derived from Bazerman (2002) where the nature and derivation of each bias can be found. This list and the comparison can be used to emphasize core issues as well as to act as an aide-memoire in decision-making. First, one has at some level to accept the validity of the optimizing and prescriptive template against which the illusions are measured. Nothing in the empirical work of the Carnegie Mellon School would indicate that decisions are made this way. Second, the list of illusions themselves has no cohesion or even weighting. One could not *ex ante* say which of the illusions is most dangerous, or whether their effect in combination is additive or compensatory. Again, Gigerenzer (2008: 89) uses the analogy of chemistry and suggests we need to move from this list to a 'periodic table' where the properties of, and interactions between, heuristics can be more clearly understood.

The dangers of operating with a list are nowhere clearer in the management field than in the area of 'behavioural finance'. As we discuss more fully in Chapter 8, economic theory has produced elegant models of how financial markets work, relying on very strong assumptions about rationality, which unfortunately do not have an excellent record of predicting market phenomena such as volatility. In response to this, behavioural finance has adapted and developed the cognitive illusions literature to explain market anomalies. The process is as follows. Empirical market events such as stock selection by investors, unusual trading volumes ('noise trading'), and seasonal or even diurnal trading patterns, which should not occur if investors are rational, are identified at the level of the market, then retrofitted to a decision heuristic that is claimed to generate them. To give a very specific example, investors purchase stocks in companies well known to them, particularly from their country of origin, to a disproportionate degree, and this is seen as availability bias (Item 1 in Figure T4.2 (a); for a review, see Willman, 2000). This retrofitting of an individual bias to an aggregate phenomenon without addressing the mechanisms of aggregation is then said to explain or even 'predict' the anomaly in question. The timing and frequency of anomalies is not explained in terms of any theory about the frequency or valence of the bias (see Shefrin, 2000; Shleifer, 2000).

The problems with this literature are immense. For our purposes, it simply illustrates the non-cumulative and non-predictive nature of the illusions literature. Fama, whose dominant efficient markets theory is not displaced or even tested by this work, refers to it as 'anomalies dredging'. It treats heuristics as irrational, which begs the very broad question of why, if heuristics are irrational, are there so widespread? Gigerenzer (2008) shows that heuristics exist because, most of the time, they work in the sense that the decision-maker achieves the objective by using them. In the more limited context of financial markets, those with illusions have been seen to profit at the expense of those without (though not consistently so; for a review, see Willman et al., 2006).

Illusions of Grandeur

Here is an example of how heuristics work in practice. In the 1990s, at the London Business School, my colleagues and I became interested in how traders in financial markets worked. We mistrusted the hyper-rational models of our finance colleagues, not least because many traders were our former students and they had shown to us little evidence of being hyper-rational. We studied traders in four big investments banks (Fenton O'Creevy et al., 2005).

Traders have to believe two contradictory things at once. They have to believe that prices give them all the information they need, and they have to believe that despite the fact everyone has the same information, they can beat the market. We wanted to see if they had a bias called illusion of control— an unrealistic belief that they can control events (Langer, 1975).

We asked our traders to play a computer game. Here are the instructions:

> When the game starts you will see a chart, similar to the picture shown below. The vertical axis represents an index with values between −2000 and 2000. The horizontal axis shows time. The index starts at zero and every half second for 50 seconds the index is increased or decreased by some amount. Changes in the index are partly random, but three keys on the keyboard may have some effect on the index. The possible effects are to raise or lower the index by some amount to increase the size of the random movements or no effect. There is some time lag to the effects. The keys are 'Z', 'X', and 'C'. There is no advantage to pressing keys more than once in any half second. Your task is to raise the index as high as possible by the end of 50 seconds. At the end of the game the final value of the index will be added to your pool of points.
>
> (O'Creevy et al. 2003: 60)

Figure T4.3 is a screenshot of how the game looked. At the end of the game, we asked the traders what the keys did, and we asked them to assign confidence levels to their verdicts. The vast majority thought the keys all had an effect (though not the same one) and were very confident in their views.

You may have guessed already what this is about. The keys did not do anything. The line movement was exactly the random walk that the efficient markets hypothesis predicts would characterize movements in stock prices.[4] The control over the line was illusory. Traders with high illusion of control

---

[4] Well, not exactly. In the efficient markets version it is a log-normal random walk since share prices cannot go negative; see Chapter 8.

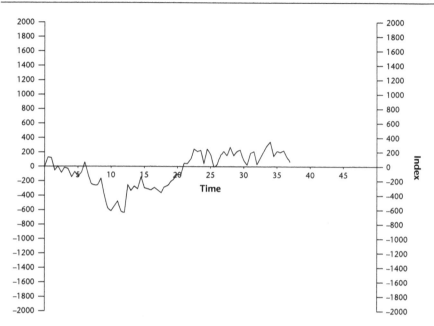

Figure T4.3. Walk on the wild side?

show less effective performance in terms of risk management, market analysis, and contribution to profits. And they were paid less. At a conservative estimate the difference in annual remuneration between a trader with high illusion of control (in the top 18%) and a trader with average illusion of control was about £100,000 per annum, which was a fair amount at the time. But what would traders do in markets if they did not believe that they could see something other than randomness in market movements (and that everybody else could see it too)? Perhaps this bias has some ecological function, in Gigerenzer's sense, in that it makes sense of a complex reality.

Conclusion: Neither Prospero nor Caliban?

It should be clear from this discussion that the first thing to do when reading the term 'bounded rationality' is to try to figure out what the author means by it. The illusions literature sees us as a bundle of error terms; a Caliban, if you will. Economists tend towards identifying agents as Prospero; omniscient and hyper-rational. Maybe they are looking in the mirror. Simon's view is something in between, and Gigerenzer is seeking to develop a theory of 'homo heuristicus' where they key variables are heuristics and the task environment, and their interaction defines the effectiveness of a heuristic; he terms this an 'ecological' approach.

It is, in my view, no accident that the theory of bounded rationality developed within the context of organizational decision-making. Economists started with rationality in markets and it may be that rationality in hierarchies has some fundamental 'ecological' differences to the extent that domain differences are significant in understanding rationality in decision-making. It is certainly the case that organizational economics ships in wholesale the market-based model of rationality. If one can identify the Carnegie School as students of business, rather than economists or psychologists, then the study of bounded rationality stands out as one of the prime examples of the benefits of the synthetic thought characteristic of academic business study.

Chapter 5

The Structuring of Organizations

Introduction

The proposition that firm structure follows from firm strategy, which originates with Alfred Chandler, is such a broadly disseminated idea in the study of management that it might seem perverse to precede the strategy chapters with a discussion of the dependent variable: organizational structure. One reason for starting with the dependent variable is chronology; it is simply the case that discussions of business organization precede the emergence of the business strategy discipline. But the main reason is that, for those unacquainted with the field, it eases discussion of the strategy issues to have established a lexicon of organizational terms. That is the primary emphasis of this chapter.

The second is to introduce some broad ideas about variance. Over time, there have been substantial variations in views about what is organizational 'best practice'. Broadly, they move from the general to the particular; specifically from the 'one best way' view to contingency theory, which is the 'best-fit' argument. Cross-sectionally, in the discussion of particular organizational categories, we see some uniformity; so for example, what we will describe as the multi-divisional organizational form came to dominate certain sectors, like cars and chemicals, and the partnership form dominated others—notably law and accounting. These two considerations introduce in the most general terms the idea of fit between organization and environment. They also raise the question of the generator of organizational uniformity within a given sector; is it efficiency, or something else?

The third reason is to flesh out the idea of hierarchy as discussed above. Organizations are about control (and power), coordination, and performance. These objectives may be in conflict. And all of these concepts are in Lukes', (1974) sense, essentially contestable, by which he means it is unlikely we can generate one agreed definition. Structures also, in a basic sense, define opportunity sets. If one has an Adam Smith organization that consists of an owner and pin assemblers only, it is likely to offer few advancement opportunities for the pin assemblers compared to one which builds in managerial roles; this may partly be a question of scale, but, as noted, whatever else the modern large firm produces, in the West at least it is a producer of substantial inequality, and greater inequality than in the recent past. This may be a function of reward policies, but I will argue that it is also a function of the structuring of jobs within the firm; if there is no ladder, you cannot climb it. So, design choices matter in a variety of ways that we will explore.

The final theme is complexity. We know that it is possible to produce an organization too complex to understand and too complex to operate. This author has been to more than one company strategy presentation over the years where the presentation of the organizational structure required to deliver the strategy relied on a hologram in three dimensions. But we need to begin with a little history, and look at one of the key concepts in organizational theory.

Welcome to the Iron Cage

The scene: a railway station in Europe. Customer and Clerk are separated by a clear glass screen.

Clerk: Good morning, sir, how can I help?
Customer: I would like to buy a railway ticket from Paris to Cologne.
Clerk: I am sorry, sir, but you have come to the 'Information' window, and you need to go to the 'Ticket' window.
Customer: Where is that, please?
Clerk: It is the next window, on your right.

Both customer and clerk walk, on different sides of the glass, to the window on the right. The customer waits. Eventually, the clerk says . . .

Clerk: Good morning, sir, how can I help?

The script is repeated.

The scene above did happen. I was the customer. It embodied what many of us think of as bureaucracy; where routines and rules take over from purpose and inefficiency results. But this is the modern, colloquial, meaning of the term and the classical meaning is very different. In the formal sense, most large organizations are bureaucracies. Some work well, and others badly. Some work well and badly at the same time. To finish the story above, I bought my ticket, and the train both left Paris and arrived in Cologne on time.

The classical approach to bureaucracy involves rationality again; it is presented as rational administration. Second (and related) it involves the application of general principles of organizational structure which are supposed to work everywhere. Third, it involves authority. Fourth, it originates in a concern, not with business, but with government.

There are those who trace the concept (but not the precise term) back to ancient China, and those who focus on its development in nineteenth-century Europe (see Albrow, 1969). A link between the two was Max Weber, who studied both. He is closely associated with the development of theories of bureaucracy although, interestingly, he never defined it precisely. He did, however, develop an outline of the ideal typical characteristics of bureaucratic operation as follows.

1. The division of labour within the organization was clear, together with the authority and responsibility attached to each position.

2. Authority derived from position, not person, and positions were organized in hierarchies, with a clear chain of command.

3. All position holders were appointed (not elected) on the basis of technical qualifications for the post, and/or formal examinations.

4. Position holders worked for salaries, and took no other form of benefit from their position.

5. Position holders did not own their posts or associated resources; they were career officials who moved up the hierarchy on principles either of merit or seniority.

6. Conduct of officials was to be governed by clear, impersonal rules and discipline.

Significantly, this form of organization . . . is, from a purely technical point of view, capable of attaining the highest degree of efficiency and is in this sense formally the most rational known means of carrying out imperative control over human beings.

(Weber; 1947: 329–33, 337).

Control and direction, lack of ambiguity, discipline and technical expertise; if this bothers you, then be reassured that it bothered Weber too. He worried about 'little men clinging to little jobs' and living in an 'iron cage' of rules in a state of 'disenchantment'. Like Durkheim and Marx, he was worried about the break-up of traditional society and its replacement by something else. But while he observed the development of this form of *government*, he didn't live long enough (1920) to see how it might develop to affect thinking about business.

Now, in one sense, this is the absolute grand design in the separation of conception from execution we saw above. You design the rational hierarchy, get the job descriptions right, hire the right qualified people, light the fuse, and walk away. It has everything in common with a nested conception of principal agent theory and almost nothing in common with some of the ideas

115

about leadership discussed above. Almost; because, as Weber hinted, if you put a charismatic leader in charge of a rational bureaucracy—and it is armed—great difficulties ensue. Two such leaders can give you a world war. Much of the development of organizational sociology in the early part of the twentieth century can be seen as exploration of the limits of bureaucracy.

Sociologists quickly began to point out the occurrence of bureaucratic dysfunction. The 'Columbia' School of Robert Merton and his associates made plain, largely through empirical work, the possibility of inefficient outcomes.[1] Merton (1940) himself was concerned with the impact of bureaucratic rules on personality (though he took no formal measures of the latter). Following rules and emphasizing prudence, discipline, and method, meant that the rules could become ends in themselves (goal displacement, as at the ticket counter above). Selznick (1943) pointed out one collective corollary of this. Within organizations, sub-units generated by the division of labour develop their own goals, which are often at odds with those of the organization as a whole; the remedy, setting up other sub-units for monitoring, basically generated an escalating situation of even more sub-unit goals and higher fixed costs.

Blau (1955) emphasized the need for discretion in the face of rules if efficiency were to be an outcome. He looked at a Federal law enforcement agency concerned to enforce laws on business. They had a rule that all bribe offers must be reported. But many officials did not comply; they kept the offer of a bribe (but they did not take the bribe) secret to exercise leverage over businesses. So the paradox is, if they obey the rule the agency seizes up, if they fully break it they are corrupt, but if they selectively break the rule in the interests of the overall objective—compliance—it works. Gouldner (1954) argued that the operation of bureaucracies depended on employees' attitudes *towards* the rules. In representative bureaucracies, people saw the rules they had to follow as necessary and legitimate. In punishment-centred and mock bureaucracies, they did not, and rule evasion or rejection led to inefficiency. In punishment-centred bureaucracies the rules were seen to serve the interests of one part of the organization, normally management, and in mock bureaucracies they were externally enforced. Of interest, of this school only Gouldner studied a private-sector business—a gypsum plant and mine.

Similar ideas about rational organization found their way into the prescriptive literature on management of private-sector firms, probably because they appealed to engineers operating with the idea of organization-as-machine. Henri Fayol, for example, stressed among his management 'principles' division of labour, authority, discipline, unity of command, centralization, clear

---

[1] For this section, see Haveman (2009).

chains of command, and stability of tenure (Wren, 2005: 215). This notion that, first, an authority structure should be preferred (over a democracy, for example) and, second that an authority structure could be optimized, tended to dominate.

Another influential management theorist, Chester Barnard, saw authority structures in a relatively neutral way, as 'an instrumental solution to the problems of cooperation/coordination that were posed by the adaptive needs of complex organisations' (Williamson, 1995: 175). Of course, this rather begs the two questions of who decides what an adaptive need is and what measures are necessary to fulfil it. In Barnard, as in Fayol, a necessary ingredient is the active consent of those subject to bureaucratic rules, and where this is problematic, many of the efficiency benefits disappear. It is by assumption rendered unproblematic, since efficiency is assumed to benefit all of those subject to the rules. Bureaucracy is a bit like taxation; both may lead to collective benefits, but I am more likely to want you to pay your taxes than I am to want to pay my own, and I am more likely to think that rules that generate predictability and performance in your work are good than I am to welcome them as governing my work. This raises some of the collective action issues I discussed in Theme 3.

A more general consideration than that about the benefits of bureaucracy is whether any general proposition about the efficiency properties of an organizational form is worth having. Particularly where structure is concerned, explaining *variance* in organizational structures may be significant. Within sectors, we need to understand at the least whether an observed pattern of variance is indicative of a pattern of lags in the move towards the optimal structure, or a set of options available about structure and efficiency. Let us turn first to academic work on variance in organizational structure.

Pomp or just Circumstance?

Once the Tavistock Institute had started to look at the relationship between organizational micro-structure and productivity, it was arguably only a matter of time before a concern with macro-structure emerged. Once it became clear that one could find fault with optimizing and general models of organizational structure, it was arguably likely that it would be empirical studies of organizational forms that would lead to new theorizing about sources of variation. Once Simon had argued against the idea of 'timeless' principles of organizational efficiency, it was likely that a contingent approach would emerge. These are arguments for the emergence of structural contingency models of organization.

There are negative ones too. Guillen (1994: 81) argues for the USA that it was the disappearance of industrial relations problems post-war that allowed a concern with micro problems—conflict and motivation—to give way to more structural concerns. There are two problems with this argument. First, an argument about why you should stop examining something is not an argument about why you should start to examine something else. Second, it did not happen in the USA first. It happened in the UK, where the industrial relations micro problems remained severe.

Joan Woodward examined organizational structure in manufacturing firms in south-east England in the early 1950s and discovered wide variations in their structure that could not be explained by size or industry, and did not have any clear relationship to performance (Woodward,1958). Firms that followed accepted principles as described above did not perform better than those that did not. However, when the firms were classified by 'technology', patterns emerged. By 'technology', Woodward meant production system, and the key distinction is threefold; small batch production, mass production, and continuous process production. These three categories involved increasing organizational complexity, and with complexity came features such as lengthening chains of command, an increase in the supervisory ratio, and a narrowing of the CEO span of control. *Within* these categories, those firms that came close to the median score on key variables were best performers.

Now, her methods, by modern standards, were not great; the measures of technology were not entirely consistent. And the association between technology and organizational structure was not explained theoretically. Rose (1988: 216–17) feels that this set of findings might reflect the fact that 'accepted principles' at the time might simply have been overgeneralizations from mass production experience, and that Woodward was simply reintroducing a more realistic set of ideas about technological differences between firms. However, the findings opened up a line of empirical research into the relationship between aspects of organizational structure and performance that displayed greater methodological sophistication and a broader set of variables, generating structural contingency theory.

Burns and Stalker (1959) undertook further empirical research in private-sector manufacturing organizations. They developed the now classic distinction between mechanistic and organic firms. Mechanistic firms are centralized, formal, and hierarchical, with fragmented division of labour and task specialization. Organic firms have loose controls, widespread discretion and initiative takings, and are decentralized. The former are highly suited to the performance of high volumes of repetitive tasks, but deal poorly with environmental uncertainty. Organic forms are suited to environmental uncertainty that generates task uncertainty and a need for creativity and innovation. This simple (but widely quoted) distinction crucially introduced the idea of a fit between an organization and its environment; different structures for different circumstances.

The way was paved for the development of structural contingency theory. In the words of one of its great defenders:

> Structural contingency theory argues that individual organisations adapt to their environment. The environment is seen as posing requirements for efficiency, innovation, or whatever, which the organisation must meet to survive and prosper.
>
> (Donaldson, 1995: 32).[2]

The organization intentionally flexes structural variables to adapt to the environment; the variables concerned included size, technology, and diversification. So, for example, product diversification is seen to fit best within a product divisional structure (much more on this in Theme 6).

This academic venture has a number of important features. First, as well as being empirically based, it was highly quantitative, both in the derivation of measures and the measurement of associations with dependent variables (usually some measure of performance). It generated large research programmes. One, at the University of Aston in the UK, became, after the Tavistock, only the second UK intellectual initiative in the study of organization to have a significant impact in the USA. The 'Aston' studies measured organizational structure in highly sophisticated ways; for example, bureaucracy becomes 'functional specialization', 'standardization', and 'specialization'. And Aston as an institution became a multiple regression factory, measuring relations between proliferating variable sets and expanded performance measures with diminishing theoretical content (e.g. Pugh et al., 1964, 1968).

Second, it generated much debate. Some concerned the measures and their definition. Others concerned the whole project (e.g. Schoonhoven, 1981). Subsequent to structural contingency theory, a wide gulf emerged between qualitative and quantitative studies of organization in academia.[3] However, it is the practical impact that concerns us for the moment. Structural contingency theory emphasizes the manager as organizational designer, not simply running an organization, but adapting it actively to environmental factors. It legitimized organizational change, and, as Guillen (1994) notes, in the 1960s and 1970s in both the USA and UK, many large firms went through thorough adaptations of their structural forms.

This was associated with two things about which I will say much more; first, the spread of multi-divisional structures in large firms and, second, the growth of management consulting involvement in structural change. Structural

---

[2] 'Whatever' turns out to be a major problem.
[3] For a rejection of the whole idea of contingency theory, see Burrell and Morgan (1979). For a spirited defence, see Donaldson (1985).

change became a constant agenda item as firms strove for successive approximation of fit to changing environments. Note one paradox in this contingent approach; though the correct 'fit' between organization and environment might involve high levels of employee discretion (as in 'organic' structures), top management tended to be seen as the architect of the change. Many of the concerns that had driven the human relations school are written out of the script. Note a second; that although contingency theory might be seen to generate organizational variety, in practice the active management of organizational change tended to have the adoption of the multi-divisional form as an outcome across sectors (see McKenna, 2006).

At the time of writing, structural contingency theory has few advocates and fewer academic practitioners. One generic problem is that it generated no robust theoretical links between structural attributes; in fact, disagreement over which variables to measure and how to measure them never disappeared. But, outside of economics, it killed off the idea of the one best way for structural design. We did not get a theory, but in the subsequent work of Henry Mintzberg, we got a synthesis.

Full Fathom Five

Here is the central Mintzberg proposition:[4]

> ...a limited number of... configurations explain most of the tendencies that drive effective organisations to structure themselves as they do. In other words, the design of an effective organizational structure—in fact even the diagnosis of problems in many ineffective ones—seems to involve the consideration of only a few basic configurations.
>
> (Mintzberg, 1983: 3).

In fact, whatever the question, the answer is five. Organizations are about first, division of labour and, second, coordination. There are five types of coordinative device, five elements of organization (though these are not present in all types), and five broad organizational types, in each of which one element is dominant. Let us look at each in turn; first, the coordinating mechanisms. They are as follows:

1. Mutual Adjustment—achieves coordination by informal communication and agreement. It operates best with small numbers, and in conditions of uncertainty.

---

[4] For precisely the reason Mintzberg himself gives in his introduction, this section relies on the 1983 'Structure in Fives' rather than the 1979 synthesis itself.

2. Direct Supervision—achieves coordination by having one person issue instructions to another and monitor their compliance. It is essentially an agency conception.

3. Standardization of Work Processes—achieves coordination by specifying and standardizing tasks.

4. Standardization of Outputs—achieves coordination by specifying outcomes, such as product dimensions and timing of delivery.

5. Standardization of Knowledge/Skills—achieves coordination by specifying worker skills or know-how.

Mintzberg argues:

> As organisational work becomes more complicated, the favored means of coord-ination seems to shift from mutual adjustment to direct supervision to standard-isation, preferably of work processes, otherwise of outputs, or else of skills, finally reverting back to mutual adjustment ...

(Mintzberg, 1983: 7).

The five parts of the organization are as follows:

1. The strategic apex looks to the mission of the organization, and to the strategies to deliver it, as well as the needs of others—owners or government for example—who control or have power over it. This apex could be an entrepreneur, or a senior management team.

2. The operating core performs the basic work related to the production of products and services. This could be assembly line workers or call centre operatives.

3. The middle line links the strategic apex to the operating core. This is the hierarchy of middle managers from first-line supervisors to heads of departments or functions.

4. The technostructure uses analytical techniques to improve the effectiveness of the work of others, by standardizing. This could include those that design processes and structures, specialists in HRM, and so on.

5. The support staff exist to provide support outside the core work flow. Examples might include the IT department, security, mailroom, and cafeteria.

These are visually displayed in Table C5.1. When one puts the coordinating mechanism and the parts together, one gets a fivefold classification of organ-izations in terms of dominant combinations of the two. Examples are included. Note that two of the types lack some parts. The simple structure has only an apex and core; the adhocracy has only an apex. The divisionalized form is essentially a photocopied version of the machine bureaucracy. Finally,

Table C5.1 Five Organizational Types.

	Method of coordination	Key part of organization
Simple structure e.g. entrepreneur-led small firm	Direct supervision	Strategic apex
Machine bureaucracy e.g. large firm in manufacturing	Standardization of work processes	Technostructure
Divisional form e.g. diversified multi-product firm	Standardization of outputs	Middle line
Professional bureaucracy e.g. large law or consulting firm	Standardization of skills and knowledge	Operating core
Adhocracy e.g. film-making firm	Mutual adjustment	Operating core (with admin support)

(*Source*: Derived from Mintzberg, 1983)

these are ideal types (and simplifications); in the simple structure, for example, there would be likely to be mutual adjustment *within* the strategic apex as well as direct supervision of the operating core.

This is essentially a static classification that provides a useful lexicon of organizational parts. It is more than a list. To use Gigerenzer's term from Theme 3, it is something of a periodic table, indicating how the mechanisms and the parts interact. The generalizations it produces are powerful. For example, professional bureaucracies dominate the professional service firm sector—particularly law, consulting, and accounting, while the fast moving consumer goods sector is dominated by divisionalized businesses. The model of the simple structure provides all the ingredients to understand the structural problems encountered by small firms when they seek to grow—that is they need to acquire and integrate parts they do not have (see Greiner, 1972). However, it does not deal with change directly, or well. The final part of this chapter will try to do this by synthesizing some of the work of previous chapters.

If Five is the Answer, What is the Question?

The purpose of this section is to address why organizations seem constantly to be in a state of flux, or change. The way I will do this is to frame central questions that organizations, implicitly or explicitly, have to try to answer; but their answers can never be permanent, they represent endemic organizational problems. In doing so, I am trying to add a little dynamism to the classification above. I will continue to pay homage to the third prime: there are five questions.

1. *Where should the organizations' boundaries be?*

This operationalizes the transaction cost question at the heart of the theory of the firm of Coase and Williamson discussed above. Organizations have to decide how vertically integrated they want to be. Where the boundary of the organization is set, firms need roles managing relationships with customers and suppliers. They also need to decide about horizontal integration—relationships with competitors. This may involve acquisition, but short of that it involves joint ventures, alliances, and networks, which in turn have their own boundary-spanning roles. Increasingly, firms need to be concerned with outsiders who have control—investors, governments, and regulators; this in turn involves concerns with lobbying, investor relations, accountability, and risk management.

In all of these boundary management activities, there is likely to be uncertainty and complexity; for example, relationships between the firm and its customers, suppliers, and competitors will, as we shall see in Chapter 6, be both competitive and collaborative. There is unlikely to be stability.

2. *How should work be divided and combined?*

Once the boundaries are decided then, as Mintzberg notes, dividing labour is the prime issue. There are essentially only two broad options. We can organize around the supply side, or we can organize around the demand side. In practice we want to do both. So, on the supply side, we might organize around a work process, such as assembly of cars, for technological reasons and economies of scale. We might organize around a skill set or knowledge base, also for economies of scale and because concentrating the knowledge base tends to improve it. So, for example, at LSE, we concentrate the economists in the economics department, not just for the benefit of everyone else, but because the conventional wisdom on how to have some of the best economists in the world is to have an excellent economics department. In administration we might organize around a function, such as payroll or security, simply because fragmentation involves more transaction costs.

On the demand side, firms often organize around some surrogate definition of the market. So for example, many multi-product firms use the product as the unit of organization. In fast-moving consumer goods firms, like Unilever and Procter and Gamble, this means organizing around the brand. A second option, where the market is segmented nationally, is to organize around geography. In Europe, for many years the default organizational form for multinational firms was the country; where the countries were either not populous enough (Scandinavia) or regarded as similar (DACH—Germany, Austria, Switzerland), they were aggregated. Third, they could organize around the customer or client. Where, as in business-to-business dealings, there are a small number of clients, client relationship managers (CRMs) can deal with big accounts; so if you are Apple or Samsung in the mobile handset business, CRMs can deal with Orange, Vodafone, and other network operators. Where one deals with mass markets, customer classifications may work. Large retail banks, for example, tend to deal separately with business accounts, high net worth individuals, and the rest of us: this is termed 'segmentation' and I will deal with it in Theme 7.

Now these organizational options—three supply side and three demand side—compete with each other at two levels. As a very broad generalization, firms have tried to move from supply-side organization (which is seen to be more mechanistic) to demand, side (which is seen to be more flexible and organic). *Within* these two categories, there is also competition. The units are also interest groups within the organization, and to be a principle of organization in this way, which may well involve control over resources, is an interest group objective (this is central to the Carnegie Mellon approach discussed above). So, if we accommodate all, the outcome is a multi-dimensional matrix too complicated to operate. So, Figure C5.2 shows a relatively simple and successful matrix, that of ABB; imagine adding more dimensions until there were three on each axis. We thus need to organize around only the most powerful or important principles at a point in time, and this is not an equilibrium. The division of labour is constantly in flux.

3. *What are the lines of authority and communication?*

There are both technical or geometrical questions about organizational design, and what one might term political or cultural ones. Let us look at them by referring to Figure C5.2.

The technical issues concern the geometry of an organizational chart. What is the span of control of a given position (how many direct reports does it have), what are the reporting relationships, how many layers of management are there in what Minztberg calls the 'middle line', what are the formal communication mechanisms—both vertical (i.e. up and down the hierarchy) and lateral (across different functions or groups within it)? These considerations obsessed classical organization scholars and they attempted to form laws or rules about them. Two broad trends occurred in organizations within the last thirty years or so. First, termed 'delayering', many companies sought to reduce costs and improve communications by taking out layers of management; this gives 'bigger' jobs lower down the organization and bigger gaps between the rungs on the career ladder. Second, as more organizations became either formally or informally matrix structures, lateral relationships— either reporting or communication—became more important in relation to the vertical. So, in Figure C5.2, if you are a graduate entrant in the Power Plant division of ABB Asia, there are going to be fewer levels between you and the director of that business but, since Asia is growing very rapidly, perhaps more need to respond to whoever is in charge of the Asia Pacific region.

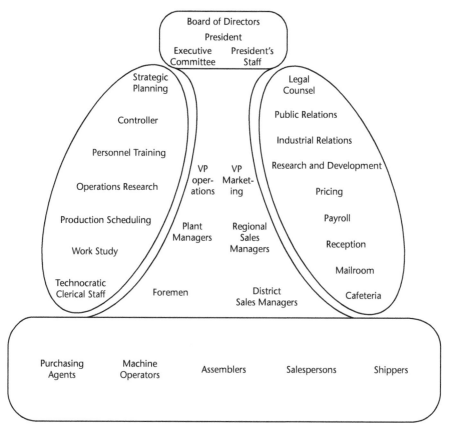

Figure C5.1. Some members and units of the parts of the manufacturing firm.
(*Source*: Mintzberg, 1983)

Technical issues are important, but organizational charts are historical documents and the real operation of an organization is somewhere between the last organizational chart and the next, which you do not have. So, as a graduate entrant, you are interested in cultural or political questions related to the organizational structure. Here are some of the questions that might interest you: Which is the best part of the organization to join? This might relate to how fast particular units are growing. How long should one stay at a given level? Most organizations have formal or informal mobility rules. Authority is delineated, but who has the real power? In the ABB matrix structure, should you spend more time pleasing the head of Power Plant or the Head of Asia Pacific; should you ever let them meet to talk about you? Is it a good idea to move between divisions or regions or to stay in one place? Put another way, if

125

you are in Power Plant in Asia, are you a Power Plant employee or an Asia employee? The same question applies to your expertise; if you join as an engineer, is it a good idea to try marketing to add to your expertise, or is the risk of failure too great?

The point of this is that organizational design is about structure, but also the implications of structure for organizational practice. Careers and power introduce flux.

4. *How much bureaucracy do we need?*

We have discussed already the efficiency enhancing or efficiency destroying properties of bureaucratic rules. In Mintzberg's terms, organizations that rely heavily on all three forms of standardization—knowledge, processes, and outputs—will feel like Weber's iron cage. Those that rely on a combination of mutual adjustment and direct supervision will feel more flexible. But there is both a light and a dark side of the force. Bureaucratic organizations are for the risk-averse, but they tend to offer forms of security; some people like an iron cage. Flexible organizations can feel political or capricious.

In designing a large organization, the ideal outcome is bureaucratic efficiency plus consummate cooperation. But the bureaucratic dynamic is such that often the emphasis is on managing the level of bureaucracy downwards. What the literature we looked at above implies is that, if I design rules to control employee behaviour, you will find ways out of that by local innovation, I will find out, instigate rules to cover those exceptions, you will find ways around those rules, and so on until the organization experiences a forest of red tape and an explosion of accountability noise. The arms race has to stop somewhere. But what this means is that the issue of bureaucracy is an endemic question.

5. *What should be the extent of centralization?*

Organizations go through cycles of centralization and decentralization; it is like a pendulum swinging. We know enough about the processes involved to figure out how this works. I don't want to take this five thing too far, but there are five issues. Let us look at them with a simple thought experiment. I am your CEO and I decide (for whatever reason) to decentralize the organization; you are a senior manager in the organization. How will this go?

1. **Consent.** This is a far more positive message than the opposite, that I want to micro-manage you. You will generally be happy (if a little worried) and so this is a good message. It is such a good message that I as CEO might be tempted to give it if I were worried about my position or your support of it. Or if I did not have another message. It is not a message you are likely to reject. I will probably have to pay you more. You will not say no.

2. **Competence**. I am in effect increasing your responsibility levels. In many organizations, decentralization means role change; you may be a middle manager responsible for implementing policies developed elsewhere and now you have profit and loss accountability. In most organizations, some people respond and some do not. Either you, or some of your colleagues, will fail; how will I respond (i.e. is it your fault for failing or mine for setting you up?).

3. **Cost**. Decentralization affects costs. First, it raises headcount; you will want your own finance director to manage and massage your unit's performance data; she may have to torture these data until they confess you are succeeding. You may want to increase headcount in marketing, sales, and other functions too. Second, you will perform functions previously centralized, so economies of scale may be lost.

4. **Communication**. Unless I instigate mechanisms to counter it, decentralized businesses fragment. Senior managers cease to communicate effectively with each other and the chances of the same business problem being solved on multiple occasions within the firm increases. The chance of really good ideas being generalized decreases.

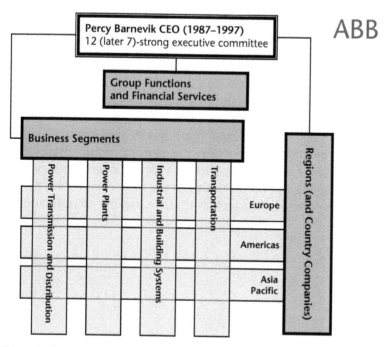

Figure C5.2. The matrix at ABB. Image/Illustration/Matrix, courtesy of ABB.

5. **CEO angst**. Once I decentralize, I have to figure out what to do. Perhaps in the past I managed you closely. Now, I need to leave you alone. What do I do? Well, I probably should spend my time thinking about the strategic issues we will discuss below. This might be both difficult (if that is not the strength I brought to being CEO) and dangerous (ditto).

I have deliberately framed these issues to indicate what I think is an underlying dynamic. The positives are omitted. They include the fact that organizations that decentralize can generate huge motivational benefits and that decentralized decisions may be much better informed, for example about customer preferences, channels to market, price/volume decisions, and people management. But there are forces that keep the pendulum swinging. And if we add the external (and noisy) signal of the business cycle (firms tend to decentralize in a boom and centralize in a recession), we can see why it might continue to swing.

So much for the dependent variable; we will look at strategy, the independent variable, in the next chapter.

Conclusion

In this chapter I have tried to provide a lexicon of organizational terms and some grasp of the dynamics of organizational change and development. I have focused on formal structures—that is those that are normally designed with intent. These are subject to intermittent redesign, and they do not always operate as planned. Moreover, they interact in complex ways with informal structures and practices about which I will have more to say in Chapter 9. Hierarchy is not, as economists imply, a unitary concept; there are varieties of organizational form, even across firms that do roughly the same thing.

In one sense, the organizational chart that depicts structure is always a historical document; it tells you what the plan was before events got in the way. But it provides important parameters for and constraints on organizational actions, and I will return to this in the next chapter. But first, in the following theme, we need to look at how we measure performance within organizations.

Theme 5

Measuring Performance: Scorecards and League Tables

Introduction

Performance measurement engages all of the sub-disciplines of management; but in different ways. Accountants measure costs and revenues; finance academics measure share prices; operations people measure efficiency; human resources measure labour productivity and issues such as retention; marketing guys look at revenues, margins, and market share; and strategy people look at profitability and return on equity. The measures are only part of the story. The issue around this theme is the dynamics of performance measurement. It is an activity that should in itself be valuable, given the time it takes to do it.

The first question is the unit of analysis. One can measure the performance of individuals, groups, departments, business units, divisions, firms, industries, or economies. In part, the unit of analysis choice reflects prior beliefs about what the drivers of performance are. A pervasive issue in performance measurement is whether the unit being examined really has control over its own performance. The pragmatic assumption is often that it does. The truth is that it seldom does entirely.

The second issue is: what does one measure? An observation more or less as old as the hills everywhere except in economics is that what gets measured gets done. Another way of expressing this is to say that the establishment of measurement distorts the underlying activity it seeks to measure. If I reward a salesperson on volume of sales, she will ship unordered goods, discount prices, sell things customers do not want and then send back, and ignore all other aspects of the role. If I reward a trader in financial markets on profitability of trades, I will generate the crisis of 2008 (and every other financial crash). So I will try to set performance targets that are reflective of a broad range of activities I would like a job incumbent to pursue, but then the issue is how I manage the trade-offs that agent will make. Cognitively speaking, being subject to very large numbers of performance measures makes it hard for an individual to both pursue and balance them. On the other hand, one measure will generate a level of focus that may be detrimental to organizational performance.

In the broadest possible sense, one can only measure three things. They are, coincidentally, the three things Minzberg says we can standardize.

- **Outputs**. We can look at the outcomes of an activity, such as, at the firm level, return on capital employed or, at the micro level, individual productivity. But not all desirable outcomes have easy measures. And some are definitely in conflict. If I am a management consultant, for example, is my best measure current year revenue (short term) or client retention and repeat business (long term)?

- **Process**. One can (and does) measure the efficiency of delivery processes in both manufacturing and service businesses. This often involves attention to reducing the unit cost of a component or transaction. But should one also measure other dimensions, such as quality? Since the answer is, mostly, yes, there is the issue of how one manages the trade-off, which is ultimately a question of what the process is there to do. So, in a call centre for a mobile phone provider such as Vodafone, you will want the system both to minimize the costs of dealing with customer queries and complaints **and** maximize customer retention.

- **Inputs**. In some cases, the output data are problematic and the economic aspects of the process secondary. If I am having heart surgery, I want the best surgeon. If I am going to a concert, I want the best orchestra. If I am buying a two-year degree in management at my own expense, I want both the best faculty and the best placement service. Particularly where the service or product is consumed as it is produced, one tends to measure inputs.

So, one issue here is: what is the mix of performance options? How does one design performance measurement systems?

Some performance measures are endogenous to firms. Most management accounting measures are. Others are required by external agents such as governments or financial markets. So, financial statements are best described as outcomes—requirements of both regulators and markets. Yet others are influential because of reputational issues; they are broad signals to markets. League tables exist in a variety of non-sporting contexts, such as law firms, business schools, wine vintages, and asset management. They send signals to prospective consumers about price/quality combinations that are often difficult accurately to perceive without actually experiencing the product. Increasingly, consumers of products in areas such as health and education, where markets are often imperfect and costs are high, require such signals.

A (Very) Short History

The appliance of scientific management brought with it a concern to measure costs. Already in the nineteenth century, textile firms and then railways had developed internal administrative controls to manage complex processes. Railways in particular had to record and summarize massive volumes of (often small) transactions; in addition to financial statements, they also developed the reporting of operating statistics, such as cost of transport per ton mile, and operating ratios (normally income divided by sales) (Kaplan, 1984: 392). As I showed in Chapter 2, the railroad legacy was significant for the emerging mass production and distribution business in the USA, and this was true also of accounting practices. A central problem was the separation of operating or direct costs from fixed or overhead costs. There was little concern for returns on capital invested (Chandler, 1977: 269–79).

Scientific management advocates may be credited with two changes of emphasis. The first was to start the practice of allocating overhead costs, but not capital costs, to products or periods (Kaplan, 1984: 394). The second was concerned with labour and as we have seen had two aspects; the first was to develop standard labour and material costs per unit of output, and the second was to use these standards for devising piece rates and bonus payments (Braverman, 1974). A key point here is the integration, at least for production workers, of organization-wide measures with individual performance pay. There were many issues to deal with (see below) but this, the link between individual and organizational performance, has arguably been a holy grail for performance measurement ever since.

As organizations became larger and more complicated, developing a set of performance measures that could operate across the entire firm became more problematic. Thanks to the work of Chandler (1977), developments of considerable significance at Du Pont and then subsequently General Motors have been well documented. Faced with the problem of measuring the outputs of functionally diverse departments such as purchasing, manufacturing, and sales, Du Pont developed the measure of return on investment (ROI), which could also be used as a measure of corporate financial performance. Capital could thus be allocated to activities generating the highest return. In turn, the ROI measure could be decomposed into the product of the sales turnover ratio (sales/total investment) and the operating ratio (earnings/sales). In this functionally organized business, then, we have local profit measures evaluating departmental performance in a way directly analogous to the ideas of cost or profit centres used much later (Kaplan, 1984: 398).

In 1984, Kaplan felt that the development of management accounting had rather stagnated since the achievements of General Motors (by 1925) in adapting these ideas to the emerging divisionalized form. As we shall see, he was to do something about this, but it is worthwhile summarizing his account of the four key elements of the system (1984: 399–401).

1. The overall objective was to achieve an average satisfactory ROI across a business cycle, not to achieve year on year increases.
2. There developed a pricing system to determine target prices that would yield the desired ROI when production and sales were 'normal' (operationally defined as 80% of capacity).
3. An explicit senior manager incentive scheme, based on an explicit profit formula, linked divisional and firm performance to individual rewards.
4. A sophisticated market-based transfer-pricing system priced interdivisional transfer of product.

Much of this became 'normal' practice in large US firms. Its capacity to give senior managers centralized control with decentralized responsibility, and the emergence of financial and accounting considerations such as ROI as central to the firm's strategy, make it key to Chandler's argument about the emergence of the M form organization and of the strategy discipline more generally, which I will deal with in Theme 6. It also ultimately raised significant questions about managerial capitalism. If a measure such as ROI could be used to allocate capital between divisions, it could be used by investors to evaluate performance between firms; I will return to this below. For now I turn to the dynamics of performance measures, and the complexity of combining accounting measures with non-financial ones.

The Goals of Performance Measurement

> The task at the heart of the performance measurement problem is finding the precursors of future cash flows—or, equivalently, the long-term viability and efficiency of the firm.
>
> (Meyer, 2002: 113)

Meyer begins,[1] as I did, with the Adam Smith example of pin making. If the pin makers are each independent businesses, there is no performance measurement problem, because each has revenue and costs, but there is an efficiency problem in their coordination. If they are coordinated in a hierarchy, we solve the efficiency problem but create a performance measurement

---

[1] This section relies heavily on Meyer (2002).

problem by substituting one revenue stream for several. The larger the firm, the worse this gets, and we seek in many cases to use a combination of financial and non-financial performance measures. There is also the problem of the use to which we put performance measures. We may collect performance measures:

- to account for our past use of capital or materials
- to reward employees for past performance, or to give feedback on it
- to guide strategy[2]
- to guide the allocation of capital or other resources in future

Deliberately, two of these purposes are backward looking and two forward looking. The endemic problem in performance measurement is that we have to use past data and/or models built on statistical relationships between past data to guide decisions about the future. This is most likely to work where we have substantial amounts of past data and good reasons to believe that the future will be like the past. Where no such data exist, or where rapid change is expected, we need beliefs about relationships between variables that have high plausibility. For example, in the dot-com boom, when many firms with rising share prices were not making profits, it was common to use hits on the website as a performance measure, broadly in the belief that this was a proxy for future cash flows; much money was lost.

Meyer describes five properties of ideal performance measurement, and the problems in attaining them, as follows (2002: 6–7).

1. *Parsimony*. There should be few measures carrying a lot of information. The advantages would be that individuals could understand the relationship between their performance and the performance measure (the two are conceptually distinct), and that the time taken to collect and collate performance data would be minimized. In practice, firms are often swamped with performance measures and individuals deafened by accountability noise.

2. *Predictive ability*. Specifically, non-financial measures *would* predict subsequent financial performance as implied in the quote above. Non-financial indicators would be leading indicators and financial indicators would be summary measures. In practice, this does not work well; web traffic was not a good predictor of future profits and commonly collected data on items such as employee and customer satisfaction has a modest and uneven effect on financial performance.

---

[2] This was the original purpose of the balanced scorecard discussed below.

3. *Pervasiveness.* The same measures *would* apply everywhere within the organization. One could thus compare across departments and areas both for allocative efficiency and equity reasons. In practice, only financial measures can be pervasive and, even here, they have to be high-order measures such as ROI.

4. *Stability.* Measures *would* be stable in order to pursue long-term goals and consistent behaviours. In practice, for reasons we discuss in more detail below, performance measures often degrade over time; specifically, they lose variance. They thus change frequently.

5. *Applicability to compensation.* People *would* be rewarded for performance on the relevant measures, thus maximizing their contribution to the organization. In practice, there are two distinct problems. First, as noted above, single measures distort behaviour and multiple measures confuse individuals. Second, where there are simple performance measurement formulae, people game the formula, and where the measures are subjectively combined, people lose the connection between measured performance and compensation.

Performance measurement is thus endemically problematic, but the purposes of measurement, depicted here in Figure T5.1, are so important for firm functioning that it absorbs much effort. These purposes include reporting past financial performance for shareholders and predicting future performance for investors. They are dominated by financial accounting measures to which, as Kaplan (1984) has noted, internal management accounting measures have become increasingly subordinated. Such measures vary, including ROI above, but also return on assets (ROA), earnings per share (EPS) or, increasingly since

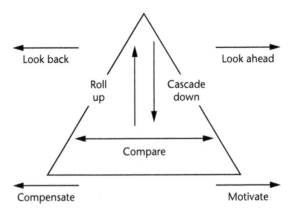

Figure T5.1. The purposes of performance measures.
(*Source*: Meyer 2002: 31)

the 1980s, the difference between the rate of return and the cost of capital, known as economic value added (EVA).

They also include internal cost and revenue-based data for allocation and compensation decisions, and a variety of non-financial measures that benchmark, motivate, and, ideally, predict. Such non-financial measures include defect rates, machine utilization and downtime, and various measures of output, as well as employee and customer measures such as satisfaction and turnover. A firm collecting all the mentioned forms of data is making a sizeable investment in its performance measurement system and will look in turn for specific benefits from that expenditure. This activity takes place in what we termed the 'technostructure' in the last chapter, which for Mintzberg is the key element of the machine bureaucracy. In the next section, we look at three specific problems the technostructure encounters: the correlation problem, the variance problem, and the control problem. In each case we look at a practical application.

Harsh Measures

The Correlation Problem

If all performance measures are highly correlated, then we gain little by adding more. It may be that we can gain all of the information we need by using a single measure. In trading floors in investment banks, for example, traders are predominantly rewarded on the basis of the profitability of their trades; however, this arguably causes other important measures to be ignored, and there is empirical evidence to show it creates intractable management problems (Fenton O'Creevy et al., 2005). We may seek a more balanced approach using multiple, uncorrelated measures. This is in fact a common approach, as Meyer notes:

> Common sense measures used to gauge the performance of a firm are generally uncorrelated . . . look across a large number of firms or their business units and you will find that profitability, market share, customer satisfaction and operating efficiency are weakly and sometimes negatively correlated.
> (Meyer, 2002: 2).

Performance is not a single construct, and the choice of uncorrelated performance measures should have some logic in terms of the long-term objectives of the firm.

This is the central logic underpinning the development by Kaplan and Norton (1992, 1996, 2000) of the 'balanced scorecard approach' that has come to dominate performance measurement. The scorecard has developed multiple variants but in the original form sought to compile measures in four domains: financial, customer, internal business, and learning and innovation.[3] In the terminology we have used above, the scorecard is a mix of financial measures and non-financial ones that predict cash flows in the future. There may be low correlations between measurement categories, but probably higher ones within categories.

The analogy often used for the scorecard measures is that of an aeroplane cockpit, with various dials showing separate indicators all-important for the safe flying of the plane. The unifying idea for a set of measures, which becomes more central to the argument in the later (1996 and 2001) versions, is that this is not simply a performance management tool, but a device for communicating and tracking business strategy; the organization's mission is operationalized as a set of performance measures. In the latter, strategic, case, there is an argument for multiple measures covering a wide range of business outcomes, but the argument reverses where the scorecard is used for compensation and appraisal, due to the cognitive limitations of individuals in understanding the link between effort, performance, and reward. Meyer (2002: 82, 108) argues that large numbers of US corporates use balanced scorecards for appraisal and compensation, and that they should not.

Figure T5.2 shows an example of a balanced scorecard in the market-leading UK retailer Tesco. In this version, twenty broad measures across five domains (the additional one is 'community') are used explicitly for performance management at store level; this is not a strategic tool. Employees are asked to develop objectives and action plans consistent with the wheel, which are then discussed in twice-yearly appraisals. The wheel standardizes performance measures in a relatively homogeneous firm (all stores are essentially the same) for a large, dispersed, and high-turnover workforce (with major induction and socialization issues) where the set-up costs can be justified by scale.

There are many customized versions of scorecards but the generic problems of the approach are:

- finding the right measures that apply across the business
- combining them effectively
- establishing their legitimacy and effectiveness in setting compensation

Proliferation of measures is also an issue, as it is often easier to add an additional measure or even a domain than it is to remove one.

---

[3] The last two are sometimes depicted as 'process' and 'people'.

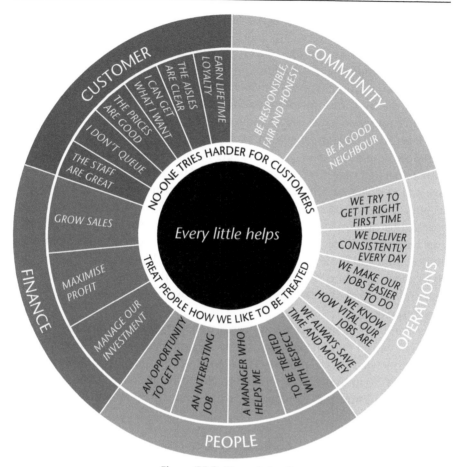

Figure T5.2. Tesco 'wheel'.

The Variance Problem

Performance measures tend to lose variance over time to the point where they do not discriminate between good and bad performers. Meyer (2002: 51–80) cites several datasets on baseball, automotive defects, nuclear safety, and hospital performance to show examples of left-editing of performance distributions as imitation of higher performers and market exit of lower ones reduces the standard deviation of performance distributions. In such circumstances, newer, more discriminatory, measures are required.

However, there may be other effects that restrict variance without improvement. We saw in Chapter 4 that in the Hawthorne studies social pressures led to output restrictions that reduced intra-group performance variance (see also Roy, 1952). More generally, collective organization in trade unions tends to lead to a reduction in wage dispersion (Metcalf et al., 2001). In such circumstances, merely changing the measures is unlikely to impact the social bases of output control.

Two widely cited examples concern grading compression in higher education and in employee performance appraisal. Meyer (2002: 61–2) cites grade inflation as a compression vehicle for Harvard undergraduates; since A+ remains the maximum grade, inflation must lead to compression. The performance appraisal issues are illustrated in the widely cited example of General Electric, a version of which is depicted in Figure T5.3. In individual employee appraisals, managers were often reluctant to use the full scales in both axes. First, very low ratings were avoided because of an unwillingness to give bad feedback or deal with the employment consequences of low scores. Second, high rankings were avoided because of fears that 'stars' would be poached by other departments. As a result, performance and potential rankings tended to cluster in zone X, and variance was low. The GE approach, termed 'rank and yank' was to implement forced rankings in the ratios 70–20–10 in zones X, Y, and Z respectively. This tackles the issues of both compression and inflation directly: 20% of employees were well rewarded, 10% were shown the door.

There are arguments both for and against this. It provides differentiated data on talent within ranking domains, but it does not guarantee it between them. Put another way, a poor employee (10%) in one department may be close to the median (70%) in another. Iterated annually, it means that better and better employees fall into the 10% bracket, which may be more appropriate where

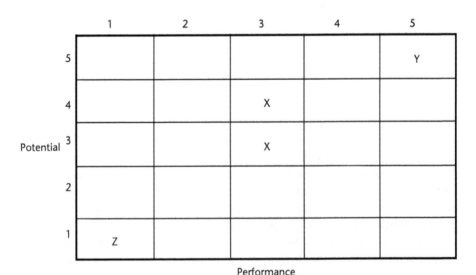

Figure T5.3. GE's 'rank and yank' system.

(*Source*: Mintzberg, 1983)

continuous improvement is possible or where the organization is downsizing. However, the primary drawback is that it individualizes performance, which may be inappropriate where there is team-based production, and by emphasizing appraisal as a win–lose game it makes team formation less likely.

Control and Legitimacy

Performance measures are problematic where the individual either does not feel she can influence the measure, or the measure itself is not accepted as legitimate. In both cases, gaming of the performance measure is likely, leading to improvement in the measure but not necessarily in underlying performance.

The expectancy theory of motivation (Vroom, 1964) depicts a cognitive process in which individuals become motivated when

- they can see a clear relationship between effort, performance, and reward, and;
- the reward on offer is desired.

In many cases, it may be that the organization of work frustrates a clear link. For example, individual and team-based performance measures and rewards have been used on assembly line technologies, even though the output and quality figures are often defined by the speed of the entire line (Willman, 1986).

Many of the issues here are similar to those we touched on in the discussion of agency theory, and agency considerations point to some difficulties. Principals control agents by monitoring and giving instructions and by providing incentives. How does the management of performance measures relate to this? In an extreme case, one could avoid monitoring, and simply align rewards with principals' interests. The most extreme case of this I am aware of is in market trading in investment banks, where the Profit and loss account (P&L) of the trader and the rewards attached to it are the prime managerial tool. However, even here agency considerations mean that the approach is dominantly, but not entirely, formulaic; managers keep discretionary control over a portion of bonus to reward 'other behaviours' (Willman et al., 2006; Fenton O'Creevy et al., 2005). To frame this in the terms used above, one is controlling inputs (picking traders) and incentivizing outcomes (profit) but not monitoring process closely. The problems with this have been evident in the fallout since 2008.

Let us explore this with a more extended case, that of British Petroleum (BP) since 1990. The case is intended to explore the costs and benefits of managing with financial performance indicators.

Roberts (2004: 186–9) describes several key reforms introduced by BP in the 1990s; let us concentrate on exploration and production for the sake of brevity. Key organizational changes he identifies include:

- Exploration and production operations were divided into forty business units termed 'assets'.
- 'Asset managers' reported to the executive committee through a pared-down management structure.
- They signed explicit individual contracts to deliver performance defined in terms of volume, costs, and capital expenditure. Within this, they could decide where and how to drill, and what to outsource.
- These contracts were extended to all individuals within the asset and compensation was defined by asset performance.
- Advisory 'peer groups' were set up to share expertise and to compete with one another on individually negotiated targets.
- Outsourcing increased, and outsourced activities did not directly employ capital.

This process began in the 1990s and was applied from the appointment of a new CEO in 1995 across the company. They were deemed a success.

> This organizational model led to BP's remarkable success. New fields were found and developed, many in areas that were previously thought to be technically too difficult to be economically feasible. The costs of developing fields was reduced substantially and kept being squeezed, and the productive life of assets was extended long beyond what had been believed possible.
>
> (Roberts, 2004: 188–9).

Then two of these 'assets', a refinery in Texas and the Deepwater Horizon rig in the Gulf of Mexico, blew up. BP's reputation generally, but particularly in the USA, was destroyed. Compensation and legal bills ran to billions (still growing at the time of writing), which outstripped the cost savings of the asset management programme. Major issues arose between BP and those responsible for outsourced activities over liabilities.

Simple explanations for complex technical failures are usually flawed, but it is at least tempting to see a protracted return-on-assets approach as pushing BP beyond technical and safety limits. While generating short-term returns, its enthusiastic embrace by those whose compensation was linked by performance measures to such returns could easily result in dangerous cutting of corners. And there are two ways at least to increase return on assets; one is genuinely to increase revenues, the other is to reduce the capital employed by outsourcing competitively. The lesson is clear; managing solely by performance measures is problematic, and probably generates precisely the agency problems it seeks to avoid.

Our second example concerns legitimacy; the imposition of performance measures that are not deemed appropriate by those to whom they are applied.

In several publications (e.g. Marsden and Belfield, 2006), Marsden has explored the application of performance-related pay to the teaching profession in the UK. The intention was to reward good teaching (and the corollary to eradicate bad). But introducing performance incentives to professions often cuts across established values and practices, and may raise questions about the legitimacy of activities. In teaching, the performance measures tended to relate to inputs (e.g. inspecting teaching quality) but also outputs (the performance of pupils), and this led both to disaffection (some felt the measures were wrong) and gaming (some felt they could be manipulated). If a teacher is paid by the performance of his pupils, then the following forms of gaming are likely:

- Paying attention only to 'smarter' students capable of getting good grades.
- Trying to exclude 'less smart' or problematic students from the school.
- Moving oneself to a higher performing school.
- Inflating student grades where this is possible.

These are all, in Meyer's terms, 'perverse' in that they increase performance measures without increasing performance.

This raises some very broad issues about the incentivization of professional work, particularly in not-for-profit organizations (Hudson, 1999). There is some evidence, for example, that merely publishing data on the success rates of surgeons (not compensating them on it) leads some to avoid difficult surgical procedures. There is even a (probably apocryphal but revealing) tale within management circles of a small European country that experienced a fall in mortality rates when doctors went on strike (because all operations were postponed). However, these examples once more reveal the difficulties of managing through performance measures. An additional feature of the teaching and medical examples is that the performance measures were exogenously set, by governments not the professions themselves. And this is an increasing feature of performance measurement in a variety of sectors. As Kaplan (1984) notes, internal management accounting measures become subservient to external financial accounting standards in firms. I turn to ranking and rating in the next section.

Accountability Noise

Ratings and rankings abound. Financial markets evaluate companies on market valuation for inclusion in indices (FTSE 100, S&P 100). Rating agencies such as Fitch and Moody's rate corporate and sovereign debt. Law firms are ranked by earnings per partner, and trade publications in law rank individual

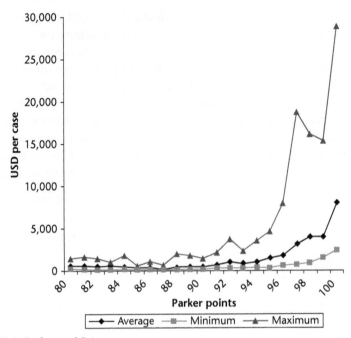

Figure T5.4. Parker and Price.
(*Source*: <http://www.wine-searcher.com/>)

lawyers by specialization. Business schools and universities are ranked on scorecard-type criteria. Even products are ranked; Robert Parker, a US wine critic, has produced a very influential ranking of wine (which the French hate). In this section I look at what rankings do and why they exist. I examine their impact on organizations and sectors, but I start with the producers and consumers.

Let's start with wine (I have always wanted to write that in a text). Figure T5.4 shows the simple relationship between a Parker score and a US case price for wines. Parker scores run from 50 (don't take it internally) up to 100 (the most excellent wines).[4] Particularly at the top end the figure shows that Parker scores matter for price; what might this mean? Let's try a few options.

1. **Parker scores simply reflect quality reliably**. In the price correlation above, the Parker score is the dependent variable and wine quality is the independent. The Parker score is simply a highly reliable signal. However, it is very useful, since particularly for the occasional wine drinker, the market can be complex; there are many brands, varietals (of grape), blends, regions,

---

[4] There are other rankings using the same scale, but not the same evaluations.

and combinations with food. If a Parker score reduces the necessary information, it will encourage consumers into wine drinking *and* reduce the power of the relatively more knowledgeable. After all, once you open the wine, there is no going back; it is an experience good. But this is simply a model of faithful reporting and reduction of information asymmetry.

2. **Parker scores actually create the perception of quality.** In this approach, a Parker score not only faithfully reports but also over time shapes the perception of what 'good wine' is. In this conception, a high Parker score is influential in shaping consumer tastes, and creating status concerns about product consumption. One would not like to say to friends one preferred an 80 to a 95 (although in blind tastings many do). This is a model of the shaping of consumer taste by ranking.

3. **Parker scores do both of the above, *and* cause ambitious producers to change what they do to conform to Parker tastes (or their perception of them).** In this conception, the ranker shapes the industry, specifically causing a focus on certain types of output and the search for ways to game the rankings. Lobbying the ranker becomes an important marketing effort. This is a model of the shaping of industry structure by ranking; specifically, it is a model of variance reduction as producers converge on a specific output type.

These are typifications, but they illustrate increasing influence from 1–3 of the ranking over the industry or product. They raise concerns over whether rankings homogenize industries and prevent innovation; an industry which uses ranking data as its only performance measure is likely to be highly protective of incumbents. Let us use the wine example to illustrate the kinds of industries where rankings are likely to be influential with consumers.

1. The price/quality trade-off is opaque. There are no standardized versions of product quality other than the rankings.
2. The market is differentiated, so that both good and bad offerings are available and they are not completely discriminated by price.
3. The market has no one dominant producer.
4. Individual consumer choice requires considerable outlay.
5. And it is difficult to go back on a purchase decision; switching costs are high relative to the value of the purchase.

Let us turn to a different industry to pursue this. Figure T5.5 shows the ranking of the top ten business school MBA programmes in 2014, published by the *Financial Times*. This is an annual survey, and it is by no means the only one; rankings compete. The survey is a sort of primitive balanced scorecard where measures are taken of student entrants, student exits, faculty, and some governance and other measures. The combination is formulaic, so it can be

Rank 2014	Rank 2013	Rank 2012	Schoolname	Salary today (US$)	Weighted salary (US$)	Salary percentage increase	Value for money rank	Career progress rank	Aims achieved rank	Placement success rank	Employed at three months (%)	Alumni recomme rank	Female faculty (%)	Female students (%)	Female board (%)	International faculty (%)	International students (%)	International board (%)	International mobility rank	International course experience rank	Languages	Faculty with doctorates (%)	FT doctoral rank	FT resea rank
1	1	2	Harvard Business School	175,994	178,300	113	86	4	50	24	89	1	23	41	50	40	34	14	48	52	0	91	2	1
2	2	1	Stanford Graduate School of Business	182,054	184,566	100	99	1	2	14	89	2	20	36	18	43	41	21	54	23	0	95	4	10
3	4	4	London Business School	155,624	156,553	107	84	12	3	27	95	4	22	32	32	86	91	82	2	7	1	99	24	17
4	3	3	University of Pennsylvania: Wharton	170,567	170,472	99	98	27	30	31	93	3	21	42	12	36	34	47	42	35	0	100	1	2
5	5	5	Columbia Business School	165,898	164,181	116	93	39	53	23	90	8	14	36	12	61	44	34	47	82	0	97	21	7
6	6	6	Insead	147,676	148,183	87	10	18	33	41	87	7	16	34	16	88	96	79	4	1	2	95	25	24
7	7	9	Iese Business School	141,873	143,168	125	65	5	4	61	90	18	20	26	23	56	78	86	8	6	1	100	76	54
8	9	7	MIT: Sloan	155,408	157,262	101	97	14	63	26	87	5	20	34	12	37	53	57	45	31	0	100	20	4
9	10	12	University of Chicago: Booth	156,623	156,004	100	94	46	16	2	91	9	16	35	13	37	48	40	55	60	0	97	10	7
10	14	20	Yale School of Management	149,790	150,880	114	83	20	5	32	85	17	21	39	20	32	40	38	58	40	0	100	44	23

Figure T5.5. *Financial Times* Global MBA ranking 2014 (top ten).

gamed, and the weights and combinations are stable year to year. Over the decades that this ranking has been produced, there is much year-to-year variation in school ranking, except at the top. Finally, this is a *product* ranking; this one is for MBAs but there are different ones for various types of executive programme. What does the experience of this kind of exercise do for and to the industry?

The Parker issues apply; it reduces information asymmetry for an experience good and it provides a status ranking which in turn indicates price and quality access points for prospective students. It probably publicizes and maybe expands the product demand. But this one does something more. It makes no sense to take Harvard on at its own game because they will always have more resources, but it may make sense to take on lower-ranked competitors using an approach that imitates Harvard. Alternately, it may make sense to differentiate. Some second-rank US schools are lucky to get students with out-of-state licence plates, much less international students, so the FT ranking is a good one for non-US schools in which to emphasize internationalism over, say, starting salaries after graduation, on which they may lose out to US schools. On the other hand, if one recruits students in relatively low-salary economies and sectors and moves them to higher ones (like India to London or Singapore) then the value added looks good. In short, the rankings promote segmentation as well as imitation.

This section closes with four general observations, all of which relate directly to more theoretical issues we will take up in later chapters.

1. There has been a substantial growth in the public accountability requirements of organizations, particularly in the West, on a variety of financial and non-financial matters.

2. This has developed to the point where many internal systems of performance measurement are defined by operational external reporting requirements to governments, media, or international markets (see Power, 2010).

3. There is a substantial academic debate about whether this homogenizes and stultifies industries. If everyone is chasing the same business model operationalized in a ranking system, where do change and diversity come from?

4. Markets are also status systems in which there are relatively stable performance rankings. This may be solely because economic power solidifies market position, or it may also be because status systems have their own dynamics. This relates to the power of brands, which we also discuss below.

Conclusion

Performance measurement is a necessary and resource-intensive nightmare. The measures are hardly ever good proxies for what we want to measure, mainly because we want to measure the future using the past. Mistrust of internal performance measures has developed to the point where we look for external and verifiable measures, but these measures are of necessity high-order market valuation methods.

People react to measures. The reaction may go either way. The goal-setting literature shows us that if one sets people stretching and accepted goals their performance will improve independent of reward (Locke and Latham, 1990). On the other hand, there is widespread evidence that people game both performance management and compensation systems where they see it in their interests to do so; they are more likely to see it as being in their interest either where there is principal agent conflict or where they deny the legitimacy of performance criteria and the consequences attached.

An outcome of these considerations is that many managers spend much of their time on performance issues. But performance measures really only matter if they lead to the capture of future cash flows and the pursuit of the firm's strategy; so let us turn to that.

Chapter 6

Strategy as Competition and Cooperation

Introduction

Business strategy has, compared to some other of the sub-disciplines, a strange history. First, there is a greatness in its lateness. Although there have been writings about military strategy for almost as long as there have been writings, business strategy is a post-World War II phenomenon. This is in stark contrast to the transfer of military ideas about *organization*, which as we have seen originated in the late nineteenth century. The second peculiarity is that the originator of several core ideas about strategy was a business historian. Chandler developed his ideas about the relationship between strategy and structure in the early 1960s by describing developments in Du Pont and General Motors in the 1920s. This raises several questions. Did no one else notice the link at the time? Or did a different language describe it? Either people were doing strategy in GM and Du Pont at the time and calling it something else, or this is seriously revisionist history. A third feature is that it has less unity than some other sub-disciplines. The sub-discipline of OB has cohesion, both intellectual and as a community. So, arguably, does finance. But in strategy there are distinctive traditions that root on the one hand in economics or, on the other, in organizational sociology (or just nowhere).

But business strategy is influential. This influence is strong among practitioners. John Kay has remarked that to add 'strategic' to a venture, whether that is strategic marketing, strategic operations, or strategic human resource management, is to increase its price. And business strategy academics tend to be less coy than some others about their wishes to influence practice (e.g. Bromiley, 2005). So the strategy literature in particular is a useful focus for any attempt to describe interactions between theory and practice.

The following three chapters will address strategy. This chapter will look at some economic approaches. The reason for starting this way is that Porter, the most significant figure in the strategy field, essentially adapted industrial economics to kick-start the field. However, it will not look at all economic approaches. Another way of looking at the strategy literature is to say that there are, on the one hand, approaches that ignore the theory of the firm. Specifically they treat the firm as a simple and single decision point that operates rationally to maximize self-interest. So strategy is about what you do to others, mostly competitors. Other theories about strategy look at sources of advantage internal to the firm that need to be leveraged and, rather differently, about what it means to say that firms *do* strategy; this includes a concern with the strategy process. These theories borrow from sociology and from psychology, but some economists get involved too. We will look at these in the next chapter. Between these chapters there is a theme devoted to the multi-divisional organization. This is talismanic to all approaches to strategy. In fact it is probably the most extended thematic case study in the management literature and I will use it to try to integrate different approaches.

Arguably, the difference between these two broad sets of approaches has a long history. Consider the following two definitions of strategy both from the 1960s. For Chandler, strategy is:

> The determination of the basic long-term goals and objectives of an enterprise and the adoption of courses of action and the allocation of resources necessary for those goals.
>
> (Chandler, 1962: 13).

However, for Ansoff:

> Strategic decisions are primarily concerned with external rather than internal problems of the firm and specifically with the selection of the product-mix that the firm will produce and the markets to which it will sell.
>
> (Ansoff, 1965: 18).

The first implies a link between the study of strategy and the study of organization. The latter sees strategy almost as a field within portfolio analysis. In fact, Chandler was primarily concerned with the role of top management in his case-study firms, specifically, to describe structures that ensured that they *did* think about the 'destiny of the entire enterprise' (Chandler, 1962: 309). Ansoff has a notion of strategy influenced more heavily by economics. Significantly, these two approaches tend to have different units of analysis: the firm vs. the market(s).

The Big Sleep

The heading is from Chandler; Raymond not Alfred. And this is a brief detective story. If Du Pont and GM went to a divisional structure in the 1920s to implement a strategy that (allegedly) required a divisional structure, why did it take forty years to figure out that strategy was the issue? Alfred Sloan himself (1963), who was at GM at the time, refers only to 'policy'.

Here is a short account from the best strategy text.

> The evolution of business strategy has been driven more by the practical needs of business than by the development of theory. During the 1950s and 1960s, senior executives were experiencing increasing difficulty in coordinating decisions and maintaining control in companies that were growing in size and complexity. Financial budgeting provided the basic framework for annual financial planning, while discounted cash flow (DCF) approaches to capital budgeting provided a new approach to appraising individual investment projects. Corporate planning was devised as a framework for coordinating individual capital investment decisions and planning the long-term development of the firm.
>
> (Grant, 2005: 15).

At the time, during the Cold War, it was not clear that planning the allocation of resources was an inferior mechanism to market allocation. In fact, influential commentators such as Clark Kerr (1962) and J. K. Galbraith (1968) were arguing that all industrial societies were converging on a model dominated by firm and governmental resource allocation decisions. Recall too, this was the age of managerial capitalism when investor oversight was not offering any dominant views of the 'destiny' of the large enterprise. The relationship of early strategy with improving financial management techniques became highly significant.

Grant goes on to argue that inflation and oil shocks in the 1970s and the advent of Japanese competition in the 1980s meant long-term corporate plans became useless. Others, such as Mintzberg (1994), took the view that it had never been a particularly good idea to rely on a top-down process in any case. What emerged was a focus on the markets in which a firm competed, the competitors involved, and the maximization of profitability. New ideas such as 'competitive advantage'—which is very different from the economic notion of comparative advantage—emerged, and the major initiative came directly from industrial economics.

Prêt à Porter

Michael Porter may be the most famous business academic around. His impact has been enormous, not only on the academic development of business strategy but also on practice. His framework is so well known that many readers may be able to skip this section to the next, where an evaluation and critique is given. Here I begin with a short account of its intellectual origins and the core framework.

Porter was by training an industrial economist and published in academic economic journals in the tradition of the 'Structure–Conduct–Performance' paradigm. In this tradition, industries were analysed in terms of their structure: the number of firms, the homogeneity of product, and entry and exit conditions (i.e. were firms coming into, or leaving, the industry?). Conduct referred to the strategies firms pursue; within economics, this tended to be discussed in terms of price–volume trade-offs. Finally, performance was examined largely as an outcome variable, and performance indicators tended to include data not only for the firm but also industry and welfare indicators; so some industries might be more profitable than others, and some might need regulation, for example if they became oligopolistic or even monopolistic.

The simple insight that generated the famous 'Five Forces' framework was to focus on the firm. Whereas the traditional concern of economic structural analysis was to assess where on the continuum between monopoly and perfect competition an industry stood, Porter looked at the firm's choice of industry and, within that, emphasized the need for the firm to position itself best to appropriate economic rents. So:

> The essence of formulating competitive strategy is relating a company to its environment. Although the relevant environment is very broad, encompassing social as well as economic forces, the key aspect of the firm's environment is the industry or industries in which it competes . . .

And the key challenge of strategy is:

> To find a **position** in the industry where . . . [the] company can best defend itself.
>
> (Porter, 1980: 137).

Some industries are more profitable than others. Grant (2005: 70) quotes figures for US industries that indicate how much. The return on capital employed in pharmaceuticals 1999–2002 was 26.8%, for airlines it was *minus* 34.8%. These differences are often enduring; for example the *Financial Times* once famously argued that

> In the first hundred years of the US air travel (1903–2003), the industry made exactly zero cumulative profit.
>
> (22 November 2003).

Pharmaceuticals is characterized by highly differentiated products, consumers who are not primarily concerned with price, and a patent system that gives decade long protection of returns to innovation. Airlines are characterized by undifferentiated products, price competition, low margins, and competition from other forms of travel. So firms should choose profitable industries, and profitability is defined by structure. For Porter, there are famously five

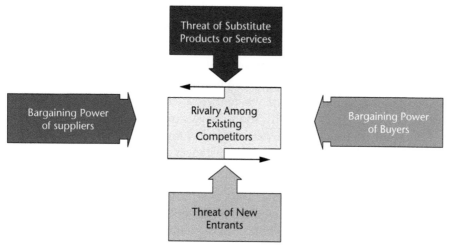

Figure C6.1. Porter's five forces.
(*Source*: Porter, Michael E. 'The Five Competitive Forces That Shape Strategy'. Special Issue on HBS Centennial. *Harvard Business Review* 86, no. 1 (January 2008): 78–93).

competitive forces within an industry that define profitability:[1] three are 'horizontal' relating to existing rivals, new entrants, and possible product substitutes; and two are 'vertical' relating to suppliers and customers. They are depicted in Figure C6.1 and we will look at each in turn.

- Supplier power is high where they are large and few and switching costs are high. Their importance to the firm also matters; suppliers of a key product component usually have more power than suppliers of catering.

- Substitutes are threatening (powerful) where there are low switching costs for the firm's customers and where the substitute has a good price/ performance balance.

- Rivalry is high where the industry is growing slowly, the product is homogeneous, customer-switching costs are low, there are lots of players, and fixed costs are high and you cannot recoup them by getting out. This analysis generically suggests that *differentiation* from your competitors is a potentially successful strategy whereas competition on cost is likely to lead to a race to the bottom.

---

[1] Porter tends to define profitability like an economist; not simply as return on capital employed but as economic value added, that is rate of return on capital relative to cost of capital. A recent accessible summary is Porter (2008).

- Buyers are powerful where there is excess supply, where they can switch between firms easily, where there are few of them, and where the product is relatively unimportant to them.

- The final 'force' is different. Whereas the first four are identifiable entities, probably other firms, the last is an industry property. Where it does not cost much capital to set up, where there are few scale economies, where the product is a commodity and so buyers can switch easily, and where there are no regulatory barriers, it is easier for new firms to come into the market (although under such circumstances it is difficult to see their logic for doing so).

Analysing the five forces does at least two things for the firm. It allows an estimate of current profit possibilities and it opens up the prospect that the firm can alter its industry position to its own advantage. This requires examination of a number of variables concerning industry which are listed in Figure C6.2. The axes are measured and positions plotted; when the axes are joined, the larger the enclosed area, the more attractive the industry. The

Bargaining Power of Suppliers
- Number and size of suppliers
- Switching costs
- Unique service or product

Bargaining Power of Buyers
- Number of buyers
- Buying volumes
- Price elasticity
- Brand identity
- Switching costs

Rivalry Among Existing Competitors
- Number of competitors
- Exit barriers
- Differentiation and diversity
- Switching costs of customers

Threat of Substitute Products or Services
- Customer loyalty
- Substitute performance
- Switching costs

Threat of New Entrants
- Cost and time of entry
- Economies of scale
- Relative cost advantages
- Technological know-how

Figure C6.2. Key industry variables.

position can then be managed in order to generate competitive advantage. At the extreme, this might suggest exit behaviour, but it can be used as an indicator of what to protect, and where the major competitive risks lie. It is not simply about defence, it also points to what aspects of the industry structure the firm might try to influence. For the diversified firm, it points towards effective portfolio management, guiding market entry as well as exit considerations.

Yes … But

There are at least two lines of criticism available; one focuses on what Porter does, the other on what he does not. Unfortunately this is not quite the watertight distinction it might seem. Let us first focus on what is done.

This is essentially a framework for the firm to accrue rents. Competitive strategy is about sustainable competitive advantage and, paradoxically, the term used refers to a situation where the firm has, in economic terms, successfully avoided price competition and erected barriers around its rents. The analysis supports a rent-seeking missile in identifying 'differentiation' possibilities. Where at least oligopolistic competition is not feasible, the industry looks relatively unattractive. So, Porter-based recommendations to a firm designed to sustain competitive advantage are likely to be orthogonal to the recommendations emerging from industrial organization about industry structure. To take a simple example, if entry barriers are low or falling, incumbent firms would, within the Porter framework, be rational to lobby government to raise them; in fact this is exactly what happened in the US auto industry at the advent of Japanese competition. The consumer interest that prevailed was to allow the competition (on the advice of industrial economists).

The dependent variable of choice is a measure of profitability. Those organizations that do not have this as their primary measure and those that have multiple performance measures are not considered. If we recall the Carnegie Mellon approach, firms are coalitions of interests based around multiple performance measures, some of which are mutually exclusive.

The outcome of an industry analysis is mainly a picture of the past; firms look for positions to 'defend'. True, analysis of prospective new entrants or substitutes might lead to scenario building, but the picture emerging from a five forces analysis is essentially of a legacy. There is no model, for example, of how to implement, following industry analysis, policies or practices that might lead to competitive advantage.

The reason why the division between what Porter included and what he omitted above does not work neatly is that these three problems relate to the underlying model of the firm. The minimalist approach inherited from economics sees the firm as a chess piece to be moved around the board. Who is to do this, how they should do it, and in whose interests they should act are not considered. Strategy processes are not considered. Internal capabilities are not considered.

Some of this criticism applies only to this framework and not to Porter's later work, and it is presented here less to diminish the achievements of the industry analysis approach than to indicate why much of the subsequent work in strategy minimized the importance of the industry, and returned to Chandler's earlier focus on the internal operation of the firm. I will look in depth at this in the next chapter.

However, there is one other major omission to be remedied before I do. The industry analysis looks outward at rent opportunities, but it does not explicitly consider the fact that all the other firms in the industry are likely to be doing the same. To incorporate that into strategy we need to understand the theory of games.

Game On

Nobel Prize-winning economist, Paul Samuelson, once remarked that the inventor of game theory, John Von Neumann, was the only mathematician to have made a major contribution to economics. He did so rather in his spare time, since his contributions to mathematics were far broader. There is little evidence that he regarded it as his major achievement (Bernstein, 1996). However, the *Theory of Games and Economic Behaviour* (Von Neumann and Morgenstern, 1944) transformed thinking in microeconomics, and was probably his most widely read work. Its route into business strategy was not direct. The canonical game, the prisoner's dilemma (see below), was developed at the Rand Corporation in the early 1950s, and many of the major early contributions were from political scientists (Axelrod, 1984, 1997). Solving two-party iterated games had a natural appeal to political scientists concerned with the dynamics of the Cold War.

In strategy, the impact post-dates Porter, and the logic of incorporating game theory does depend on industry analysis to some extent. Once one has analysed the forces, it makes sense to think how counter-parties will react to moves on the part of the firm to enhance its competitive position. Game theory gave at least two major opportunities. First, it could add dynamism to the static Porter framework. Second, it could include strategy options other than competition, notably cooperation, a high-profile option in the essentially oligopolistic contexts Porter envisaged.

However, the impact is uneven. For economists who study firm strategies, game theory *is* strategy. Nothing else in the field simplifies the world so radically and enables such mathematical rigour. However, for many academics in the field, it has merely a walk-on part. The most significant US and European strategy texts pay slight attention; Grant (2005) covers it in seven pages of 530, Whittington (2001) in under one (of 128)! There is a British yeast-based sandwich spread called Marmite which is advertised on the basis that people either love or hate it. Game theoretic models of strategy seem to elicit a similar response.

This section will present in non-technical terms two basic examples of games applied to the firm; the one-shot version of the prisoner's dilemma and an iterated version with a game tree. This will introduce the key ideas and terms. Those who know their games can skip to the next section, where we assess its contribution to the field.

The setting for the prisoner's dilemma has two prisoners in separate cells who have the option to confess their crime or remain silent. If both stay silent, they both get short sentences; if both confess, they both get a much longer one. If one confesses and the other does not, the confessor goes free and the other gets a *very* long sentence. They are mutually aware, but they cannot communicate. The silent option is termed cooperation. The confess option is termed defection. If both prisoners follow individually rational strategies they will both confess since this offers the best pay-off. This option gets them both long sentences. So rationality leads to an inefficient and Pareto-inferior outcome, which is why economists got interested. If both prisoners are Mafia members, with a code of silence, then they will profit from that by remaining silent.

Let us play the game with a business example, but using game theory language.[2] The *players* are Colgate Palmolive and Procter and Gamble. They

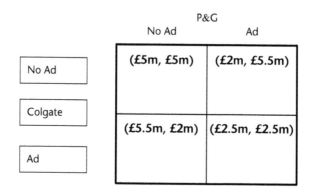

	P&G	
	No Ad	Ad
No Ad	(£5m, £5m)	(£2m, £5.5m)
Colgate		
Ad	(£5.5m, £2m)	(£2.5m, £2.5m)

Figure C6.3. The prisoner's dilemma.

[2] I am indebted to Professor Tobias Kretschmer for this version.

		Company B	
		Low	High
Company A	Low investment	(4,3)	(2,4)
	High investment	(3,2)	(1,1)

Figure C6.4. The one-shot game.

sell competing brands of toothpaste. They have to decide whether to run an advertising campaign or not (their *strategies*). The *rules* are that they decide simultaneously. The *pay-offs* are as follows. If they both do not run one, they make £5 million each. If one runs a campaign and the other does not, the runner makes sales of £8 million (80% of the market) and incurs £2.5 million costs, leaving a net benefit of £5.5 million. The other firm makes £2 million (20% of the market). If they both advertise, then, since the total market is fixed at £10 million, they each net 2.5 million. We can now construct a *pay-off matrix*, as in Figure C6.3. What this figure tells us is that both will advertise since advertising is a *dominant strategy*; that is it does better than the others for any strategy the other player chooses. However, if the parties can reliably collude, they would not advertise.

This is known as a one-shot game. There are also iterated games with very different implications; here is one. The *players* we will call Company A and Company B; they are both consumer electronics companies developing high definition DVD recorders. The first company to produce a recorder will set the industry standard. Both companies would like to minimize their investment in the new design and are preparing for entry into talks on developing a joint venture. Company A is currently slightly ahead in the technology.

In a one-shot game as in Figure C6.4, there is a *Nash equilibrium*; that is a combination of strategies such that no one player can improve their own pay-off by a unilateral move (or more colloquially that no one will move given the other's strategy). But Company A is not happy with the beautiful mind solution. It can improve the situation by moving to an extensive, multi-period game. A simple representation is in Figure C6.5. Here, A makes an initial choice to constrain the choices B has.

If A can commit itself (credibly) to invest high (by moving first), then they can induce the (3,2) outcome—a definite improvement relative to the (2,4)

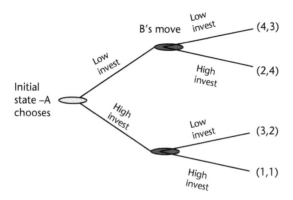

Figure C6.5. The Iterated Game.

result in the simultaneous game. Knowing this, B may announce: 'We will pursue a high-invest strategy if A makes high investment'. This could lead to the highly negative outcome (1,1). This is a *deterrent threat*. If A invests high, and they believe B, then they are assured their worst outcome.

Fun and Games

For people who like this sort of thing, this is the sort of thing they like and it can get much, much more complicated and formalized than this (Binmore, 1991). I have done enough to turn to the following question: what are the benefits of using game theory in the study of business strategy? (Dixit and Nalebuff, 1991).

First, it offers a formal way of analysing competitive situations, predicting equilibrium outcomes, and, in these terms at least, identifying optimal choices. Second, it allows us to examine the mix of competition and cooperation in business relationships. Businesses such as Apple and Microsoft have combined cooperation with fierce competition, and game theory gives us an avenue towards explanation of observed patterns. It explains other phenomena too, such as the clustering of competitive businesses in Silicon Valley, Hollywood, the City of London, and so on. It provides mechanisms for explaining why firms in oligopolistic industries avoid price competition. The notion of deterrence explains phenomena such as the guarantee many retailers give to make refunds where customers find lower prices elsewhere; this deters price cuts (and may provide useful competitor information). The idea of commitments explains why we have frequent-flyer programmes on many airlines.

But if we want to understand the low profile this form of analysis has in the major strategy texts, the limitations need also to be addressed. First, to repeat, this approach sees the firm as a single decision point. Firms are just individuals in this literature. More specifically, in game theoretic language, all the players are the same. Differences in strategy arising out of differences between internal structures or capabilities of firms cannot be considered. Second, as the games above indicate, the approach is best in highly stylized situations where one can identify players, rules, and pay-offs. This allows the mathematical rigour that the above examples have spared you, but as Grant remarks, the necessary conditions are considerable.

> If we identify the players in a game, identify the decision choices available to each player, specify the performance implications of each combination of decisions, and predict how each player is likely to react to the decision choices of the other, then we have made huge progress in understanding the dynamics of competition.
>
> (Grant, 2005: 112).

To use the language of military strategy, this is an approach to battles not to wars.

Another of the difficulties about game theory in strategy is rooted in the problem of common knowledge rationality. Common knowledge rationality refers to a situation where we all know x, we all know that everyone else knows x, we all know that everyone else knows we all know x . . . and so on. Consider the following repeated game variant of a prisoner's dilemma.[3]

> A king assembles his prisoners. He says to them 'At least one of you has a red spot on the top of her head. If that person comes forward, I will free her. However, if a person steps forward who does not have that spot, they will be executed.'

As in the prisoner's dilemma, it is a condition that the prisoners cannot talk to each other. By induction one can see that people will step forward on the nth occasion if this is a repeated game, where n is the number of red spotted people. If $n = 1$, the person will recognize that he or she has a spot (by seeing no spots on the others) and step forward on the first play. If $n = 2$, no one will step forward on the first play. The two spotted people, seeing only one person with a spot, *and* that no one left on the first play, will leave on the second play. It can be reasoned that no one will step forward on the first $n-1$ plays if and only if there are at least n spotted people. Those with spots, seeing $n-1$ spotted people among the others and knowing there must be at least n, will reason that they have spots and step forward. On this logic, they will live.

---

[3] This is taken from an Oxford University interview question when the author was conducting undergraduate entrance.

Three people are sitting on a long-haul flight from London to Johannesburg and they can't sleep. Jacko is an eccentric millionaire who flies economy. Terry is a British business traveller. Francois is a South African student flying home for the holiday. Jacko is bored stiff. He plays a game. He pulls out 10,000 rand in cash from his wallet and puts it on his tray table. He says; 'here's the deal—if you two can agree how to split this money within ten seconds you can keep the split, okay?' They agree.

Jacko says to Francois; 'you start'.

How should this come out? If Francois is rational and thinks Terry is, he should wait nine seconds and then offer Terry ten rand (or less). The logic is that Terry is then presented with a choice between something and nothing and he will take something. But if Terry is not rational, or does not want ten rand, Francois loses out. You have probably figured out we are back in the cognitive biases literature again. This is a version of a Kahneman game and in fact the outcome is often closer to a 50–50 split because Francois factors Terry's utility function into his bid (Bazerman, 2002). The key point is that if you are uncertain about the rationality of, or information possessed by, the counter-party, gaming becomes more complex. In the red spot example above, you *really* need to know that among the other prisoners there is no one who just wants to die. Where there is uncertainty about rules and rationality, economic gaming does not work in practice. Arguably, relationships between firms involve fairly severe uncertainties, particularly in volatile markets, which are simply not captured. Which is one of the reasons strategy texts don't use it much.

What is the point here? First, one must in real-life games not only act rationally but also assume that counter-parties will do so and that they have figured out what you will do. These are quite severe assumptions, even in game theoretic terms. Consider the following.

Game theory is not particularly predictive, and although it might appear dynamic, as Porter himself noted, game theory 'stops short of a dynamic theory of strategy... these models explore the dynamics of a largely static world' (Porter, 1991). This is perhaps less true of modern game theory. But Camerer, generally a fan, suggests that in the context of strategy research there are four reasons why adoption has taken some time (Camerer, 1991: 149).

- The 'chopstick' problem. His reference is to the argument that chopsticks are harder to use than a fork, and that game theory is too hard to use. My guess is that it depends which implement you are used to, but his argument holds in that prior to the impact of game theory, there was little mathematical sophistication in strategy research.

- The 'collage' problem. By this he means that game theory models are not additive to any general theory of strategy (there are parallels here with the decision bias literature discussed above).

- The 'testing' problem—that is models are hard to test. This implies empirical strategy research.

- The 'Pandora's box' problem. Like many hidden-information approaches in economics, game theory can predict outcomes that do not reflect actor preferences (as in the prisoner's dilemma) so rational actors can do apparently foolish things. The 'Pandora's box' problem is that game theoretic models can explain almost anything. Entertainingly, in the same volume, Postrel (1991) demonstrates, mildly convincingly, that you can articulate a model that explains why bank executives could rationally set fire to their trousers. The fact that there are few documented instances is not the main issue here. Let's take a look.

Liar, Liar

Postrel sets up a two period game in which:

- There is an equal number of high- and low-quality banks.
- Customers only discover bank quality after depositing (i.e. it is an 'experience good').
- Presidents of high-quality banks set their trousers on fire to signal that their bank is of high quality. It is rational to do so since the benefits of customer acquisition exceed the cost of flaming trousers.
- Presidents of low-quality banks do not have a positive pay-off to pant firing since this requires customer retention across two business periods.
- It is known by customers that presidents of both high- and low-quality banks have this pay-off, and that they share in bank profits.

He establishes that there is 'a subgame perfect Bayesian Nash equilibrium . . . in which bank presidents publicly set their trousers on fire' (Postrel, 1991: 154).

Now one might see this as comic. However, writing in 2013, the idea of bank presidents doing something as ostensibly stupid as firing their trousers does not perhaps seem too far-fetched. And there are historical examples—for example in medieval Europe—of rich people destroying wealth or giving it away in ostentatious consumption to send signals (Keen, 1984). But Postrel is concerned to show how game theory works, and that models are extremely sensitive to assumptions about information, the sequences of moves, the pay-offs, and constraints on action. One starts with the phenomenon one wishes to explain, then specifies a game in which this phenomenon emerges in equilibrium.

His key point is that game theory is not a theory of business competition since it contains no substantive account of behaviour. It is a set of logical tools that helps us explain what happens if all actors (firms) behave rationally. It might work better in some circumstances than in others. Where rules are unclear, pay-off matrices uncertain, and the sequence of movement of actors uncontrolled, game theory models may become intractable. In auctions in bond markets or for broadband spectrum, where all is clearly defined, they predict (sometimes). But if the models in these cases predict, they do so not because they simply describe reality but because they design it. Auctions, for example, often have clear objectives: they are performative. This is an important point to which I will return.

Conclusion

In this chapter, we have introduced two significant brands of economic thinking about strategy. There are other varieties which we will discuss below, but what these two approaches share is an approach to the firm; the firm is a unitary decision-making actor, similar to an individual and, most of the time, the actor is assumed to be rational. We can question this (or not) but one consequence of it is that the models of the world are complete. For Porter, the industry has boundaries and competitors can be identified. In game theory, the rules and the players need to be clearly defined.

Another consequence is that because there is no theory of the firm, there is no analysis of the relationship that interested Chandler; the relationship between the nature of the firm and the performance of strategy. Both sides of this relationship have been analysed. Scholars have looked at the internal capabilities and resources of the firm, and argued they are central to the search for competitive advantage; for many such scholars, industry structure is not a key variable and competition is a consequence of strategic decisions, rather than the reverse. Other scholars have concerned themselves with the processes of doing strategy. They have concerned themselves with how it is done (e.g. is rationality a useful assumption?) and with who does it (e.g. is the Chandler argument that top managers should do it the right one?). I will examine these in the next chapter. But first, let us look at the M form.

Theme 6

A Short History of the M Form

Introduction

Few phenomena have attracted more attention in the business literature than the multi-divisional business. It is central to the works of historians (Chandler), economists (Williamson, Teece), organizational theorists (Mintzberg), finance academics (Jensen), and accountants (Kaplan). Although Williamson describes it as 'The most significant organisational innovation of the twentieth century' (1985: 279), it is not clear that it is completely a modern phenomenon (Anderson et al., 1983), but its proliferation internationally in the modern era implies it has substantial properties of efficiency or legitimacy or both. It is often presented as an American gift to the world.

There are approaches that treat it as an undifferentiated entity. So, for Chandler it facilitated strategic thinking and for Williamson it is an internal capital market. Mintzberg sees it as fostering bureaucracy. But many who have investigated the internal operation of divisionalized structures stress their diversity. Some divisionalized structures are vertically integrated; oil companies would be a good example, with 'upstream' and 'downstream' operations. Others are diversified, with divisions operating in different sectors; banks, for example, have (for now) retail and investment banking divisions. Diversification was once fashionable; at the time of writing, at least for public corporations, it is less so. Other internal dimensions of diversity include relations between head office and divisions, degrees of decentralization, relations between divisions, divisional performance measures, and mobility of resources between divisions.

In this theme, I will look at the general propositions before turning to variance, and an attempt to explain the sources of variation. First, I describe in basic terms what it is and how it works.

The four forms (a)–(d) in Figure T6.1 are all divisionalized structures. Head office in each stylization oversees four divisions. I will deal with *how* it does so later. The structure involves a number of principles.

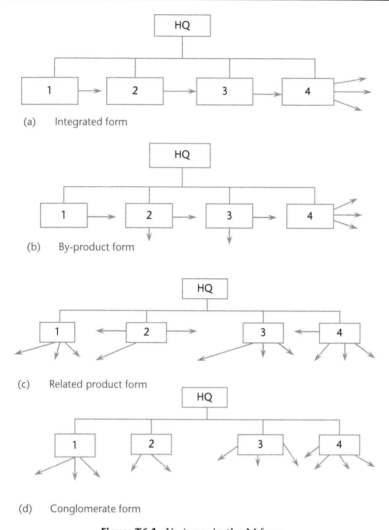

Figure T6.1. Variance in the M form.

1. In strategic terms, the separation of conception from execution. Head office oversees the business, and divisional managers run their divisions: grand-scale Taylorism.

2. Divisions have some performance target set by head office. It may be the same for all divisions, or there may be variance.

3. There is some mechanism for distributing surpluses created by divisions.

4. Head office decides the basis of divisionalization in two senses; first, the internal boundaries between divisions (they could be, for example, product, brand, or geographically based); second, whether to own a division or not (the 'make or buy' decision).

Then comes the variance; again, consider Figure T6.1.

(a) Presents a single value chain where the divisions are parts of a vertically integrated business. The divisions are likely to be cost, not profit, centres and only division 4 faces the market. Key issues are the relative economies of scale of the divisions, since upstream divisions cannot produce more than downstream divisions can eat, and transfer prices; that is how we account for movement between divisions where there is no external market. Because of this level of integration, the level of autonomy of divisional managers is likely to be limited. Although it might use divisional terminology, this is really a functional structure with decentralization generated by scale.

(b) Presents a single value chain where some of the pressures of (a) are reduced by allowing upstream divisions access to market, sometimes component markets. This allows transfer prices to be set with some market reference, and allows for each division to produce close to optimum scale. It probably permits more divisional discretion. However, issues emerge about prioritizing internal vs. external customers, about allowing downstream operations to buy outside if upstream can sell outside, and about product development for external vs. internal markets.

(c) Takes disintegration a stage further and raises the question of whether divisions that are linked (3–4) should be treated differently from those that are not (1), particularly in performance measurement terms. Compared to the single value chain examples (a) and (b), it also raises an information asymmetry issue; can head office know all about what divisions do? What if they compete with each other?

(d) Is the completely diversified business, which in practice replicates an investment portfolio since the chances of independent division performance being highly correlated are reduced. Divisional autonomy and information asymmetry are increased. Investors may (and did) come to ask what the added value of head office is over and above an independently invested portfolio in similar assets.

This is neither an observable historical sequence nor a representation of a clear dynamic. But it does serve to emphasize that the internal dynamics of the M form structure contain some general issues and some that vary by firm. Let us look at the general ones first.

Long Division

The reasons Chandler gives for the success of the M form are as follows.

> It clearly removed the executives responsible for the destiny of the entire enterprise from the more routine operational activities, and so gave them the time, information, and even psychological commitment for long term planning and appraisal...
>
> ...this new structure left the broad strategic decisions as to the allocation of existing resources and the acquisition of new ones in the hands of a top team of generalists.
>
> (Chandler, 1962: 382–3)

Divisionalized structures were both an innovation and an end point. The Chandler argument, developed in later works, was that the move to divisionalization would happen in every industry and geography; it was to be, as Whittington et al. delightfully put it, 'the final resting place of corporate development' (1999: 546).

It certainly became common. Students at Harvard working with Chandler studied the spread of divisionalization in the USA (Rumelt, 1974), the UK (Channon, 1973), and continental Europe (Dyas and Thanheiser, 1976). Rumelt (1974) found 77% of Fortune 500 firms were divisionalized in the USA. By 1993, surveys of large firms in Europe were discovering very high densities of divisionalization; 76% in France, 70% in Germany, 90% in the UK (Whittington et al., 1999: 543). The growth in Europe was steady, starting at a very low post-war base.

The spread induced economists, and particularly Williamson, to develop a theory of the M form. If it was common, it must be because it is efficient, driving out less efficient forms; and if it was efficient, it ought to be possible to specify the efficiency properties. Williamson develops Chandler's ideas, and interestingly relies more on agency theory and information asymmetry arguments than on transaction costs. For Williamson (1985: 281–4), the M form has

1. a strategic planning and resource allocation capability;
2. a monitoring and control apparatus;
3. a cash flow allocation process to incentivize and reward high-yield uses.

The M form is for Williamson in fact an efficient internal capital market in which information asymmetries are reduced by effective monitoring and agents (divisional managers) have their

> goal structure altered in favour of enterprise-wide considerations... A concept of the firm as an internal capital market thus emerges
>
> (Williamson 1985: 284)

Referring back to Figure T6.1, this is more likely to be (b) and (c) above, where it makes sense to talk about the coordination of diversity. In (a), which approximates what Williamson would term a 'J' form or functional structure, monitoring and control are likely to be head office priorities, but strategic planning will be crowded out. By contrast, in (d), which approximates what Williamson would call an 'H' form (a holding company), there is likely to be poor monitoring and a simple earnings retention approach, which raises questions about whether the corporate is more than an investment shell.

Now this too is quite a Chandlerian conclusion, but with a different logic. In particular, the conglomerate 'H' form that became a popular form of division-alization was a target in his later writings. For Chandler, divisionalization was a mechanism allowing firms seeking growth opportunities to exploit econ-omies of scope and learning opportunities. They should only do so by explor-ing *related* diversification where existing skill sets are relevant. *Unrelated* diversification by conglomerates has no such benefits; rather it indicates failure in the search for good diversification (for a good summary of the issues, see Whittington et al., 1999: 525–8). For Williamson, unrelated diversification is only a problem to the extent it impairs the operation of activities 1–3 above, otherwise the internal capital market will prevail. The causal relationship between divisionalization and diversification has produced a monstrous literature to which we will return below.[1]

Now, the basic problem with the efficiency argument for the diffusion of divisionalized structures is that it has proved difficult to torture the data into confession. Armour and Teece (1978) found first-mover advantages to division-alization only in the USA; this is difficult to reconcile with broad diffusion. Moreover, even this effect disappears in other countries (Mahajan et al., 1988), and this has prompted at least two other types of explanation worth mentioning.

1. Institutional theorists such as Fligstein (1985, 1990) argue that it is about power. In the course of development of large firms, power resides initially with manufacturing personnel capable of coordinating large-scale production. The search for growth opportunities then shifts power to sales and marketing personnel who pursue related and unrelated product opportunities.

2. At least for second-movers, imitation and the search for legitimacy may have been important; if first-movers profit, others may be encouraged to adopt. This imitation may be encouraged by high-status agents, such as McKinsey (McKenna, 2006) or even Chandler himself via the Harvard alumni network (Palmer et al., 1987: 107)!

These three types of argument are not mutually exclusive and perhaps effi-ciency, power, and imitation effects need to be compounded to achieve the

---

[1] But for a useful summary, see Kogut and Parkinson (1998).

dominance that this organizational form has among large firms. But there may also be unobserved heterogeneity: specifically, what if the existence of a divisional structure is consistent with the operation of a variety of different organizational arrangements? I now turn to variance in the M form.

A House Divided?

For both Chandler and Williamson, the key issue for the effectiveness of the divisional structure is the operation of the 'general' or head office, and the structure itself facilitates its effective performance but does not guarantee it; one may have decentralization without strategy and an internal capital market with no reallocation between divisions. So a useful way into the variance that may underpin divisional forms is to look at what head office does.

1. *Manager of the Strategic Portfolio.* There are two broad issues here. The first is to decide on and develop the portfolio. This involves purchase and sale of divisions but it also involves forming or splitting divisions. It is clear from the Chandler approach to the pursuit of growth opportunities that divisionalization is a process—perhaps a self-perpetuating one—rather than an event. In this particular respect the diffusion studies quoted above underestimate the amount of divisionalization taking place since they operate with binary categories. There is probably variance between companies in the *rate* of ongoing divisionalization. There is also variance in the extent to which these processes are systematic and formalized. The most widely quoted formalization was developed in GE in collaboration with McKinsey in the late 1960s, which spelled out criteria under which divisions (there were about 50) should be built up, simply held on to, or 'harvested'—either managed to maximize cash flow or sold (Grant, 2005: 477–9). But many corporations use either different or no models to manage this portfolio balance.

2. *Owner of Performance Control System.*[2] Head office will devise, monitor, and develop measurement systems for divisional performance. There may be more than one, since it may not be sensible to measure divisional performance in the same way if divisions are different. For example, one might not wish to measure a new start-up division in terms of profitability; revenue growth or market share considerations may be important. Options include:

• *Cost centres.* These are useful in vertically integrated divisions such as (a) above where it is not sensible to allow divisional managers control over quantity or quality, but one wants them to focus on maximizing the efficiency of the production process and not worry about demand conditions.

[2] This section relies heavily on Jensen (1998: 345–61).

• *Revenue centres.* These are useful where HQ wants managers to focus on marketing and sales efforts, although it is unwise to focus solely on revenues since managers will be tempted to push to the point where marginal revenue is zero. More common are calculations of gross margin where costs are netted off against revenues.

• *Profit centres.* This is a more extreme form of decentralization where divisional managers are in charge of product mix, quality, and quantity. This only works well in example (d) above where there are no interdependencies since this is the only circumstance where the firm's total profits are maximized by maximizing the profit of each division. Where divisions are buying or selling to each other or where they are selling complementary products (e.g. DVD players and DVDs) interdependencies may reduce the overall profit of the firm.

• *Investment centres.* This relates the achievement of profit to the cost of the assets necessary to produce them. They thus take into account the efficiency of asset utilization. Common measures are ROA (return on assets) or return on equity (ROE); both are problematic where managers have discretion over the level of assets, since one way to increase ROA or ROE is to sell all assets except the ones with the highest return (i.e. manage on the denominator). One way to overcome some of these problems is to use a measure such as economic value added, which is cash flow minus a cost of capital charge. This tends to be more desirable in capital-intensive businesses.

• *Expense centres.* Some support functions, such as human resources and public relations, have no external market referents. They produce services for the rest of the organization and consumers generally do not pay. These departments tend to overproduce because there is no charging, and consumers tend to demand quality that is too high. Expenses thus tend to escalate. Outsourcing is a clear possibility, particularly if the service is not central to the firm's purpose and there are economies of scale (e.g. payroll administration).

The choice of performance measure mix is likely to vary by firm, depending on the precise mix of divisions and the demand for support services.

3. *Monitoring Divisional Performance.* As we saw above in Chapter 5, one can monitor inputs (decisions), processes, or outcomes. Divisionalized corporations differ in how much monitoring they do, as well as the way they do it, and what they monitor. Goold and Campbell (1987) studied large multi-business firms in Britain, looking at what they termed 'parenting style' (it is Britain after all); what they meant was the texture and intensity of HQ–divisional relationships. They found that the portfolio structure was influential in the balance between a 'strategic planning' approach that emphasized

monitoring intensity and a 'financial control' approach that emphasized output monitoring. The elaboration is as follows:

- *Strategic planning* firms tended to have closely interlinked businesses with high-capital requirements. They were exposed to strong competition for technological advantage. The style was one in which the HQ was involved in detail in divisional strategy and coordination of implementation. Vertically integrated firms were typical. Divisions were not autonomous; linkages were important.
- *Financial control* firms tended to be conglomerates giving a 'go away and make money' approach to divisions. They tended to be in mature industries with low marginal capital requirements. Simple measures such as ROA were used across diversified businesses, and divisions were bought and sold. The HQ weapon of choice was the divisional budget.

In these categories, the firms looked very different. Strategic planning firms needed big head offices, since exerting this level of control requires man-for-man marking of divisional senior managers. They needed quarterly intervention. They needed to own the careers of senior divisional managers who will move from division to division at the whim of HQ so that they do not 'go native' in any division. They needed to avoid acquiring any difficult-to-integrate operations. Financial control firms could survive with a small head office in which the sale and acquisition teams were important. They need a uniform performance-measurement system; the only people who would move between divisions would be finance directors.

There is an important Chandlerian point here. Strategic planning firms require a lot of monitoring costs, and this is only justified if the Chandlerian benefits of economies of scope are being achieved (Chandler, 1990). Where they are not, or they are perceived to be absent, you can *always* save a lot of money in the short term by moving to a financial control model. And, for much of the post-war period, McKinsey would come and do it for you. You can measure the savings, but the opportunity costs of abandoning the pursuit of long-term synergies is less observable. Two things become important. The first is the difference between short-term returns and long-term growth. This is related to the second, which is the embedded conflict between shareholder return and managerial pursuit of growth. We shall return to this in Theme 8.

4. *Allocator of Financial Resources.* Once a division is seen to make profits under the relevant accounting system, the issue is what to do with it. The Williamson model implies all surpluses moving into head office and being reallocated on some rate of return basis, net of dividends. This is more likely in a 'Strategic Planning' firm, where it would be reallocated in the direction of

growth opportunities. In a 'Financial Control' firm, reallocation in this way might attenuate the pursuit of profit; why would I make profits as a divisional manager if you take them away? The balance here is about the Matthew principle (Gospel according to Matthew; 25:29 'Unto every one that hath shall be given...but from him that hath not shall be taken away'). One reallocation mechanism is to return the bulk of surplus back to the profitable division, another to use it for growth opportunities elsewhere. There are many complex issues here, which I will discuss below, but the point to mark here is that M form organizations differ in their allocation mechanisms and the transparency with which processes of reallocation and cross-subsidy are formalized.

These considerations open up the issue of internal conflict over resources within the M form. Williamson considers these better than Chandler. For Williamson, as we have seen, opportunism is endemic. For Chandler, a much more benign model of managerial behaviour prevails. Let us look in some detail at an example of transition from ownership to managerial control in a divisionalized business to explore this further.

Here for the Beer

Some of the oldest surviving firms are in the beer business. The technology has not changed very much in many years, the brands are important, and beer drinkers are quite loyal. Whitbread[3] was founded in London in the late eighteenth century; it brewed beer and sold it through pubs. It was a family firm, and remained so until the 1990s. Over the years, it expanded across Britain, building breweries and opening pubs. The law in Britain allowed pubs to be 'tied'; that is, they were often in effect franchises, but they had to buy their beer mainly or exclusively from the brewery that owned the property. Properties had licences to sell alcohol that depended on a local magistrate deciding that someone should be allowed to do so, and the large breweries in the UK dominated the ownership of licences. In Porter's terms, this was a barrier to entry.

By the early 1990s, the family had retreated from running the business. There was a share structure containing two kinds of share. The greater part was openly traded; the smaller part, owned by the family and possessing most of the voting rights, was not. The share structure thus protected this company from takeover in an industry in which very large international players were acquiring smaller businesses because there were major economies of scale in

---

[3] The data for this story were gleaned both from published sources and from conversations with senior managers at Whitbread in the 1990s when the author was fortunate enough to direct their senior management programme.

brewing and distribution. This pattern, of family retreat from involvement in commerce over generations, has been well documented for the UK (Wiener, 1985), and the family in this case wished to exit, not least to free up capital for other things. Those not from the UK (and/or not interested in beer) will recognize the Whitbread name in association with literary prizes and a round-the-world yacht race rather than pubs. When the family did exit, the protection from takeover disappeared, and the senior managers running the business found themselves both answerable to more focused shareholders and vulnerable to takeover; in the jargon of the market, they were in play.

In these circumstances, senior management teams often want to know what they are in play *with*. This involves looking at assets, revenues, and markets and as we have seen above, the divisionalized structure facilitates doing so and Figure T6.2 shows in simplified form what divisional structure they adopted in the early 1990s—a type 'a' structure from Figure T6.1. The brewing division had assets, naturally, in brewing capacity; in pubs and retailing divisions, the main assets were in property (outlets) but since many of these properties were held at book value over a very long period, calculating a return was not straightforward. To take one example; a very highly priced property in the City of London (now a successful conference centre) housed a beautiful set of old English dray horses. These horses had been used to pull carts (though hardly in living memory) and were beloved of some family members. The last division was a collection of businesses acquired opportunistically to generate increased revenue; it contained amongst other things two restaurant chains franchised from their US owners (Pizza Hut and TGI Fridays), an acquired set of coffee shops (Costa Coffee), and the Marriot Hotel chain in the UK (again franchised). Once the divisions were established, it became clear using ROI measures that the brewing division was profitable, the pubs were not, the retail selling of alcohol was a market leader on certain measures, and no one could figure out quite what was happening in the final division because the accounting systems were not uniform. But the margins were obviously good. There was no company-wide system for assessing alternative uses of capital.

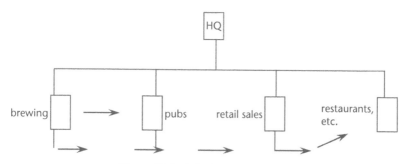

Figure T6.2. Whitbread (1) 1992.

Several of the senior managers had come in from Unilever. Unilever knows about brands, and it knows about consumers. This expertise was to prove important. Most consumers know about Unilever's products but they may not know that Unilever owns them. (Dove, anyone? Ben and Jerry's?) Unilever accounting systems focus on brand profitability and performance. The examination of the organization's performance was influenced by this. Let us look at it by division (Figure T6.3).

Brewing

The figures were confusing because they were good. First, by international standards, the breweries were small and there are substantial economies of scale in the industry, both in production and distribution. Second, Whitbread had a number of beer brands such as 'Trophy' and 'White Label' that were not well regarded. For any beer drinkers among the readership, faced with a pint of Whitbread Trophy there was a real dilemma about whether to take it internally or not. The most profitable *brands* were Heineken and Stella Artois which, you guessed it, were franchises; Whitbread owned the licence to sell them in the UK. This raised an interesting make-or-buy decision. Whitbread used its own brewing capacity to make these brands, but there was plenty of opportunity to supply the franchised brands by purchase from their owners. And if one did this, the investment in the breweries came under question.

Pubs

By 1992, Whitbread had several hundred pubs across the UK. Many were in high-value city centre locations, having been in the 'estate' (the name for the property portfolio) for many years. Two forms of franchise existed. 'Tenants' ran pubs on a revenue-sharing basis, many with incumbency rights. 'Managers' were on a salary. Incentives were very difficult to apply to the former. Many pubs ran at a loss. The company had no clear, centralized view of the market value of the 'estate'. Did one judge it by local property prices, by the revenue stream it generated, or by a calculation of the opportunity costs of current use? In practice, the company looked at revenue per square foot. Old city centre pubs that just sold beer did very badly. Those that also sold food did better. Distressingly, those rented out to other organizations as offices or shops did best. These factors explained performance variance.

However, the underlying problem was that the cost of purchasing beer from within Whitbread was much higher than purchasing it from outside. The profitability of the brewing division was sustained by very high transfer prices that allowed that division to extract the rents from this and other divisions. The firm thought of itself primarily as a brewer, and brewing dominated its internal accounting and pricing systems. This affected all divisions, but pubs most. The review indicated that profitability in pubs would go up substantially if beer was bought from outside. It was not simply a cost issue; the product range could be expanded.

Retail

In the UK you are allowed to sell alcohol in retail almost anywhere, but the tradition before the dominance of big supermarkets was for specialized alcohol stores known as 'off licences' (i.e. licences to sell for consumption off the premises). In this period, local off licences became important (you were hopefully not going to drive). Whitbread developed a brand of store called 'Thresher' that had the highest sales per square foot in the industry. It was a cash cow.

Now there are two obvious ways to increase sales per square foot. You can work on the numerator and offer a varied product at good prices. Or you can work on the denominator and get small sites packed with produce. Whitbread did both. Now if you are going to walk out to buy a bottle of wine, you might want something else, like a pint of milk or cigarettes. You might be willing to visit a couple of stores on a high street to do this, but what if there is no supermarket on the high street? After all, most large supermarket chains rely on scale economies, so move to bigger sites that might be further away. In the 1990s, Thresher became, in US parlance, a 7–11 (off licences were allowed to stay open for very long hours) and those stores that sold the greatest range of products generated the best revenue per square foot. So Whitbread discovered that developing liquor stores into 7–11s (which could still sell liquor) was the best option.

The Rest

In the final division, Whitbread had coffee shops, restaurants, hotels, and health clubs. Think of a residual in a regression equation. There were data problems, but the returns looked much better than elsewhere. This division was hardly exposed to the brewing issue. Some of the brands here were acquisitions, but many were franchises, particularly the profitable (in the 1990s) TGI Fridays, Marriot, and Pizza Hut. It was something like an investment portfolio for the business, in that the returns were uncorrelated. It was not an integrated operation, like the other three divisions, since it had no single market focus.

It was bringing in different types of managers to the business. Brewers are manufacturing managers. Pub owners are small business managers. Those who run chains of restaurants tend to think about things in a different way.

The Points from All of This

1. Exposure to capital market oversight triggers strategic change.

2. Divisionalizing a business tends not to be an event but a process. Since divisionalization helps transparency on costs and revenues it facilitates decisions on the make-or-buy decision, and the exit decision. It is thus a process that can migrate a company across industry boundaries.

3. An n-1 rule tends to operate in the divisionalization process in which n-1 divisions make sense in product and market terms, and the Nth division is a residual of businesses that may be legacy, or growth potential, or both.

4. The Nth division will probably contain the next CEO.

5. It is difficult to use the same performance management metrics across all divisions, particularly nth. Which raises questions about which is the Nth and then what measures to use.

What Happened Next?

Whitbread began to close its breweries and allow its pubs to buy in beer and other alcohol from outside the firm. The franchises on Heineken and Stella Artois expired. It made money from selling some factory sites. It also sold pubs that were not making any money. But some other pubs were in valuable locations that could make money if you made them into something else, like a Pizza Hut or TGI Fridays; it is a well-known fact, and a barrier to entry, in the UK restaurant market that you have to be able to sell alcohol to succeed, so having the licences already was an advantage. The company developed a piece of software that allowed them to select the optimum usage for a property given location, size, distance from the nearest other property, and data on local disposable income (proxied by house price) and they changed the usage of properties to maximize revenue.

They also went shopping; their targets were retail brands that could be made more profitable if they had access to the Whitbread estate. In some cases, such as Café Rouge, a pseudo-French brasserie chain, they bought the brand. In others, they tried to get franchises for the UK on international brands. They streamlined their distribution system so a single distribution operation serviced all their properties. The trucks had multiple brands on their sides. The Whitbread brand itself disappeared from customer sight.

To do this, they had to disrupt the divisional structure. Property had to be 'owned' centrally and allocated to brands on a revenue basis. The same was true of distribution. The culture changed. Historically, the men of power in the firm had been brewers; in fact running a brewery was the path to higher management. It became a company of hoteliers and restaurateurs. Alcohol generally and beer specifically became unimportant to the business. In the late 1990s they described their business as depicted in Figure T6.3. Within the circle are the assets and skills they seek to leverage; on the outside are the brands through which they do so. The brands are disposable, and have been disposed of; Whitbread has sold Café Rouge and no longer has Marriot or Pizza Hut.

In 2013, Whitbread is a company focused on 'hospitality'. The brands are budget hotels, coffee shops, and 'pub' food. All three are successful, but particularly the first two. It no longer has all of the franchises listed in Figure T6.3, and it got out of the fitness business. Here is the strategy statement:

> Our strategy is to create value for our shareholders by focusing our investment and growth in the expanding areas of the hospitality industry, with a particular focus on value-for-money hotels and Costa coffee shops. This is how we manage to deliver outstanding performance across all of our businesses.
>
> (<www.whitbread.co.uk>)

The Points from All of This

1. The assets, or competences, Whitbread is trying to leverage are not products and are tied to very broad ideas about industry, such as hospitality, rather than narrower ones, like selling alcohol.

2. The focus on budget hotels and coffee is a contingency that delivers value for shareholders. If other contingencies arise, they can be pursued.

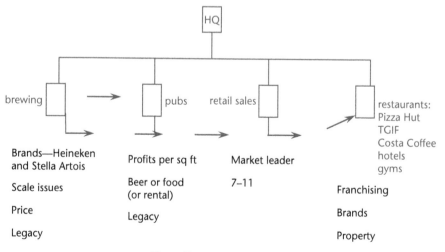

Figure T6.3. Whitbread (2).

175

3. This lowers risk in the sense that the costs are not entirely sunk; if we drink less coffee, Whitbread could use those outlets for something else. The risk exposure to the UK economy remains huge, since the business is in revenue terms only international to a limited extent.

4. By stressing the assets it is leveraging, Whitbread can sell itself to financial markets as having a cohesive strategy even where the products are diversified.

Conclusion

The M form is totemic in business research. Its examination by Chandler kick-started business strategy. As we shall see in the next chapter, it strongly influenced many approaches to strategy that focus on matters internal to the firm. Chandler examines the origins of a US phenomenon close to the start of the short twentieth century that was exported to Europe during the apogee of US dominance. By the end of the short twentieth century, it was the dominant form of organization for large firms and this in itself offered encouragement to those searching for empirical generalizations and a positivistic approach to organizational theory.

Its spread raises questions for many other business disciplines such as accounting, finance, organizational theory, and marketing, for all of which it suggested innovation, and it may even have stimulated their development. It raises key questions in both sociology and economics; indeed one may argue that economists have come closer to developing a theory of the M form organization than they have to a more general theory of the firm. It is argued by some that it is a stable end point of corporate development, although those

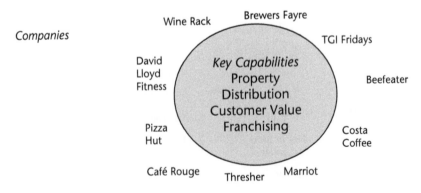

Figure T6.4. Whitbread after divisionalization.

who do so differ in their justifications for this proposition, which is in any event an implausible proposition in social science. It was once made for the Roman legion in the context of military development. In the absence of more substantial evidence on the comparative economic advantage of the M form, one may doubt its permanence. If the diffusion logic *is* sociological, relying on legitimacy, power, or imitation, then transience is more or less assured.

Chapter 7

Strategy as Organizational Theory

Introduction

As the previous theme indicated, Chandler's focus on the M-form organization has generated an enduring fascination with the operation of this widespread phenomenon. But his impact goes beyond this. Though not a theorist, he was influenced by the work of sociologist Talcott Parsons, who analysed social structures by looking at the functions of their constituent elements and their interactions (Chandler, 1971; Teece, 2010); he narrowed this focus to an analysis of the internal dynamics of the firm, from the perspective of senior management, in analysing key case studies in the USA (Chandler, 1962).

In this respect, his work embeds three features which have affected the strategy discipline. First, that the legitimate object of study for strategy academics is top management. Second, that the ways in which these managers generate and mobilize assets *internal* to the firm can generate sustainable competitive advantage. Third, that it is reasonable to use the method of comparison of detailed case studies to sustain 'non-historically specific generalizations' about firm behaviour. The fact that all three propositions have more recently become contestable in the literature should not distract from either their substantial role in the discipline's emergence nor their continued influence on much of its practice.

Having looked in Chapter 6 at the competitive positioning view of strategy—that sustained superior firm performance requires effective product-market positioning—I now turn to examine a range of theories that advance versions of the broad proposition that it is what is inside the firm that matters; sustained superior firm performance requires unique resources, routines, capabilities, or competences (we make the distinctions below), *and* their effective deployment by managers. So, whereas Porter and the game theorists look at cost positions, products, brand features, and market share, other schools within strategy look at business processes, skill sets, innovation, and organizational culture. The unit of analysis changes from the industry/

market to firm-specific assets, and the concern moves from optimizing a position to generating or appropriating a benefit.

In this chapter, I trace the roots and contribution of this literature. The roots lie in both economics and sociology, often in creative conflict. The contribution is both academic, particularly towards the theory of the firm, and practical, in its impact on firms and the consultancy industry. At the root of many of the questions posed is the broader one of whether business strategy is, or should aspire to be, a rational process.

The Mother of All Strategists

Some of the theorists we have already encountered used terms such as capabilities and routines to denote organizational aptitudes. For example, Selznick's (1957) work on leadership refers to organization-specific capabilities that are difficult to transfer from one firm to another. The Carnegie Mellon school of decision-making discussed in Theme 4 described organizational learning processes in which business processes are seen as storage for the collective memory of the firm (Cyert and March, 1963). But the largely unsung heroine here is Edith Penrose.

There are (limited) parallels between Penrose and Coase. Both were interested in the distinction between firm and market. Both saw the firm as a hierarchy coordinated by authority and with clear boundaries. More personally, both were economists whose seminal contributions were largely ignored by economists before being picked up by business academics. But, whereas Coase emphasized the firm as an alternative resource allocation mechanism in the event of market failure, Penrose sees the firm also as a resource *creation* mechanism. Markets may allocate resources but firms make them. Market failure and resource creation approaches are not mutually exclusive; indeed they have been combined to explain the multi-product firm (Teece, 1982).

The core work is *The Theory of the Growth of the Firm* (Penrose, 1959, 2009 edition). In it, the firm is depicted as a bundle of productive resources, both tangible and intangible. Intangible resources are important, and human resources, particularly managerial resources, are vital. This is in effect a similar approach to Chandler—though it precedes it—in emphasizing managerial actions to create, develop, combine, and appropriate resources in the pursuit of growth and profit. In this respect Penrose is in the tradition of classical economists such as Smith and Marx, but distanced from neoclassical economics. As Pitelis puts it, her major insight was to identify:

> ...the endogenous production side growth advantages associated with the knowledge creation process through specialization and division of labour, in an evolving,

cohesive shell called a firm. This is not efficient allocation of scarce resources under conditions of perfect knowledge, it is not static, it is not equilibrium; in a word, it is not neoclassical.

(Pitelis, 2009: xxix)

There are a number of specific attributes of the firm for Penrose.

1. Resources are firm specific; effective managerial resources in particular are difficult to acquire in the market.

2. There are always unused resources in firms that offer opportunities for growth and expansion; this is a similar view to the Carnegie School.

3. Firms are thus heterogeneous in at least two respects; first, apparently similar firms can contain different bundles of resources, and second, similar bundles of resources may be combined and developed in different ways.

4. Firms are not defined in terms of products or industries, but resources, and thus diversification is a normal condition of firm growth.

5. Firms create knowledge; this can be formal (easy to transmit) or tacit (hard to transmit).

6. Firms pursue growth and total long-term profit (Penrose, 1959/2009: 26); Penrose does not put any emphasis on agency issues or intra-firm conflict more generally.

7. There are limits to growth, defined by the rate at which managers can implement growth and innovation.

8. But there are no limits to firm size.

9. Firms 'choose' their environments based on productive opportunity; it is implicit that the firm, not the environment, is the primary object of study.

10. Firms try not to compete; growth and long-term survival depend on establishing 'relatively impregnable "bases"' (Penrose, 1959/2009: 121) from which to adapt and extend operations.

Now a cynic (and you have one here) might see the subsequent literature in strategy concerned with resources and capabilities simply as an extended playing out of these ten commandments. This refers to both the strengths and weaknesses of the above list and is at its most extreme in those writings that treat the firm as a cornucopia of possibilities for senior management action unconstrained either by other stakeholders or by ethical consider-ations. For example, prior to its collapse, several strategy authors saw Enron as a fine example of extending resources developed on an impregnable base to a wide range of growth opportunities (see Theme 8).

However, one would not judge the worth of the real Ten Commandments by the actions of those claiming to follow them, and it is in Penrose that one finds the theory of the firm that is of most significance for modern academic strategy work. Let us trace the route from her to here.

To Infinity, and Beyond . . .

The specific trigger for the import of these Penrosean ideas into strategic management theory was the reaction to Michael Porter. Barney's seminal (1991) article is titled 'Firm resources and sustained competitive advantage', stressing the importance of the unexamined former to the latter Porter concept. Resources are defined as 'the tangible and intangible assets that a firm controls which it can use to conceive of and implement its strategies'. Resources may be financial, physical, human, and organizational, and resource combinations are important. The term 'capabilities' is used to refer to that sub-set of the firm's resources that enables a firm to take full advantage of the other resources it controls. Apparently similar firms may possess different bundles of resources and resource differences between firms may be long lasting; the history of a firm matters to the accumulation of resources.

Much of this is clearly from Penrose, but the advance is to be much clearer about resources and competitive advantage. Taking the firm as resource base idea as given; the concern becomes to classify those resources most central to the firm's sustained success. What in Penrose appears almost as a stochastic process of resource identification and development based on spare capacity, in Barney emerges as a forensic strategic process, by use of the 'VRIN' framework, which runs as follows. To generate competitive advantage, resources must be:

- Valuable—that is create more value (rents) than the costs of exploitation.
- Rare—that is not commonly available to other firms.
- Inimitable—that is not capable of being copied by other firms.
- Non-substitutable—that is there is no different resource that can perform the same function.

If a firm has no valuable resources, it cannot compete. If it has valuable but not rare resources, it is in competitive parity and price competition will ensue. If it has valuable and rare resources, but they can be copied quickly or a substitute found, the competitive advantage will be transient. Sustained competitive advantage in this framework emerges only from resources with all four properties.

The approach has generated a wide literature, and some criticisms. It is clearly consistent not only with Penrose but also with the Carnegie views on exploitable organizational slack. It is essentially a theory of rents based on the idea that there are resource market imperfections (Amit and Shoemaker, 1993). It also had substantial practitioner appeal; managers could mine their existing resources to generate future profits. But, conceptually, it is vague; what is a 'resource' independent of the value it creates? Is the association of resources and value simply tautological? Does competitive advantage flow from resources, or are resources built from competitive advantage; for example, if a firm does a lot of marketing and is successful, which is logically prior? How could one falsify the hypothesis that firm-specific resources are important? Practically, how could managers *create* VRIN resources? Some of these could potentially be empirical questions, but in the absence of conceptual clarity the empirics may be difficult to perform (Williamson, 1999; Priem and Butler, 2001). In addition, it retains the Porter notion of sustained competitive advantage; what if, particularly in dynamic markets, this is not possible? In these circumstances, seeking increasingly to leverage one's historical resources might be positively damaging for the firm.

The question was quickly asked about resource-based theories—do resources have value independent of their deployment? In Penrose, resources are combined and mobilized to some productive purpose and the capability or competence to do so became a focus of attention.[1] In particular, reviving Selznick's old (1957) idea of a distinctive competence, Prahalad and Hamel (1990) developed the idea of a *core competence* to identify those capabilities central to a firm's performance and strategy (see also Hamel and Prahalad, 1996).

This is a distinctive and influential contribution to the literature on the firm and it emerged from a criticism of US businesses, specifically their focus on product rather than the capability to generate product; for these authors, this is to mistake cause for effect. And given the timing of the idea in the early 1990s, it was often accompanied by examples showing US business behaviour in an unfavourable light compared to Japanese. They define a competence as:

> ...the collective learning in the organisation, especially how to co-ordinate diverse production skills and integrate multiple streams of technologies.
>
> (Prahalad and Hamel, 1990: 81)

Core competences are those central to the creation either of customer value or the efficiency or quality with which that value is delivered. But, crucially, they provide a basis for entering new markets; so an examination of core competences (retrospective) is central to market entry and diversification strategy (prospective). They are **not** products, nor the physical and financial assets that might generate products, nor are they patents or intellectual property rights. So, for example, a core competence of Sony would not be any element of its

---

[1] As Grant (2005: 144) notes, in much of the strategy literature these terms are used interchangeably. The literature on *dynamic capabilities* is somewhat different and discussed below.

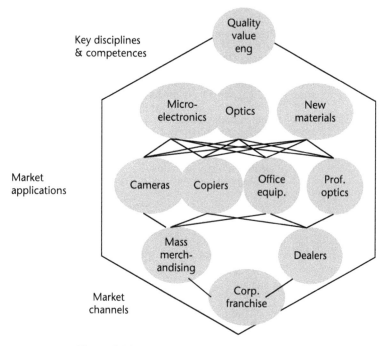

Figure C7.1. Canon portfolio of competences.

product portfolio, nor its ownership of music rights, but the capacity to miniaturize personal electronics. Figure C7.1 takes this further by showing the relationship between competences and products at Canon (see Grant, 2005: 146). In this approach, the key disciplines and competences underpin the products, which are simply market applications of the underlying competence. It thus follows that other market applications of these competences should lead to competitive advantage.

Now this approach develops out of the resource-based view of the firm and has some of its strengths and weaknesses, both conceptual and empirical. Identifying competences *ex ante*, and the reliance on the rather casual empiricism of case studies, are two particular difficulties. But, in the specification of competences as market entry devices, it provides a theoretical justification of (and indeed a practical injunction for) diversification. If products do not matter then presumably industries do not either. Figures C7.2 and C7.3 show how the analytical approach was applied in a large US corporation, Disney. Disney began with animated cartoons, and developed other forms of film and TV products before moving into bigger investments such as theme parks, hotels, and golf courses. It then augmented its content with distribution by adding TV stations and channels, stores, and records and DVDs.

1923 – Animation
1930 – Mickey Mouse books
1950 – Live action films – Treasure Island
1954 – TV series, Davy Crockett
1955 – Disneyland
1971 – Walt Disney World – golf courses and hotels
1982 – EPCOT community of the future
1983 – Disney Channel, Touchstone Pictures
1986 – Videos of back catalogue
1988 – Caribbean beach resorts, Disney Store
1993 – Hollywood Records, NHL
1995 – Pixar Toy Story
1996 – Celebration – city in Florida
1997 – Lion King on stage, ABC TV
1998 – Cruise lines

Figure C7.2. Disney—growth and diversification.

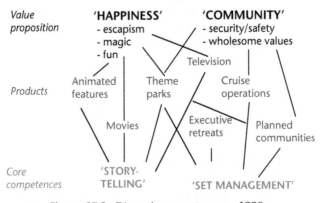

Figure C7.3. Disney's competences—1990s.

By the mid 1990s, Disney is apparently a highly diversified company if viewed in product terms. Naturally, by then, it has a multi-divisional structure. A diversified portfolio business might be very sensible for such a family- or owner-managed firm. There are many examples of such firms; for example, the Mars organization from the USA, Virgin from Europe, and Hutchinson Whampoa from Asia. However, by the mid 1990s, Disney had a much wider shareholder base and, in publicly-traded corporations, diversification was unfashionable. Further diversification would be even more unfashionable. However, if one could show that, so to speak, underneath the ephemera of product, there was an underlying strategic glue underpinning the business, then diversification can be re-coded as deployment of core competences. It both makes sense of the corporate history and indicates avenues for further diversification.

Figure C7.3 tries to simplify the core issues. The originating idea of the company is a package of content that represents certain sentiments which are the value proposition. Disney content has a clear positioning, both culturally and generationally. The more products that can embody such content and the wider the customer base, the greater the long-term profit opportunity; the person who goes to see the *Lion King* as a child can buy their kids the video at a theme park, take their grandchildren to the musical, retire to cruise and play golf and pass away in a planned community. The brand is associated with a style and quality of experience throughout, and in order to deploy the brand optimally, industry barriers do not really matter, provided the story and the 'set' are right. And the 'story' is not only for customers but for securities analysts and investors.

Conversely, the analysis points to things that any diversification strategy should avoid; that is anything that does not leverage the core competences (e.g. a zoo) or that might damage the value proposition (e.g. distributing the Tarantino film *Pulp Fiction*). In fact Disney did both. But the strength here is that looking at core competences is a form of visceral factor analysis that can point to the direction of a diversification strategy. It opens up to firms a mechanism for leveraging sunk costs and recovering stranded assets which is likely to be particularly relevant for large firms who are, so to speak, in 'bad' Porter territory—poorly positioned in low-growth industries or markets. Though not explicitly a dynamic approach, it goes beyond the resource-based audit to focus on options for the future. But to find a truly dynamic approach, we need initially to go back to economics.

Capability and God-like Reason?

It is all very well to have resources and competences, but quite another thing to deploy them into profit. Sony probably had all of the technologies necessary to make an iPod, but they did not; interestingly, Apple at the outset owned very few of these technologies, but they did make it. So writers in the resource and competence traditions began to concern themselves as much with how the knowledge was leveraged as whether it existed. As Rumelt (1984: 561) put it, the strategic firm 'is characterized by a bundle of linked and idiosyncratic resources and resource conversion activities'. This built on work in economics in the Schumpeterian tradition that argued firms have 'repertoires' of 'creative routines' that generate innovation (Nelson and Winter, 1982). Other writers, such as Leonard-Barton (1995), argued that what Penrose termed the impregnable base could be a disadvantage; in her terms, core capabilities could become core rigidities, discouraging or hampering change.

Change was the issue, as strategy writers sought to understand, in the late 1980s and 1990s, why some firms appeared capable of change and adaptation (had routines), while others, perhaps endowed with substantial resources (having rigidities), did not. To call 'ability to change' a 'core competence' was pushing the limits of credulity and there emerged a need to identify more specific firm attributes that sustained change and profitability. Teece, whose writing is the core of this approach, came up with the idea of 'dynamic capabilities', defined loosely as:

> ...the firm's ability to integrate, build and reconfigure internal and external competence to address rapidly changing environments.
>
> (Teece et al., 1997)

Clearly, more specification is necessary. In a later paper, he argues that the concept explains:

> How a business enterprise and its management can first spot the opportunity to earn economic profits, make the decisions and institute the disciplines to execute on that opportunity, and then stay agile so as to continuously refresh the foundations of its early success, thereby generating economic surpluses over time.
>
> (Teece, 2007: 1347)

There isn't really anything else in business strategy to worry about. It is thus somewhat a theory of the universe, explaining how to boldly go and split infinitives as none previously has. But writings in this tradition have tried to show what dynamic capabilities are, rather than simply what they can do. And that venture proves interesting for ideas about competitive advantage. Eisenhardt and Martin stick with the idea of capabilities as routines and identify several.

- Some integrate resources, for example in product development.
- Strategic decision making is a dynamic capability.
- Some move processes around within firms, by combining existing knowledge in new ways.
- Some create knowledge.
- The ability to secure new knowledge through acquisitions and alliances is a dynamic capability.
- As is the ability to get rid of uncompetitive resources.

(Eisenhardt and Martin, 2000: 1107–8)

Their list is not presented as exhaustive, and one might reasonably add at least two more:

- The ability to learn from failed ventures; what Leonard Barton splendidly describes as 'failing forward'.
- The ability to absorb and use knowledge from other competitors; what Cohen and Levinthal (1990) call 'absorptive capacity'.

The subversive element in this list is that these are generic rather than idio-syncratic capabilities; they have common characteristics and there is no obvi-ous reason why they should be sources of sustained competitive advantage. Naturally, the conclusion drawn by those in the dynamic capabilities litera-ture is not that they have not yet found the sources of sustained competitive advantage, but that such advantage is ephemeral, particularly in dynamic markets. Pursuit of an exhaustive list would presumably gene-rate parameters of generalized, and generalizable, excellence. However, the approach does focus on the need to identify specific business processes that are key to success, and it is reasonable to assume that these might vary by firm and industry. For example, product development becomes more important in rapidly changing industries, and the ability to get rid of stranded assets is important in mature ones.

But Teece also argues,

> Dynamic capabilities reside in large measure with the enterprise's top manage-ment team.

(Teece, 2007: 1346)

This is highly unlikely; the market for ideas about dynamic capabilities might be strongest at CEO level, but the nature of dynamic capabilities is such that they are likely to rely on knowledge and skill dispersed throughout the organ-ization, and the rationality requirements for top management to know every-thing relevant about such capabilities (even if everyone was charitable enough freely to tell them) are, as I showed in Theme 4, implausible; which leads us to the final issue to consider in this chapter. If a large part of strategy is about leveraging capabilities in the firm, why would top management be important to the exclusion of others? Is strategy making a top-down process, analogous to caricatures of military decision-making, or is it a more diffuse and emergent process, summarizing the knowledge of the whole organization? We need to turn to the strategy process.

Is it Strategy?

Since there is no firm to speak of in Porter's and the game theory approaches to strategy, characterization of the decision-making process is implausible but unproblematic. The conception of the firm as a single decision point sits very well with the idea of the top management team as the only focus of interest. But the cognitive demands of resource and capabilities approaches are more severe. We can consider this by looking at Figure C7.4, which typifies a 'classic' model of the strategic process, indicating in the process that it is possible to combine both the externally focused and resource-based analytics. Top managers consider the external environment and internal capabilities (not necessarily in that order), formulate strategies that synthesize the two, then implement them. Do people really do this? Some have their doubts.

Mintzberg (1978; 1985) feels that this model of the strategy process describes only one aspect. He distinguishes three types.

- *Intended strategy* designed by the top management team; this is primarily a rational and planned approach, but even here Mintzberg envisages bargaining and compromises reminiscent of the Carnegie Mellon School.
- *Realized strategy* is that fraction of intended strategy that is implemented.
- *Emergent strategy* refers to the sets of decisions made by managers trying to work within the intended strategy.

Mintzberg feels that most realized strategy is emergent and the processes he describes would be familiar to Cyert, March, and Simon. Put another way, it would not have been necessary to say this if the strategy field had not already developed an unhealthy obsession with top management rationality in designing strategies.

What Grant refers to as the 'battleground' (Grant, 2005: 24) between design and emergence arose in the case study of Honda's success in dominating the US motorcycle market with small, 50cc bikes. For the Boston Consulting Group (1975; writing for the British government!) this was an example of superbly planned market entry exploiting economies of scale and scope to establish unassailable cost leadership; the Japanese had developed huge production volumes in their domestic market and volume-related cost reductions had followed. This resulted in a highly competitive cost position which the Japanese used for penetration of world markets with small motorcycles in the early 1960s. Here is what a key Honda manager had to say about it:

'In truth, we had no strategy other than the idea of seeing if we could sell something in the United States. It was a nice frontier, a new challenge, and it fitted the "success at all odds" culture that Mr Honda had cultivated...

Throughout our first eight months, we had not attempted to move the 50cc Supercubs.... They seemed wholly unsuitable for the US market where everything was bigger and more luxurious.

We used the 50ccs ourselves to ride around LA on errands. They attracted a lot of attention. One day we had a call from a Sears buyer...But we still hesitated to push the 50cc bikes out of fear they might damage our image in a heavily macho market. But when the larger bikes started breaking, we had no choice. We let the 50cc bikes move. And surprisingly, the retailers who wanted to sell them weren't motorcycle dealers, they were sporting goods stores.'

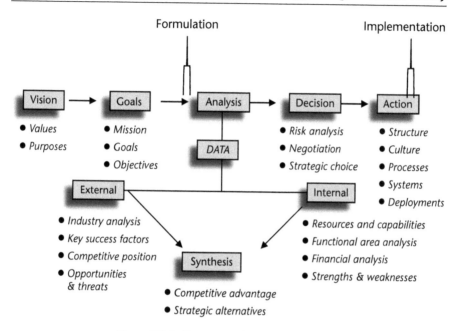

Figure C7.4. Strategy as (rational?) process.

Whittington takes this approach further in what he refers to as four 'theories' of strategy, as depicted in Figure C7.5. Deliberate processes and single objectives characterize only the classical strategy school focusing on rational top management engaged in long-term Chandlerian planning. In the other cases, strategy seems to be presented as some non-specified sub-set of organizational decision-making in general, or—as in the Honda case above—a post-hoc rationalization of organizational decision-making in strategic terms. He gets to the heart of the matter in remarking:

> . . . the very notion of "strategy" may be culturally peculiar. Arising in the particular conditions of North America in the post-war period, the Classical conception of strategy does not always fit comfortably in other cultures . . .

But this does not mean that it has not been influential.

> Whether or not formal planning in the Classical mode is economically effective, if that is how key elements of the institutional environment expect business to be done, then it is sociologically efficient to at least go through the motions.
>
> (Whittington, 2001: 28–9)

This raises some very big questions, and not just about strategy. If business tools of any sort 'work' merely to provide some form of legitimacy for managers and firms in the eyes of governments and investors, then they are performative, but do not directly impact firm performance; I will return to

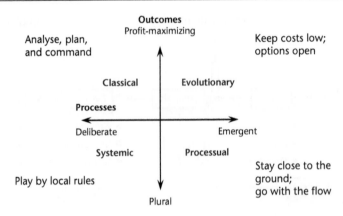

Figure C7.5. The assumptions of different strategies.
(*Source*: Whittington, 2001: 10)

this in Theme 9. But Whittington's key question is 'does it matter?', and the answer given is that it matters what you think strategy is, since there are at least four broad ways of doing it. Where does this leave us?

Conclusion

> Her Majesty the Queen, on the occasion of the opening of a new LSE building in 2009, to an eminent LSE Professor...
>
> Why didn't you see the crash coming?
>
> (The immediate response is not recorded)[2]

In the last two chapters and intervening theme we have ranged across a wide variety of approaches to strategy. At one extreme, strategy is about formal games. At the other, it blends into more general fields of organizational analysis. Advocates of different strategy schools find it difficult to communicate. They tell practitioners very different things. Because the field developed relatively late, we know that for much of the short twentieth century, both firms and the managers within them did without it.

But these diverse views do have some things in common. Strategy authors generally think that, whatever definition of strategy they are operating with, it is better to do strategy than not to do it. Economists such as Williamson, by contrast, think it is actually a bad thing to do, and sociologists who work in institutional theory or organizational ecology think it does not make any

---

[2] But a collective letter was sent later. As Mike Power has remarked, when economists write to the Queen, you know you have a problem.

difference whether you do it or not (Donaldson, 1995). Strategy authors further tend to assume that it is the top management team that has the power of agency; even for the more 'emergent' authors, whatever ideas emerge blinking into the light are subsequently to be addressed by the top team. Some independence of action by this team is thus a pre-condition for strategic action. Third, and slightly more depressingly, all find prediction difficult. Qualitative approaches to strategy abound with case studies which are often just-so stories; quantitative approaches in game theory or industry analysis use historic assumptions and data.

But debates in the business strategy literature often turn on the issue of rationality; is it possible, or even desirable, to run a business on the basis of a rationally thought out plan, whether that plan focuses externally on the industry or internally on competences or capabilities? In the next chapter I will discuss the emergence of the academic finance discipline, in which such concerns are muted, to say the least, but which in many ways seeks to usurp some of the intellectual turf of strategy writers. However, first we need to take a look at markets which, within the management literature, are not to be endured or perfected, but managed.

Theme 7

Managing Markets from Hierarchies

Introduction

The chapters about strategy dealt with circumstances in which managers within firms are seeking to control, protect, or predict what markets are doing; the premise is that this is possible. For many economists it is neither possible nor desirable. Managers simply need to maximize profits by setting output at the profit-maximizing level—where marginal costs equal marginal revenues. Those that do will survive in the long run and the others will fail.

In practice, early empirical evidence seemed to show not only that managers did not act this way, they did not even know what their marginal costs and revenue curves were (Hall and Hitch, 1939, cited in Whittington, 2001: 16). Large firms looked both to differentiate products to avoid direct price competition and to rely on measures other than cost to figure out prices. They looked to understand differences between the preferences of groups of consumers and they sought to access those consumers through distribution channels. In short, they needed to understand the four 'P's of modern marketing: product, price, promotion, and place.

Modern marketing emerged from economics, beginning around the turn of the twentieth century. There is some debate about the location of its roots, but little argument about where it flourished best—the USA. The economists who fostered it were primarily interested in the *distribution* of goods produced by the then new large-scale firms, and the primary criterion in distribution was efficiency, which gave new marketing ideas an affinity with scientific management. However, neoclassical models of the consumer did not appear useful to practitioners concerned with net revenue, and economics petered out as an influence (Jones and Shaw, 2002: 44, 55). The discipline has developed 'sub-disciplines' that rely on mathematics (e.g. distribution), social psychology (e.g. consumer marketing and sales force management), and organizational theory (e.g. channel management). It has some claim to be the precursor of the strategy discipline, since, without a basic understanding of product markets, most of the tools of strategy do not stand up. These claims have been made forcefully by developers of the 'marketing concept' such as Drucker (see below).

However, marketing operates with a different conception of the market from economics. For economists, a market is a collection of buyers and sellers who contract for a particular item, as in the housing market or the equities market. However, the marketing approach sees only the buyers as the market; the sellers are an industry. So Kotler defines a market as 'the set of all actual and potential buyers of a product or service' (Kotler, 2004: 14). Market share, a key concept, describes the share of buyers 'owned' by sellers.

In most marketing, managers in firms are seeking to do something to buyers, who may be other producing firms (business-to-business) or consumers. It is about managing the relationship between hierarchy and market. As Webster (2002: 67) puts it:

> Marketing exists both within the firm and outside it. It is both a set of organisational management activities and a set of institutional actors and functions within the marketplace, external to the firm, in which the firm participates.

In this theme I look at the things such managers do.

Origins and Implications

Fligstein (1990: 116–61) relates the rise of what he calls the 'sales and marketing conception of control' roughly to the great depression of the 1930s in the USA. Where demand was depressed and collusion on prices illegal, firms could see only mutually assured destruction in severe price competition.

> Instead of price stability, managers and entrepreneurs began to focus on selling goods ... Firms differentiated their products from their competitors' and appealed to buyers with price differences based on quality. An extension of this tactic was to establish brand names and build consumer loyalty through advertising.
>
> (Fligstein, 1990: 118)

The role of the large organization here is not passively to respond to demand conditions, but actively to create and control markets. New products, price differentiation, and the identification of and access to new markets become vital. Managerial activities such as new product development, pricing, advertising, and channel management become highly valued. Marketing management—which is what I primarily focus on here—is about the stimulation of demand. It seeks to optimize performance on a dependent variable, such as sales revenue or market share, by flexing performance on the 'four Ps'.

Investment in such managerial activities implies sufficient stability and structure in markets to generate a return. Markets have 'segments' (distinct groups of consumers within which tastes are homogeneous) that may be accessed through 'channels' (distribution processes with distinctive properties) and with the support of communication devices (advertising) based on specific product or service propositions (brands). The implicit conception is of markets as social structures with stable properties. A corollary is that where such stability is absent, marketing activities seek to create it.

A second implication is that marketing is not primarily transaction focused. As Kotler puts it, firms often try to create marketing 'networks' consisting of the firm and its surrounding profitable business relationships:

> Increasingly, competition is not between companies but rather between whole networks, with the prize going to the company that has built the best network.
>
> (Kotler, 2004: 14)

Stability allows the generation of information about customers and other counter-parties, and also avoids the transaction costs of customer acquisition; Kotler remarks that the costs of acquisition are often much higher than those of retention. Marketing contains, but is different from, selling. Marketing may thus be seen from our perspective as a bundle of techniques designed to create social structures within markets to sustain revenues.

From its humble origins in concerns about distributional efficiency, the academic discipline of marketing generated somewhat imperial ambitions, most notably in the idea of the 'marketing concept'—seeing the whole firm from the customer perspective. This was most notably articulated by Drucker, who argued:

1. The sole purpose of the business is to create a customer.
2. The customer's view of what she is buying is more important than the firm's view of what they are making.
3. All firms are only about marketing and innovation.
4. Marketing is *much more* than sales.
5. Marketing is the whole business, seen by the customer.

(Drucker, 1954: 39; Webster, 2002: 71)

This is one of two ambitiously reductionist views of the firm—I will look at the finance version which attributes primacy not to the customer but to the investor in the next chapter. It defines the firm's purpose in ways that leave substantial space for the subsequently emerging strategy discipline; it does not say how to satisfy customers, or which customers, or whether doing so will generate profits. It articulates the importance of the demand side (consumer behaviour) while leaving the supply side (competitive positioning) open.

But marketing has developed a number of tools to analyse and attempt to manage markets. In the following sections, we will focus on what managers do when they seek to manage markets, under the conventional headings of product (including market structure), price, promotion (including branding and advertising), and place (channels and distribution).

Segments and Cycles

Consider the following.

> Market structure is an idea, like a demand curve or an attitude, that cannot be observed; it can only be inferred. It represents the aggregation of individual consumer choices within some specified product domain over a given time period...
>
> Product market definition seeks to identify the set of 'product' alternatives or competitors...a product market can be thought of as the totality of product alternatives that could be actively considered for purchase or use.
>
> (Shocker, 2002: 107)

The quotes point to a central concern in the management of markets; designing products targeted at distinct market segments, and understanding how those products and segments behave over time. It is not self-evident.

One might, for example, think in producer terms that one car competes with another, or one wine with another. But there are more general market categories like personal transport (including motor bikes) or alcohol (including beer) that might be in the consumer mind. Once, mobile phones and cameras were discrete markets, so these things change over time. In addition, at the most general level, everything competes with everything else for a finite amount of purchasing power; for example, a consumer considering a Christmas gift list probably has a very flexible set of product preferences. Marketing managers approach this by analysing market segments—relatively homogeneous groups of consumers who can be targeted—and product life cycles—the growth and subsequent decline in demand for a product. I will look at each in turn.

(i) Segmentation

In 1929, Harold Hotelling, an economist, produced a simple spatial location model with an equilibrium solution (Hotelling, 1929). Imagine two ice-cream sellers on a beach; their ice cream is identical in quality and price. Rational consumers of ice cream are spread evenly along the beach. Where should the ice-cream sellers locate? The equilibrium is in fact that they both locate in the

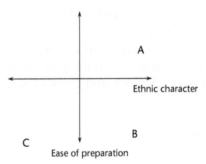

Figure T7.1. Spatial representation of market structure. (Adapted from Shocker, 2002: 111.)

centre to access consumers equally. Any move away from the centre yields market share to the other seller.

Here, the competitive space is one-dimensional and the product undifferentiated. If we speculate that the space could be N-dimensional, and the products differentiated with respect to these dimensions, we can begin to understand how marketers think about segmentation. The N dimensions might be generic product attributes such as price, quality, status, or ease of use, and we can calculate the 'distance' between products on these dimensions. Then the firm can move, like the ice-cream seller, better to deliver to customers. The key empirical questions then are: how many dimensions are relevant, how stable is demand, and how easy is it for the firm to move to satisfy it?

A simple model is presented in Figure T7.1. Products which are closest together may be deemed to be more in competition. Products A and B might be an uncooked and pre-cooked chicken dinner respectively; product C might be a pre-cooked Chinese meal. A and B compete on content and B and C on convenience. Product development activities within the firm may move the 'position' of a product to intensify or avoid competition. It is very important to generate knowledge of consumers in these approaches because the observed 'distance' between products is defined by consumer preferences (Cooper and Inoue, 1996). Information on the stability of demand can be established by asking prospective consumers *ex ante* ('judgemental' methods) or by analysing purchasing decisions *ex post* ('behavioural' methods) (Shocker, 2002: 110). Although simple, conceiving of markets as multi-dimensional spaces moves away from the traditional notion that each firm faces a simple downward-sloping demand curve to the idea that positioning and differentiation may be sources of revenue and profitability.

How do we deal with the 'Christmas gift' problem above, in which every product can compete with any other? One way is to use simple decision tree analysis. Imagine that the products are Diet Pepsi and Coke respectively.

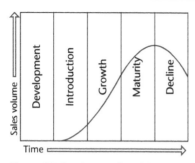

Figure T7.2. The product life cycle.

We can consider attributes sequentially rather than simultaneously (as in the game theory example in Chapter 6). Individual consumers might consider first purchasing a soft drink, then whether to buy diet or not, then whether it is cola, and finally the brand.

(ii) *Product Life Cycles*

As well as differentiation of markets in space, marketing concerns itself with differentiation in time. The product life cycle, presented in stylized form in Figure T7.2, is the conventional approach to this. It specifies four broad phases of post-development product lifespan—introduction, growth, maturity, and decline—with attendant implications for sales volume. Acceptance of these phases has implications for new product development, for spending on product launches, and for pricing. In the early phase of introduction, costs exceed revenues and the main concern is to stimulate demand. In the growth phase, revenues increase and unit costs tend to fall, often leading to product profitability. Sales volume peaks at maturity, but prices are likely to fall as competitors imitate the product. Further price falls may occur in decline; in particular, discounting may be an option to flatten the curve in the 'decline' phase. Although the curve is widely accepted as an ideal type, it is not empirically well verified (Lambkin and Day, 1989); in particular, the precise metrics for the axes are difficult to identify across broad product ranges, and the relationship between sales volume and sales revenue may also be indeterminate.

The product life cycle hints at the imperial ambitions of the marketing concept. If marketing managers see the firm's portfolio of products as a series of life cycle curves, then they have a legitimate interest in the entire product development process. New products need to arrive early enough to replace old ones before consumers have the chance to switch to a competitor's product, but not so early that they cannibalize sales of existing products. New technologies come to market not because they can (technology-push) but because there is or can be consumer demand (market-pull). And this demand may be differentiated, so that 'early adopters', such as the young, are targeted at product launch, while conservative consumers who may be risk-averse can wait until the product has substantial market presence. So, Apple considered the sales of iPhone 4 and 4S in timing the launch of iPhone 5, and many technology companies consider product profitability by date of product launch; for example, for many years in the Hewlett Packard Annual Report there was a graph indicating how much of the current year's profits came from products launched one, two, or three years ago.

This line of thought has been taken further by several writers in the operations management tradition who take the product line and its associated production process as the unit of analysis (termed the 'productive unit'—Abernathy and Utterback, 1982: 102), and analyse both process and product innovation. As with the product life cycle approach, this leads to a stylized (and not always accurate) life cycle model of the sort depicted in Figure T7.3.

The logic is as follows. In the early stages of a productive unit, product innovation is high and there is no industry standard, so product variation is high. Processes are fluid and inefficient. Subsequently, product design stabilizes and a 'dominant' design or industry standard develops; processes become more standardized and economies of scale emerge as competition focuses on price and product differentiation. Competition focuses on sales maximization.

> It becomes increasingly difficult to better past performance, users develop loyalty and preferences, and the practicalities of marketing, distribution, maintenance, advertising etc demand greater standardisation.

(Utterback and Abernathy, 1975: 644)

Much of the evidence for this life cycle approach is based on US manufacturing, particularly cars, so let us use that example to illustrate. In the early days of car production, there was no standard model. Powered vehicles had two, three, or four wheels, were steered by steering wheel or handlebar (like a

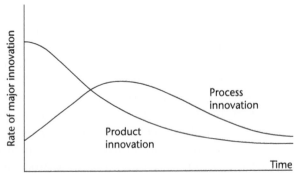

Figure T7.3. A model of process and product innovation.

bicycle) and might be powered by steam, electricity, or internal combustion engine. Eventually, a standard design of four wheels, steering wheel, and internal combustion engine emerged and the key competitive question moved from what to make to how to make it. We are now roughly at the curve intersection of Figure T7.3.

I have used the Ford example before; here I am concerned not with labour strategy but with the creation of the car market.[1] In 1905, when Ford started to make cars, the market was small, and cars were a luxury. His vision was to create a mass market. He did so by standardizing and simplifying design, applied assembly line technology to achieve scale economies, and achieved massive cost and price reductions; assembly times collapsed (from 12 hours in 1908 to 1.5 in 1913), and prices were halved to $450 (across the same period). Volume of output increased from 10,000 to 730,000 (over approximately the same period).

By 1925, the new head of General Motors, Alfred Sloan, noted that the market was saturated and the technology of the car—the Model T—obsolete. He introduced the idea of product differentiation in both (market) space and time. GM introduced model variety and market segmentation; luxury cars were developed. It also introduced annual model change so that consumers could trade up not only on price but on novelty. Ford could not respond quickly, since his highly dedicated production system described in Chapter 3 was inflexible. GM's market strategy worked and in three years it became market leader, a position it held until 1986.

The key themes here are:

1. The firm (Ford) creates the market, not vice versa.

2. Economies of scale in production not only drive down cost, they create barriers to entry.

3. The successful response to this by GM is not lower costs, but differentiation, segmenting a mass market.

4. GM designs the (annual) product life cycle.

5. In Fligstein's terms, the 'sales and marketing' approach outdoes the 'production' approach.

Show me the Money

In perfectly competitive markets, firms take but do not make price. In economic terms, each firm faces a perfectly elastic demand curve unaffected by any production decisions. There are no brands, no advertising because of perfect information, and no barriers to entry or protectable rents. In short,

---

[1] I am indebted to Prof. Rafael Gomez for this articulation of the example.

you neither need nor have marketing. Marketing requires imperfect competition. Whether one can infer the existence of imperfect markets from the growth of the marketing discipline is a large question, but one is on safer ground in saying that the activities of price setters in marketing management are designed to sustain market imperfection.

Models of imperfect competition came along later (e.g. Bain, 1956) and, as we saw in Chapter 6, were incorporated into thinking on competitive strategy, but early approaches to pricing often focused on the idea of what the market (i.e. the consumer) would bear. Eventually, though with some delay, marketing developed theories concerning consumer behaviour, many of which relied on consumer psychology (Jones and Shaw, 2002: 55). A key feature of the marketing approach is to put emphasis on both of the economic functions of price. Economists tended to emphasize the market clearing function; marketing academics paid equal attention to the informational function; that is what the price tells the consumer about the product.

In marketing, the idea that consumers will in general prefer lower to higher prices is complicated. Early research implied the existence of price 'thresholds'. Consumers judged very low prices as indicating low quality, and very high prices as simply too expensive. There emerged the idea of an inverted U-shaped price acceptability function linking subjective price acceptability and actual prices. This has prompted a large literature, much of which is concerned with measurement accuracy, since it becomes very important to know by product and consumer segment what the upper threshold is. As Ofir and Winer put it,

> Understanding price thresholds and willingness to pay is critical to marketing managers' being able to price appropriately and not succumb to extreme pressure to drop prices.

(Ofir and Winer, 2002: 278)

An associated idea is the 'reference price', that is some standard of comparison against which the observed price is compared by the consumer. Again, as with reference groups in sociology, this is unfortunately an empirical question and it may be the price last paid, the expected future price, the reservation price, or some idea about a 'fair' price. This is naturally an area to which Kahneman and Tversky's ideas about prospect theory discussed in Theme 4 have been applied; consumers are much more unhappy when the reference price is exceeded than they are happy when the observed price falls short.

The bias literature has also been deployed to look at what are termed 'odd prices'. Prices ending in 0 or 5 appear very often; this may be retrievability bias. Prices ending in 9 appear *very* often. This may be because, for example, consumers sense £4.99 is much less than £5.00. In the UK retail wine market, for example, £4.99 is seen as a key price point around which sales cluster (Figure T7.4). Whether the price here is the independent variable (based on

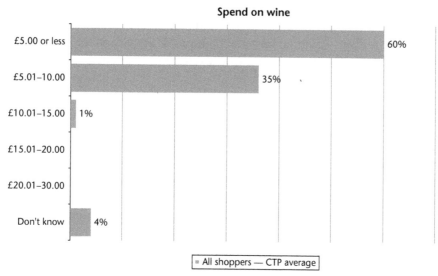

Figure T7.4. Wine prices and sales, UK.

consumer preference) or dependent (based on industry conformity), there is no doubt that the price point impacts merchandising, discounting, and supplier management.

Greater complexity is introduced when we consider price changes. There is good evidence that consumer perceptions of appropriate price (and wages) become hazy where inflation has an impact; consumers are slow to adjust their reference points upwards (Willman, 1982). In other cases, such as high-technology product innovations, consumers may seek to delay purchase in the expectation that prices will subsequently fall through discounting. There are also inter-industry variations in the extent to which prices are transparent to the consumer. Supermarket prices (both within and between stores) tend to be much more transparent to consumers than airline prices where yield management techniques may generate substantial seat price differences on the same flight and class.

In several papers, Zbaraki and others have examined the importance and complexity of the price-setting process within the firm (Dutta et al., 2003; Zbaracki et al., 2004; Zbaracki and Bergen 2010). They argue that price-setting capabilities are important rent-appropriation activities for the firm but that they are both complex and costly. Economists (e.g. Blinder et al., 1998) have argued that price stickiness may follow from the costs to the firm of price change but that the 'menu costs' of price change (i.e. producing a new price 'menu' and labels) do not appear high in comparison to the benefits of price increases. Zbaracki et al. (2004) argue for the existence of two other sets of costs; managerial costs of information gathering and decision-making and customer costs of communication and negotiation. These dwarf menu costs; the ratio of menu to managerial and consumer costs is 1:6:20 in their data. Price-setting is an important and high-profile activity endogenous to the firm, in which competitor prices are only one consideration.

Cheap Talk

Kay (2004: 215–16) uses the above term to describe advertising, remarking that it is often almost content free. He uses the example of the Coca-Cola company simply stating 'Coke is it' to argue that costly and wasteful communication serves mainly to demonstrate commitment to product and thus to customer. He compares it to the mating display of male peacocks; but some peacocks finish the job.

Many businesses advertise, and mostly what they advertise are brands. The American Marketing Association yields the following broad definition of a brand.

> A brand is a customer experience represented by a collection of images and ideas; often, it refers to a symbol such as a name, logo, slogan, and design scheme. Brand recognition and other reactions are created by the accumulation of experiences with the specific product or service, both directly relating to its use, and through the influence of advertising, design, and media commentary. A brand often includes an explicit logo, fonts, color schemes, symbols, sound which may be developed to represent implicit values, ideas, and even personality.
>
> (<https://www.ama.org>)

The same site defines advertising slightly more poetically as 'persuasive messages in time or space' purchased in any of the mass media.

Some firms have many brands. For example, Unilever has Ben and Jerry's, Dove, Flora, Lipton, Signal, and Surf. This is common in the packaged goods sector; its main competitor, Procter and Gamble, also has many. Some brands have many firms. For example, the Virgin brand does not only involve the Virgin organization itself, but also Singapore Airlines, Stagecoach, EMI, and Royal Bank of Scotland, among others. This approach is known as 'brand extension', with the positive market value (brand equity) of the brand extended across different sectors as a low-cost way of effecting market entry. Brands are market differentiators, but are not differentiated in production. Currently, a visitor to a major UK supermarket such as Tesco may buy a branded tin of soup (e.g. Heinz) or a lower-price own-branded (i.e. Tesco) one which may have been made in the same production process. Coca-Cola branding signifies nothing about the production process. Some very big brands such as Coca-Cola, but also Nike, Apple, and Microsoft, can be identified simply by their logo.

Brands are said to have properties. Some of these, such as awareness, are subject to quantitative measures, such as how many consumers have heard of the brand. They have more qualitative attributes such as image, association, and personality which are essentially measures of the recognition or affective response the brand evokes with consumers. Some even argue that brands give consumers 'identity' (Holt and Cameron, 2010). However, in business terms, brands are revenue streams and profit opportunities. Companies develop brands mainly so that they can charge more, increase new and repeat purchases, and differentiate an increasing set of products. Brands are bought and sold independently of the capacity to produce the product or service they represent.

Brands are promoted mainly, but not exclusively, by advertising. Others have defined advertising more pithily than the AMA as 'salesmanship mass produced' (Hite and Fraser, 1988: 203). It is a species of marketing promotion and as such has the following functions (Stewart and Kamins, 2002).

1. To inform customers about products or offers.
2. To persuade customers to buy.
3. To remind customers of a product or brand.
4. To act as a barrier to entry for potential new entrants by raising entry costs.

This combination of possibilities helps explain why many already high-profile brands are supported by high levels of expenditure on advertising. However, not all advertising supports brands. There are cases where firms in an industry collude to increase demand for the industry's product; that is they increase *primary* demand, as opposed to increasing *secondary* demand for a specific brand within the industry. A good example here would be advertising for milk products which in the UK and USA is funded by an industry body. In the USA at least, there is evidence that this form of advertising works; Chung and Kaiser (2000) found that over the decade 1984–93, advertising increased demand for milk by just over 1% and, more significantly, the price of milk by more than 14%. This is theoretically interesting since it is an example of advertising paying off where all products are perfect substitutes.

Mostly, though, advertising is about differentiation to increase demand, and as such competes with the conventional way to increase demand, which is to cut prices. So the decision as to how much to spend on advertising is potentially a difficult one since it is an attempt to increase demand at constant or increasing prices. It thus turns into a calculation about the price elasticity of demand. Dorfman and Steiner (1954) developed the basic prescriptive formula as follows:

$$\frac{\text{Advertising expenditure}}{\text{Sales revenue}} = \frac{\text{Advertising elasticity}}{\text{Price elasticity of demand}}$$

So, if advertising elasticity = 2, then, for a given price–advertising combination, sales will increase by 2% if advertising expenditure increases by 1%. The same applies in reverse for prices; a price elasticity of 2 means that sales increase by 2% if price decreases by 1%. The theorem shows that the sensitivity of prices depends on advertising, and the sensitivity of advertising on price. The best position for the firm is where price sensitivity is low and advertising sensitivity high; substantial price rises can be sustained by moderate advertising expenditures.

There are three implications to point out.

1. The more productive advertising is in raising sales, the higher will be its proportion of sales revenue.

2. The greater the price elasticity, the less effective advertising will be and the smaller the percentage of sales revenue. High-price elasticity implies many substitute products.

3. Advertising should be highly effective for new products where there are few comparable offerings, so the advertising to sales ratio will be high at product launch. As the market becomes saturated, advertising elasticity will fall, and one would thus expect the advertising to sales ratio to fall across the life cycle of a product or brand.

This is essentially an equilibrium model, and one would expect advertising expenditures to be triggered by external events. For example, we have noted that advertising expenditures are used by incumbent firms as a barrier to entry for new firms, and there is evidence that when there are new entrants into markets, incumbent advertising expenditures spike.

Channelling your Energy

Distribution was a core concern of early marketing theory, and it remains so, not just in terms of logistics and efficiency, but also in terms of market structure. On the cost side, US data show that margins in distribution channels account for on average over 30% of the ultimate selling price; advertising by comparison typically costs around 5% (Stern and Weitz, 1997). But also, structurally, channels turn potential buyers into orders and thus revenue. Channels *make* the market. They do so by performing a number of functions (Anderson and Coughlan, 2002: 223). They take ownership and physical possession of goods, they promote products and brands, and they may negotiate price and finance purchase (as car dealerships often do). Channels take much of the inventory risk in many businesses and this may require substantial margins. This author's partner once took a job in a high-end jewellery store in London, in which one of the main employee benefits was to purchase jewellery at cost; this revealed 100% mark-up on many items, and was used to support the argument that since the nominal savings of jewellery purchase often exceeded her monthly salary, more should be bought.[2] Channels also take orders and secure payment (though on highly variable terms).

Three literatures we have already encountered are used to examine channel structures. First, transaction cost economics; should the channel be vertically integrated? Second, agency theory; how does, for example, a manufacturer monitor and incentivize the downstream channel to market? Third, game theory; how do we settle conflicts over transfer prices and quantities? We deal with each in turn.

The transaction costs approach is used to consider the make-or-buy decision. If I produce a product or service, should I own all of the steps to the end consumer? In Chapter 2 we saw that the answer to this for many manufacturing firms considering the value chain for intermediate product was yes, but the marketing literature has had to contend with the empirical regularity that outsourcing of downstream channels is common. Outsourcing is thus often considered more efficient than vertical integration, and not necessarily on cost grounds but because:

> ...a specialist (such as a distributor or sales agent) pools the demands of many producers for given distribution services. Thus, the outsider can achieve economies of scope and scale, which are all-important advantages in the competitive world of distribution channels.

> (Anderson and Coughlan, 2002: 226)

This explains why we have supermarkets, department stores, and Amazon; which 'market' themselves on the range of products they can offer in one location or site. Transaction costs analysis can also explain the opposite outcome. Where assets are very specific and intangible, the product or service provider and the customer are more likely to be linked by a vertically-integrated supply chain. One does not buy legal or consultancy services through an intermediary (although when the selling partner disappears it can feel so). The approach also, crucially, can help with the more complex case where firms sell product both through their own distribution channels and through outsourced ones. Dual channels may be preferred both when there is a need to monitor and incentivize (in agency-theoretic terms) players in the channel and monitoring is difficult because the relationship between behaviour and sales is

---

[2] Yes, I know.

stochastic, and where there is a segmented market, with consumers looking for differentiated purchase experiences; the latter case applies to big brands like Apple and Nike and we shall return to it below. Where performance is difficult to judge and consumers difficult to predict, dual channels allow benchmarking (Dutta et al., 2003).

Agency theory may be applied both to the problem of selection and of monitoring of channel members. In the marketing literature, the term *screening* is used to refer to actions taken by a product or service producer to assess an intermediary's quality, and the term *signalling* to refer to action designed to reveal its quality to the manufacturer. Consider Harrods and its relationship to the major brands it retails. It sends signals to fashion houses such as Armani and Dior of several types, relating to its reputation and customer base, as well as the other brands it does (and does **not**) carry, the physical fabric of the store and merchandising—specifically the space and prominence it will give to a branded product. Armani, which also wishes to sell through its own outlets, will screen Harrods on these matters, and on issues such as relative pricing and discounting, in decisions about which product to supply.

High-end brands often use channels to restrict or ration product availability while advertising to increase brand awareness. In the 1980s, this author was privileged to hear the late Victor Gauntlett, CEO of Aston Martin, describe how he chose on his appointment as CEO simultaneously to restrict production (because of the investment capital constraints) but to advertise in airline magazines and lend his own cars to the producers of the next Bond movie. He was deliberately trying to generate demand and simultaneously restrict supply. Demand exploded and price doubled, but waiting times on delivery increased markedly because one could only buy from Aston Martin itself. At that point, it became possible to develop a market for places in the Aston Martin customer queue.

A key issue is whether to focus monitoring and incentives on outcome- or behaviour-based contracts. An outcome-based contract simply focuses on measures such as sale or margins (or both) allowing the channel member, say a retailer, to exercise discretion in pursuit of certain targets. A behaviour-based contract relates to practices in selling a product. Take an example of UK retailing. In large UK supermarkets, the suppliers of wine (generally small) have outcome-based contracts in which they receive a percentage of the sale price without influencing either the sale price or the merchandising; if they are heavily discounted (and they often are) they suffer both in revenue and brand terms. A large supplier, like Pedigree Petfoods (the pet food market leader) will influence not only price but also negotiate 'slotting', that is the amount of shelf space the products are given. It will then support the brands heavily through television advertising. The arrangements reflect the relative power of the parties.

Game theoretic models build on this, primarily to consider transfer pricing within the channel. Consider a channel in which a manufacturer introduces a product at a given transfer price, x, and has no control over subsequent downstream prices. At each stage, prices might be set above the competitive level to generate rents to each channel member, resulting in an uncompetitive retail price, y. This is termed *double marginalization* (although it may happen more than twice). The task then for the manufacturer (or some other channel member) is to achieve channel leadership, that is control over pricing within the channel.[3] This might be achieved by the ownership of key assets or by legal rights.

However, as well as price, there is quantity, and producers may be able to affect prices by offering product returns. A good example is the market for books (Padmanabhan and Pang, 1997). If publishers do not let retailers return unsold books, the latter will order only those they are sure they can sell, and the quantity ordered may not satisfy demand. If they allow returns, retailers will order at least as many as they think they can sell, and price competition will both squeeze retailing margins and clear the market. Allowing returns may thus also influence the double marginalization problem. In economic terms, this channel management strategy shifts retail competition from Cournot competition (quantity) to Bertrand competition (price).

We close by considering the channel management strategies of four of the world's biggest brands. For Coca-Cola and McDonald's, the model is primarily franchising, although they differ in how they manage it. For Nike and Apple, they offer multiple channels to market; at one extreme one can click online, at the other, one can have an experience in Niketown or an Apple Store.

Coca-Cola makes syrup and advertises. Its franchisees add water, bottle, sell, distribute, and merchandise. It controls its channels by having 'anchor bottlers' often partially owned by the parent, who have exclusive control over the brand in particular geographies. Coca-Cola Enterprises, for example, has control over the brand in Western Europe. It also has independent franchisees elsewhere who, crucially, can add sugar to the syrup by agreement. The exclusivity of these arrangements creates a long-term relational contract of mutual dependency in which both screening and signalling are important.

---

[3] In general game theoretic language this is termed 'Stackelberg' leadership, defined as a player who can pre-commit to an action which must be taken as a given by other players in defining their own actions.

McDonald's owns properties, supplies raw materials, and advertises. Its franchisees cook the food and maintain the environment. Here is the description of the deal from the UK website.

The approval process

After several interviews, if we're both sure that a McDonald's franchise is right for you, you'll embark on your training programme which typically takes nine months. This involves visiting and working in several restaurants as well as classroom-based tuition. The training is excellent, but you'll have to support yourself throughout that period, as well as provide a refundable £5,000 training deposit.

There's more to running a McDonald's franchise than serving burgers and French fries – much more. You'll need a remarkable aptitude for connecting and communicating with people. You'll be completely committed for at least 20 years, with no other business interests. And we only offer franchises to individuals, although many of our franchisees run their businesses as husband-and-wife teams.

What does it cost?

As a guide, the cost of a restaurant typically ranges from £125,000 to £325,000. You will need to provide at least 25% of the value as unencumbered funds, the remaining 75% can be funded through a bank loan with favourable funding terms. There's also a one-off franchise fee of £30,000 and a training deposit of £5,000 which is refunded when you complete your training.

There are also ongoing fees:
Monthly rent on the premises, based on sales and profitability (usually ranging from 10% to 15%)
Service Fee for the use of the McDonald's system—5% of sales
Contribution to the national marketing spend, currently 4.5%

And the returns?

Cashflow (before debt repayment) typically ranges from £95,000 to £200,000 per year for each restaurant but this isn't guaranteed: it could be more, it could be less.

In the terms we have used above, this is a long-term (20-year) relational contract, with both outcome and behaviourally based elements. One net effect is to incentivize restaurant performance, but another is to monitor sales.

Nike and Apple are two of the world's biggest brands, and they operate similar channel structures. It is possible to buy both product sets online, either through their respective stores or through an online operation like Amazon. The products are also available in department stores and specialist generic outlets. However, they both also operate high-cost customer service operations in the Apple retail stores (394 of them in 2012) and Niketown. At the high-end operations, new products and variants are available first, and advice or customization are available. In Niketown, in particular, an 'experience' of the brand, including entertainment, is available and the ostensible purpose of the location is brand development and to stimulate purchases at other outlets; in this there are parallels to them parks such as Disney, although no admission is charged (Pine and Gilmore, 1998). In both Nike and Apple, queues form on opening or new product launches.

Why would these companies operate multiple channels? It is not primarily about price. Although one might get a discount from a channel, the prices, for example, in Apple Stores are not generally higher than through other retailers. An advocate suggests,

> ...the secret to the Apple Store success lies in the fact that employees are trained to educate, not to 'sell.' In an Apple Store, education means specialists will answer all your questions about the iPad. They will spend as much time as you need. Since Apple retail is a non-commissioned sales floor, specialists are not reprimanded for spending too much time with a customer. They will encourage you to sign up for free classes offered in the store. They will let you touch and play with the device. But they won't 'sell' you a product in the traditional sense. If you leave the store without having purchased a product, that's perfectly okay with them. They will not feel pressured to make a sale. The mission of the Apple Store specialist is to provide a great experience and to build loyal customers.

(*Forbes*, 16 March 2012)

Conclusion

Marketing is seen by some as a bundle of techniques—such as branding, distribution, pricing, and advertising—rather than a cohesive discipline with a discrete body of theory. These techniques are, however, at least integrated by the core belief that there are benefits in the active management of markets for goods and services. In economic terms, these can be seen as raising switching costs and reducing search costs for consumers, creating rents, and protecting profit margins. Firms may then come to be valued on the basis of attributes of the markets they manage—customer base, profit per customer, market share, and market growth may all be factors in the share price. These benefits operate not only for firms but also for managers within them; in most large firms it would be career limiting for managers to argue it was a waste of time to worry about the customer. Conversely, high levels of customer knowledge can be a key personal advantage.

Another way of framing this is to say that marketing tries to put social structures into markets. Marketing assumes firms can create markets, segment them, protect them from competitors, and grow them. Indeed this activity may come to be the key preoccupation of the firm, or at least its strategic apex. Many of the world's largest brands, such as Nike, Apple, and

Coca-Cola, outsource the actual production of their products and focus most of their activity on product design, promotion, and delivery. This has profound implications for the structure of the modern corporation, and I will examine it in Theme 8. First, we must understand the key elements of the most recent and most prestigious discipline in the management toolkit: finance.

Chapter 8

The Strange Rise of Financial Economics

Introduction

This chapter and the next theme both focus on finance, in different ways. The first issue concerns the rise of the academic discipline of finance. Today, finance is central to any serious management education, and its faculties are arguably the most prestigious and certainly collectively the best paid in the top business schools. However, it was not always so and, while there are some earlier roots, academic finance is primarily a post-war and US phenomenon.[1]

Modern academic finance is analytical, mathematical, and firmly rooted in economics; several Nobel laureates of recent years have been financial economists. Institutions and firms barely feature. It concerns itself primarily with markets and with tradeable financial instruments. It also borrows concepts from applied mathematics (the portfolio) and engineering (diffusion equations). However, despite its role as 'high theory' within the business curriculum, it has had a profound impact on the commercial practice of financial markets.

The second issue concerns the growing influence of such financial markets on business behaviour and specifically the modern corporation. Pfeffer, himself a trenchant critic of the growing influence of mathematical economics in organizational analysis, remarked in 1997 that one of the four key changes organizational theory had to explain was the 'increasing influence of external capital markets on organizational governance and decision making'; incidentally, one could argue that the other three—the 'externalisation' of employment, the growth of smaller firms, and increasing salary inequality are also related to this influence (Pfeffer, 1997: 18).

Financial oversight is a specific form of external regulation, and its impact on the hitherto largely autonomous senior management of large US

---

[1] The roots are mostly French. For a lively and non-technical introduction to the work of Bachelier and Levy, see Weatherall, 2013.

corporations was substantial. Two key features—vertical integration and indifference to financial markets—disappeared quite rapidly as key measures of corporate success moved from size and market share to share price and market capitalization—'ideally achieved with as few tangible assets as possible' (Davis, 2009: 13). In short, the managerial corporation died in many Western markets. Because financial markets became so important, the finance function grew in status within the firm.

There is an intriguing chicken-and-egg question about the impact of financial theory on these changes to the corporation. I shall return to it below. First, we need to be clear about what was involved in the revolution in financial economics and why it came to have such an impact. I will look at the four key pillars of financial economics in non-technical terms.

Blame it on Herb

Theme 4 dealt with bounded rationality; specifically, it looked at the attack on 'super-rational' stylized economic actors by Herbert Simon. To recap, he argued that these were unrealistic descriptions of human behaviour, and that one needed more credible models. In reaction, economists might have engaged with the proposition, or tried to make it irrelevant. They predominantly chose the latter, and set out to prove what you could do with rigorous assumptions about human behaviour and mathematical models based on those assumptions. The field in which this approach came to full fruition was academic financial economics. For Herb, the problems began at home, at Carnegie Mellon.

The Modigliani–Miller hypothesis (1958) states that, in a perfect market, neither the total market value of a corporation nor its average cost of capital was affected by its capital structure. What does this mean? Corporations raise money by issuing securities. Securities are mostly stocks and bonds. Stocks confer rights of ownership and, in certain circumstances, the right to dividend payments. In a second paper, Modigliani and Miller (1961) argued that a firm's dividend policy was also irrelevant. Bonds confer the right to a capital sum in repayment at a given date, and to pay interest up to then. Combined, they form a firm's capital structure. The argument was essentially that if two identical firms (i.e. identical in terms of expected earnings and risk exposure) had different capital structures, any difference in their market value would disappear through arbitrage in a perfect market. And perfect markets are everywhere, except where you have taxes, particularly differential taxes between stocks and bonds, brokerage fees, any costs associated with information acquisition, and any trader who can influence price (Modigliani and Miller, 1961: 412). So *empirically*, there are very few circumstances in which the proposition could hold and certainly not in the USA at the time they were writing (MacKenzie, 2006: 42).

Their second proposition, however, is that the rate of return investors can expect on their equities increases as the firm's debt-to-equity ratio increases. This seems at first at odds with the proposition that debt/equity ratios do not matter, but the answer is that any increase in expected return is exactly offset by an increase in risk and therefore in shareholders' *required* rate of return (Brealey et al., 2008: 480). The same restrictive assumptions apply.

Modigliani and Miller were at Carnegie Mellon, but followed a prevailing view in economics that models could be built on the rational expectations of actors; such actors were as rational and knowledgeable as the economist writing about them. The most famous exponent at the time was Milton Friedman at Chicago. In financial economics, this was to build a legacy of models that were mathematically simple (usually assuming normal distributions that could be summarized by means and standard deviations), sustained by strong sets of assumptions whose realism was not relevant, and indifferent to data. Indeed, as Simon himself noted, a basic concept in many models, the expected rate of return on a stock, was not directly observable (MacKenzie, 2006: 40).

So academic finance grew as part of the post-war mathematization of economics, but this in turn was part of a more general trend, as Whitley has noted, in which there was a confidence that hard sciences could be used to improve management practice (1986: 171). In particular, war mattered. The tremendous development of operations research capability during World War II was applied to a number of civilian uses (Mirowski, 2002) and it is in operations research that we find the roots of finance.

Any Portfolio in a Storm?

Harry Markowitz, who wrote one of the seminal papers in finance, was an operations researcher. He took up the point that investors would put their money in those stocks with the highest expected rates of return. But since investors did not put all of their eggs in one basket (i.e. one stock), but diversified their investments (i.e. many), he argued that they did so to control risk. He thought of risk as the variance of returns, or its root, the standard deviation. He argued that the unit of analysis should be the investment portfolio, and these portfolios could be more or less 'efficient'. An 'efficient' portfolio could be one that maximized return for a given level of risk, or minimized risk for a given level of return (Markowitz, 1952).

For his seminal paper, his own rate of return was initially low; it did not generate a lot of attention. In order to study standard deviations of returns, he had to square rates of return, so he needed quadratic rather than existing linear programming techniques. This meant his fullest version of his argument was not in a finance, but an operations research, journal (Markowitz, 1956). But a core problem was computational. The basic argument of portfolio theory was that one looked at correlations between stocks in which one invested. If they all move together, the risk is high. If they have low covariance, the risk is lower. But in an average portfolio, that is a lot of correlations; with limited computational capacity at the time it was not feasible for investors to do this.

The solution to this was Sharpe's (1964) idea that one looked at the correlation between each stock and the underlying performance of the market, normally proxied by a market index. If one looks at the correlation between an individual stock and an index, one can separate out the systemic from the idiosyncratic risk of a stock. One can get rid of the idiosyncratic risk of a stock by diversifying the portfolio, but the systemic risk remains and cannot be diversified away. High systemic risk (which Sharpe termed beta, as in a regression equation) would mean a stock had to be priced low, and thus have a high expected rate of return. Low beta means low rates of return as in Figure C8.1.

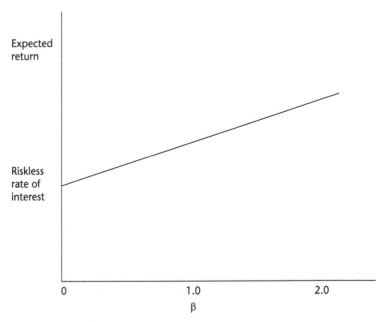

Figure C8.1. The capital asset pricing model.

(*Source*: MacKenzie, Donald, *An Engine, Not a Camera: How Financial Models Shape Markets*, figure: 'The Capital Asset Pricing Model', © 2006 Massachusetts Institute of Technology, by permission of The MIT Press.)

There can thus be only one efficient portfolio, the market index itself (MacKenzie, 2006: 56–7).

Sharpe, together with others, developed this insight into the Capital Asset Pricing Model (CAPM);[2] in a competitive market, the expected risk premium varies directly with beta. The model achieves its elegance at the price of seriously strong assumptions about equilibrium. According to Whitley (1986: 177; see also Jensen, 1972) there are seven.

> All asset holders are single period expected utility of wealth maximizers who choose their asset portfolios on the basis of the mean and variance of expected returns. They can borrow or lend an unlimited amount of money at an exogenously given, risk free rate of interest. They have identical subjective estimates of the means, variances and co-variances of returns on all assets. They are price takers, so that asset markets are perfectly competitive. The quantities of assets are fixed so that there are no new issues and they are perfectly divisible and liquid—i.e. there are no transaction costs. Finally there are no taxes.

And no death either, presumably. Needless to say, Whitley was also able to note that empirical tests of the CAPM are elusive.

Fama, I'm Going to Live Forever

If everyone is perfectly rational, and information freely available, then it is tough to make a profit trading. As an old finance cliché goes, if you see a $100 bill lying in the street, it must be a fake because otherwise someone else would have picked it up. So if everyone knows everything, then any systematic patterns in stock prices would disappear, because traders would spot and eliminate them. It is the corollary that is critical; if there are no patterns then prices follow a random walk, and if they do that, you can apply probability theory.

MacKenzie (2006: 59–66) traces this observation back to the nineteenth century. The academic who has developed the observation into the 'efficient markets hypothesis' (EMH) is Gene Fama. However, in the modern era, a British statistician Maurice Kendall (1953) is generally credited with the 'discovery' of randomness in stock and commodity price series.[3] In mathematical terms, stock price movements in this model are martingales.

In the subsequent models developed by Fama, asset price changes follow a random walk, which must in practice be modified to a log normal random walk to prevent prices going negative (because of limited liability). The essence

---

[2] The others were Lintner and Treynor. See Brealey et al., 2008: 213–18.
[3] The most popular finance text, Brealey et al. (2008) describes EMH entirely by reference to Kendall.

of the approach is that all relevant information is contained in prices, but there are three different forms of the efficient market hypothesis (Fama, 1970, 1991):

- The weak form states that present prices reflect all information contained in the record of past prices. In other words, past prices are no guide to the future.
- The semi-strong form states that current prices incorporate not only all information from past prices but also all other published information.
- The strong form states that current prices incorporate all information that could be acquired by a painstaking fundamental analysis both of the asset and of economic circumstances.

The link to the CAPM is that anomalies in the efficient markets hypothesis— stocks with 'excess' returns, are identified with respect to their level of risk. And the efficient markets hypothesis also implies that the best portfolio to hold is the market itself.[4]

The model is not meant to be a description of markets; as Fama notes:

> Like all models, market efficiency (the hypothesis that prices fully reflect available information) is a faulty description of price formation. Following the standard scientific rule, however, market efficiency can only be replaced by a better specific model of price formation, itself potentially rejectable by empirical tests.
>
> (Fama, 1998: 284)

However, there is a body of evidence that supports the hypothesis. Market prices are mostly consistent with risk profiles, stock prices (mostly) follow a random walk, past prices do not predict future ones, and fund managers do not on average outperform the market (Fama, 1991; Fenton O'Creevy et al., 2005). But there are anomalies; and all investors do *not* hold only the market portfolio.

Others are less sure of the EMH's usefulness:

> I submit that moving from the mechanics of arbitrage to the [efficient markets hypothesis] involves an enormous leap of faith. It is akin to believing that the ocean is flat, simply because we have observed the forces of gravity at work on a glass of water. No one questions the effect of gravity, or the fact that water is always seeking its own level. But it is a stretch to infer from this observation that oceans should look like millponds on a still summer night. If oceans were flat, how do we explain predictable patterns, such as tides and currents? How can we account for the existence of waves, and of surfers? More to the point, if we are in

---

[4] Which is in essence the investment strategy advised by Fama's own investment firm, Dimensional.

the business of training surfers, does it make sense to begin by assuming that waves, in theory, do not exist?

Lee (2001: 284)

The essence of the M&M hypothesis, the CAPM model, and the EMH is captured by Lee's observation. Although none of these models focuses on market imperfections, anomalies, or arbitrage opportunities, their essentially prescriptive nature enables anomalies to be identified, for example in different valuations of firms (M&M), beta values of stocks (CAPM), or inexplicable share price differences offering arbitrage opportunities (EMH). Winds, tides, and currents, to continue the analogy, are not the main focus of interest. That is left to the subsequently emerging discipline of behavioural finance, which studies anomalies using the decision bias literature we examined in Theme 4.[5] However, while there are simple and elegant theories in academic finance that describe perfect and efficient financial markets, there are no parallel intellectual developments in behavioural finance that address anomalies and crises; it remains, as Fama described it, 'anomalies dredging' (see Willman, 2000).

More Heat than Light?

In Shakespeare's *The Merchant of Venice*, Shylock loans Antonio money to fund a maritime mercantile project, with a set future repayment date, but failure to repay this 'bond' will result in Antonio giving up a 'pound of flesh'. Antonio's ships sink, he cannot repay, Shylock refuses to accept an alternative payment, and the outcome is a debacle in which Shylock cannot enforce the contract in court. So much easier, then, if they could have purchased an option or hedge against disaster.

Options are contracts in which the purchaser gets the right to buy or sell a stock or commodity at a given price (the 'strike' price) on or up to a given future date. If it is an option to buy it is a 'call' option; if to sell, a 'put' option. If the transaction can happen any time up to the future date (the 'expiration') it is an American option; if you can only do it *on* the date, it is a European option (and generally much riskier). Prices for these things are not straightforward to calculate, particularly where they are themselves tradable; you need to know the expected rate of return on the stock, and on the option itself, and both are unobservable.

---

[5] For a simple review of the behavioural finance literature, see Fenton O'Creevy et al., 2005: 32–44.

Before dealing with the pricing issue, two background points. First, the distinction between buying and selling options and pure gambling was not always clear. In Britain and the USA, for long periods, options were banned. In the USA, where options were often on agricultural commodities, you had to prove the commodity (crop) existed before an option could be placed (MacKenzie, 2006: 119). Second, there were again roots in operations research, but also in practice rather than academia; two key figures in the development of options pricing, Black and Treynor, worked at Goldman Sachs and Arthur D Little respectively.

Let us deal with five non-mathematical issues. Take a call option.

1. The higher the price of the underlying asset, the higher the price of the option to buy it.

2. The lower the price of the option to call, the more valuable it is (given asset value constant).

3. You do not need to pay the strike price until expiration. It is thus a free loan net of the option price, more valuable when interest rates are high.

4. It is asymmetric between loss and gain. If the strike price is below the asset price, everything upside is profit. But if the strike price is higher than the asset price, you do not care by how much.

5. A long-term option is more valuable than a short-term one. Particularly in an American call, a distant expiration allows for increase in the stock price both monotonically and through volatility (Brealey et al., 2008: 588).

The solution to the pricing problem above is termed the Black–Scholes–Merton formula. MacKenzie (2006: 119–42) brilliantly describes the solution to the mathematical difficulties. The solution to the two expected value problems above is to use beta. Black noted:

> If the stock had an expected return equal to the (riskless) interest rate, so would the option ... if the beta of the stock were zero, the beta of the option would have to be zero too ... The discount rate that would take us from the options expected future value to its expected value would always be the (riskless) interest rate.
>
> (quoted in MacKenzie, 2006: 132)

One then assumes that the distribution of underlying stock price changes is log normal, in continuous time, that there are no transaction costs, that you can borrow at the riskless rate of interest to buy or hold any fraction of a security, and that there are no short-selling penalties (Black and Scholes, 1972, 1973; Merton, 1973). If you do this then the equation reduces to, in non-formal terms:

$$\text{Value of option} = (\text{delta} \times \text{share price}) - (\text{bank loan})^6$$

The key term is delta, which is the ratio of the change in the price of the option to that of the underlying asset. If the delta is 1, for example, the relationship of the prices is 1 to 1. That means there is a $1 change in the option price for every $1 change in the price of the underlying instrument. With a call option, an increase in the price of an underlying instrument typically results in an increase in the price of the option. An increase in a put option's price is usually triggered by a decrease in the price of the underlying instrument, since investors buy put options expecting their price to fall.

There have been many developments of this original approach, which have enabled some of the assumptions to be relaxed, but arguably this is the start of all derivatives trading. While this equation was being developed, there was very little organized option trading. Many securities that did not look like options could be thought of as such. I will look at some in the next theme. There developed specialized option exchanges, notably in Chicago, and using options to hedge current positions became common for both financial and non-financial institutions.[7] MacKenzie quotes Fama as saying that the equation was 'the biggest idea in economics of the (twentieth) century' (2006: 31). However, others have pointed out that it is a specific form of heat diffusion equation commonly used in physics and engineering.

These four theoretical constructs by no means summarize the field of academic finance (although they are important pillars of it). But they do capture its essence—the extension of equilibrium models of perfect or efficient markets to capital markets in models that 'emphasize analytical coherence over empirical adequacy' (Whitley, 1986: 187). Whitley goes on to note that the size of the academic field grew massively in the post-war period, that it was largely a US phenomenon until the time he wrote, and that a few 'top' US universities dominated it. As we have seen, its roots lay in applied mathematics, but of a particular type. Specifically, it was addicted to normal or log normal probability models, the implications of which are, inter alia, that extreme events such as crashes and crises should be very rare (MacKenzie, 2006: 105–18). This assumption was to be sorely tested after 1987, particularly in the crisis of 2008.

[6] To see this expanded, go to Brealey et al., 2008: 600.
[7] One does this by creating a long position in the stock and a short position in the option.

All That Glisters is not Goldman's

By the 1960s, these theories had begun to influence the practice of financial management throughout the USA and Europe. Consider Figure C8.2 which shows what happened in New York between deregulation and the end of the dot-com boom. It is worth labouring the point, first, that although there were many more listed companies at the end of the period, the growth in transaction volume and value far outstrips this; and, second, that the average company's shares were traded far more at the end of this period that at the beginning. This is an operational measure of the financial market oversight that Pfeffer referred to.

However, there were two other major changes across the period covered in Figure C8.2. First, more instruments were traded. As well as 'vanilla' stocks and bonds, options and other derivatives proliferated. And the number of exchanges proliferated. Some of this was global spread; after 1980 over forty countries opened stock exchanges, including former communist countries and emerging markets (Weber et al., 2009). International capital flows massively increased. In addition, specialized options markets were established (MacKenzie, 2006). Once, using the EMH, stock prices could be seen as capturing all information on future cash flows, anything that had a definable future cash flow could be turned into a tradeable capital asset—that is 'securitized'—and priced using variants of the CAPM. As Davis puts it:

> An essential factor enabling the growth of securities markets is a technology for evaluating capital assets at low cost . . . the capital asset pricing model . . . [provides] a framework for setting prices for securities in markets.
>
> (Davis, 2009: 39)

MacKenzie shows how, within these expanding markets, a concern to justify investment practice, not least to regulators, also led to an engagement with financial economics (MacKenzie, 2006: 69–88). Lee argues that the expanding and globalizing stock markets of the late twentieth century were designed with the core tenets of financial economics in mind; in particular,

> Fama's notion of efficient markets has come to underpin much regulation concerning the dissemination of price and quote information in financial markets.
>
> (Lee, 1998: 222)

However, these proliferating exchanges also compete. The older ones, such as those in New York and Chicago, began as partnerships but have evolved into firms. These firms in turn engage in competition for investors—by setting standards for listing firms which manufacture trust—and for listing firms—by making sure these standards are attainable; firms can thus go 'regime shopping' (Michie,

2006; Abolafia, 1996). Several exchanges, such as the London Stock Exchange, engage in cross-border acquisition and have their own quoted share price.

The key point here is that the term 'market oversight' is slightly misleading, since the markets themselves are financial firms. Moreover, trading in these markets is dominated by other large firms such as mutual funds, insurance companies, and, particularly, investment banks. Since one cannot understand the evolution of modern management practice up to 2008 without understanding investment banking, let us turn to examine them.

Consider the following:

> A small number of investment bankers sat at the nexus of the contracts that allocated capital in the American economy. To many contemporary observers, the investment bankers looked like titans who had accreted an excessive degree of power, which they used irresponsibly to feather their own nests at the expense of the ordinary working people whom they had disenfranchized.
>
> (Morrison and Wilhelm, 2007: 223)

This might look like a decent description of 2008 but in fact it refers to the early part of the twentieth century, when investment banks were relatively small partnerships dominated by a few individuals such as J. P. Morgan, aggressively generating large corporations through mergers, then sitting themselves as influential board members.

Morrison and Wilhelm's excellent history of investment banking contains the following key points.

- Investment banks began as partnerships based on trust and reputation that managed networks concerned with price-relevant but tacit information. They began in Atlantic trading in the eighteenth century and thus are essentially Anglo-Saxon institutions.

- Within these networks, they create 'private institutional mechanisms that allow them to risk their reputations' (63). Two things follow. First, they are by nature opaque, since they protect information and networks. Second, their operation is highly dependent on law; for most of the short twentieth century, they were constrained by the 1933 US Glass Steagal Act that required the complete separation of investment banking from commercial deposit taking.

- In the period after World War II, two factors generated a codification and commoditization of trading activities within investment banks. First, the growth of information technology allowed codification and standardization of trading (most exchanges, for example, moved from face-to face to electronic trading). Second, portfolio theory and pricing instruments such as CAPM displaced more tacit methods for managing trading. Economies of scale became important.

- By the end of the twentieth century, investment banking was a 'bipolar' activity. On the one hand, investment banks continued with the advisory, client-based, network-driven work such as mergers and acquisition and underwriting. On the other, they were engaged in low-margin, capital-intensive trading businesses. The large banks tended to own the technological platforms for algorithmic trading, both to trade on their own account (proprietary trading) and for clients (brokerage). There were clear conflicts of interest.

- Pursuit of scale destroyed partnerships. Banks floated as public corporations in pursuit of capital to fund growth. As the Glass Steagall Act was gradually eroded in the post-war period,[8] many of the partnerships were absorbed by commercial banks possessing lots of capital. This tended to happen quicker in more commoditized trading houses, and slower where advisory work was most important, for example at Goldman Sachs; but by the 1980s, partnership had disappeared.

- The investment banking industry grew massively. The market capitalization of the ten largest investment banks increased by over 2000% between 1980 and 2000 *in real terms*. In addition, the industry became highly concentrated around the largest US and Swiss banks (Morrison and Wilhelm, 2007: 7–19). However, much advisory work migrated into smaller firms, often hedge funds.

- Key financial economists were engaged in this, as we have seen, through employment in investment banks or, as MacKenzie (2006) shows, by setting up hedge funds. In addition, the large employment expansion was fuelled by recruitment of MBAs equipped with the standardized skills of financial economics taught at the major business schools.

By the end of the century, a highly concentrated financial services industry became a significant part of GDP in many large, developed economies, amplifying the impact of the financial crash. The crash itself was triggered by the subprime mortgage crisis in the USA which itself rested on a particular piece of financial economics technology: credit scoring (Altman, 1968). However, the sheer volumes of trading globally emerging in the late twentieth century and the concentration of trading and capital in a few 'bulge bracket' institutions were undoubtedly important. These institutions were important delivery pipelines for the impact of financial economics on the real world of financial markets. Moreover, they were, as I will discuss in the next theme, central to the market for corporate control.

[8] It was finally repealed in 1999.

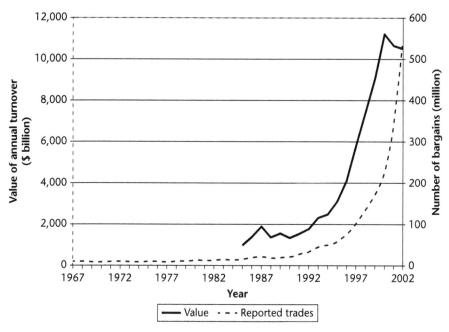

Figure C8.2. New York Stock Exchange equity turnover 1967–2002.
(*Source*: Fenton O'Creevy et al., 2005)

Conclusion

This chapter has sought, first, to document the key concepts and, second, indicate the impact of academic finance theory. It has sought to do the first by looking at key developments that share in common a commitment to rational expectations economics and indicating what they were trying to achieve; it has not attempted a summary of a vast field. It has sought to do the second by looking at markets and investment banks; the argument is that a combination of information technology and financial engineering techniques has transformed both in the second half of the twentieth century. Strictly speaking, investment banks did not survive the crash, but the institutions and the conflicts of interest are still there.

As Whitley (1986) noted, financial economics was an unlikely success story growing from the unpromising descriptive courses on banking around in the early 1950s; but a success story it definitely has been. No other business field commands the attention and shapes the behaviour of practitioners in a comparable way. There are problems. Many core theories, notably the efficient markets hypothesis, have been subjected to stringent criticism (Shiller, 2003). Indeed, the whole field of behavioural finance focuses on market anomalies that 'classical finance' cannot easily explain. It does not, however, offer any convincing general alternatives.

In the wake of the 2008 crash, one must point to two major deficiencies with the body of theory. First, there are simply too many crashes. Since the substantial deregulation of financial markets in 1984, there have been three major ones; 1987, 2001 (the end of the dot-com boom), and 2008. As MacKenzie (2006) trenchantly pointed out, even before the 2008 crash, the probability of two such events—if share price movements really do follow a modified normal distribution—in approximately twenty years is infinitesimally small. He argues that, from a mathematical perspective, the discipline took a wrong turn in sticking with this assumption; the third crash endorses his view. Second, because of the rigorous conceptual frameworks in financial economics, there is no room for firms; yet, just as financial markets exercise dominance over many corporations, large financial corporations dominate financial markets. Regulation of finance is as much about the behaviour of firms as about markets; for example, no other industry regulates itself as much as investment banking, where compliance and settlements for trading are in the same firm as the traders, and where 'Chinese walls' (which are simply firm processes) separate conflicts of interest in advisory work.

However, the impact of financial economics has been felt further than the financial services industry itself. It has gone some way to redefining the conception of the firm and the role of management. We need now to turn to what some have called 'financialization'; the increasing influence of financial considerations in the management of large corporations. For the USA, for example, Krippner (2005) shows that the ratio of portfolio income (dividends, capital gains, and interest) to total cash flow in US corporations in the 1980s and 1990s reaches five times that of the 1950s; the ratio of financial to non-financial profits behaves similarly. In fact, this influence of finance extends to governance, strategy, organizational structure, incentives, and employment. We turn to it next.

Theme 8

The Modern Corporation

Introduction

I have deliberately borrowed the title of Berle and Mean's book for this theme, which will complete the work of the last chapter and consider the impact of financial market oversight on the firm. Readers will recall that their central concern was with the separation of ownership and control—the inability of dispersed shareowners to control managers, who would then act in their own interests. As I argued in Theme 2, this was an early stirring of concern with the agency problem, which in turn embeds a strong anti-managerialist perspective. Such concerns re-emerged following the growth of academic finance, since tools now existed systematically to deal with the financial structure and performance of the firm. However, for the modern corporation, at least in the USA, shareholdings became much more concentrated in the 1980s, with pension funds, mutual funds, and insurance companies dominating (Useem, 1996).

I begin by looking directly at how the approach documented in the last chapter sees the corporation; this is the 'nexus of contracts' approach, and particularly the work of Michael Jensen. Then I will look at the impact of this view on the managerial firm itself, particularly its governance. The argument picks up the other three 'Pfeffer' themes which I introduced in the last chapter; I look at the fragmentation of the firm, the changing nature of employment relationships, and the increase in inequality within the firm. This leads us to deal with outsourcing, changing labour markets, and pay, in particular CEO pay. I do this by case study of two 'iconic' US firms, Nike and Enron—success and failure—and I will treat these two impostors just the same.

The Public Corporation

A central problem with the Berle and Means argument always was that, if dispersed shareholders were disadvantaged but rational, why was share ownership so attractive to so many? The answer, in Jensen's work, is essentially around the structure of contracts. In their seminal agency paper, Jensen and Meckling describe the corporation as a 'legal fiction which serves as a nexus for contracting relationships' (1976: 311). Agency is a cost of running a network of contracts, so networks that minimize or control agency will be more attractive, other things equal, than those which do not. The public corporation will incur serious agency costs in certain circumstances.

Jensen's (1989) argument contains a bit of revisionist history; the golden age of shareholder activism associated with J. P. Morgan gave way under 'populist' legislation to the public corporation. The latter was 'a social invention of vast historical importance' (1989: 64), mainly because of its capacity to spread financial risk across the diversified portfolios of investors. In growing industries, where profitable investment opportunities exceed cash generated internally, it can still work; in 1989, he identified computers, electronics, and financial services. However, where cash generated exceeds profitable investment opportunities, managers will waste it.

From our perspective, this is the centrally important bit—the embedded theory of management. Managers want passive investors who can't sell their shares, to hoard cash reserves, to grow companies beyond optimal size in order to provide promotional opportunities. To stop them doing this, you build highly leveraged financial structures; debt is a good discipline for managers, creditors are good disciplinarians, and, following Modigliani and Miller, the debt/equity ratio does not matter. You distribute excess cash as dividends to get it away from managers. You introduce pay for performance systems for top management involving substantial equity ownership. You introduce financial disciplines preventing the subsidizing of underperforming business units and you sell them. Managers do not need to do 'strategy' because;

> Wall Street can allocate capital among competing businesses and monitor and discipline management more effectively than the CEO and headquarters staff of the typical diversified company.
>
> (Jensen, 1989: 68)

You need an unrestricted takeover market (Jensen, 1993) in order to get rid of underperforming management teams; also, because debt is good, leveraged buyouts are good.

There are a number of both practical and theoretical issues here. Practical ones first. This approach justifies hostile takeovers, management buy-outs, downsizing, senior management stock options, breaking up of multi-divisional companies, reduction in head office staff, loss of corporate AAA credit ratings, and concentration of dispersed shareholdings through mutual funds and investment banks. All of these were features of the corporate landscape in the last two decades of the twentieth century (Davis, 2009).

The main theoretical point here relates to the efficient markets hypothesis. Markets know better than managers and they do so because the price of a stock contains all necessary information about future cash flows. What could managers be there for but to maximize stock price and shareholder value? Managerial strategies and actions could be judged in terms of their share price consequences. Jensen was an explicit fan of the EMH, and it plays a central role not only in the theory of markets but in the theory of the firm from a finance perspective. Absent the reliability of share price information, this approach rests on sand.

Davis (2009: 43–50) describes this as the 'functional' theory of corporate governance. Its elements are the primacy of shareholder value and the effectiveness of institutions to focus managerial attentions on it. He asserts its practical influence by contrasting the state of the US economy in the 1970s, prior to the development of the functional theory, with the 1980s. The latter period he characterizes as a 'bust-up takeover wave', in which over 25% of Fortune 500 companies received hostile approaches, most of them successful, and one-third of the largest corporations in the USA disappeared. Diversified firms were particularly hard hit; debt-fuelled takeovers could be profitable by buying a diversified firm and selling its component parts (Davis, 2009: 85). In Davis's view, 'The corporation has increasingly become the financially-oriented nexus described by its theorists' (2009: 63).

Within the corporation, what Fligstein (1990) has referred to as the 'finance conception of control' altered the demand for and influence of skill sets. If the firm is a bundle of contracts designed to optimize share price, then valuation of assets and rates of return become important, as do the skills associated with them. As I noted in Theme 5, management accounting measures become subordinated to financial accounting, externally referenced ones. If the functional theory of governance prevails, then it is important that senior managers can articulate to investors of various sorts how management activity is maximizing share price. Bluntly, the probability of the Finance Director becoming the CEO increases. In fact, Jensen's quote about 'Wall Street' is revealing. The role of investment banks was considerable. They played a massive role in the markets where share prices were defined. They participated in debt issues and marketing corporate bonds. Their advisory functions were key to the operation of the market for corporate control. Analysts' views on managerial performance and the functionality of governance mechanisms could affect a firm's valuation. Management of the firm's reputation in the capital markets becomes vital.

A final point to make in this section is a paradox about industry. For conglomerate firms, industry had ceased to matter through diversification. Broadly, the conglomerate public firm died in the 1980s merger wave (Davis et al., 1994). But the breaking up of conglomerates did not lead to a refocus in industry-specific issues or skills, since the pursuit of shareholder value knows no boundaries and the skills required to do it are generic financial ones. Financial engineering skills are just about the most generic on offer within the management curriculum and as such career-enhancing over a wide range of opportunities. If the next CEO needs to be the FD, she can be anyone's FD. Let us turn to the nature of the modern firm under financialization.

Into the Nexus

If market capitalization is the overriding objective, then its efficient pursuit should involve as few assets, particularly tangible assets, as possible. Anything that can be outsourced without a negative impact on shareholder value, should be. There are famous, almost clichéd, examples. Nike does not make any clothes or shoes. Apple does not make most of the components for the iPod or iPad. Most PC vendors do not make PCs. In the UK, the dominant supermarkets have their equally dominant own brands, but they buy it all in. Toyota—famously, given its recent product recalls—makes little of the car you buy. For several reasons, most notably the role of IT in monitoring outsourced relationships, you can outsource most manufacturing and a number of service (e.g. call centre) activities.

In some ways, the more interesting question is what you keep in the nexus, and what you keep closest to it. I suggest the following.

- Design; specifically the distinctive signature of the product and the innovative capacity to sustain it. Apple need the OS, the slide to unlock, and the next phone.
- The brand, and the marketing efforts and distribution that sustain it. Nike need their signature logos, advertising, and the stores.
- A reputation-enhancing set of professional service firms—accountants and lawyers and, particularly if you are one of the latter,
- high-status customers, who act as a quality signal.
- High-reputation investors and investment bankers; if Goldman Sachs and Warren Buffet publicly give you money, others will too.
- High-status executive and non-executive directors.
- Where relevant, key alliance partners, perhaps including a university or two.

This is not necessarily complete, and the optimal network of affiliations may shift by industry and geography but, in the organizational terms from Mintzberg we used in Chapter 5, it often excludes the operating core and support services. The closest of his models is the adhocracy. Stable career hierarchies are absent; skill sets tend to be generic. The 'nexus' is thus likely to be, in employment terms, much smaller than the 'managerial' variant typical of this sector that preceded it.

Employment and Inequality in the Nexus

It is likely that adopting the finance theory of the firm will increase inequality within it. Roughly, this occurs because of new practices introduced at the top and old ones shed at the middle and bottom. Let us deal with the top first.

The agency cost problem is solved by aligning the interest of top managers with investors by introducing share-based compensation. These might be direct awards of stock, but often they are put options on the share price. Senior managers are given warrants to buy shares at a set price, the value of which depends on the rise in the stock price to the expiration. In the USA, the average value of options grants to corporate CEOs increased tenfold in the 1990s (Davis, 2009: 87). The net effect of this during the long periods when share prices were rising (1990–2000 and 2001–7) was to generate large increases in CEO pay.

In the financial theory of the firm, all employees who can influence share price should have their incentives so aligned. In practice, options are often granted only to the top management team, thus decoupling executive compensation from other pay-setting devices and opening up a fault line in compensation and incentives within the firm. To illustrate this, consider a firm facing the prospect of takeover. Employees with stock options will welcome the approach since such tenders increase the share price; those without might fear the consequences.

Let us consider those without. The finance theory of the firm considers an employment contract to be like any other contract. Explicitly, Alchian and Demsetz (1972) compared the employment relationship to buying from your grocer; a simple spot contracting model without mutual obligations. Within this approach, there is no place for the institutional apparatus of the internal labour market providing long-term career ladders and pensions. Within the USA in particular, the 1990s saw the collapse of long-term employment and internal labour market structures (Osterman, 1996; Cappelli, 1999). Low-paid, entry-level jobs that launched new employees on such careers tend to be dead end jobs (Appelbaum et al., 2003). Arrangements to tie employees into organizations long term, such as pensions, collapsed. In the USA and UK, defined benefit schemes, where the employee is guaranteed a percentage of salary on retirement based on length of service, have given way to defined contribution schemes, where the employee invests in stocks and bears all the risk.

The net effect of this is that in many large firms top management pay, expressed as a multiple of average or lowest pay, has risen rapidly (Frank and Cook, 1995). Intra-firm arrangements have become massive generators of inequality. In a fascinating paper using Gini coefficients as the inequality measure,[1] Davis and Cobb (2010) show relationships between the market for corporate control and inequality. For the USA, they identify three broad periods:

1950s–1970s: where conglomerate mergers increased employment concentration and inequality declined.

1980s: when bust-up takeovers split up these conglomerates and inequality increased slightly.

1990s: when the 'shareholder value' approach dominated and inequality increased rapidly.

Interestingly, they also include an international comparison which shows much higher employment concentrations in most European countries, and lower levels of inequality.[2]

This last consideration helps raise the point that the finance model of the firm is best considered as the American way. It has provided the intellectual justification for the functional model of governance and the hollowing out of US manufacturing but it would not, for example, comply with many legal and regulatory frameworks in Europe. Nonetheless, it has global reach to the extent that it derives from market oversight. Hundreds of non-US firms are listed on NYSE and NASDAQ and are subject therefore to pressures to adopt the finance model. These may be competitive, to the extent their share price 'competes' with those of listed US companies, or regulatory, in that they are subject to oversight by the US Securities and Exchange Commission (SEC).

This is not merely an American phenomenon. Figure T8.1 shows for the UK FTSE 100 companies the ratio of CEO pay to average employee pay in 2008. Highly paid sectors such as banking do not show the greatest variance. This occurs where there is a combination of very high *and* very low pay. Reducing intra-firm inequality can occur by outsourcing the very lowest paid jobs. It is worth noting that these figures probably understate the extent of intra-firm inequality since most income distributions are log normal (i.e. the average is to the right of the median).[3]

---

[1] Gini coefficients vary with scores from 0 (where everyone has the same pay) to 1 (where one person has it all).

[2] The gap is quite big. They cite a Gini coefficient of 0.4 for the USA in 2006. The average for the five Nordic countries is 0.25.

[3] To the extent that CEO's are rewarded with capital assets and other employees with cash, these intra firm effects reflect the key driver of inequality noted by Piketty (2014), namely the tendency for return on capital to exceed GDP growth.

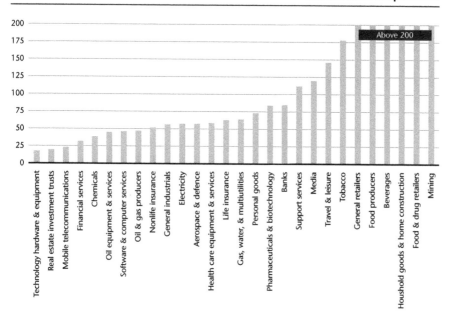

Figure T8.1. Ratio of CEO pay to average employee pay in 2008.
(*Source*: Lee, 2013)

In this section, we have tried further to show the impact of academic finance theory by outlining the association between the finance theory of the firm and changes to firm structure in the late twentieth century, particularly in the USA. However, this focus is misleading about the nature of the modern firm in at least two important respects. First, although Nike may not make anything itself, my Nike shirt still got made. We need to look at how the nexus that is Nike sits within the global supply chain that is Nike. Second, the simple presentation above might leave the reader with the misconception that market oversight worked in some unproblematic way. Enron shows it did not. We start there.

Making a Skilling

Enron is a typical but extreme business school story; a highly praised and discussed company that subsequently proves not to be viable (typical), but then a massive corporate bankruptcy that provokes legislative change in the USA (extreme).[4] Here are the key ingredients to this recipe.

---

[4] This section relies on IMD case, IMD-1-0195.

- In the 1970s, the USA deregulates its energy markets.
- A merger and acquisition wave kicks off in the 1980s, and Enron emerges as a corporate entity owning exploration, production and, particularly, pipeline capacity. Geoff Skilling, previously a government energy economist, ultimately ends up as CEO.
- Its acquisitions are funded by debt; by 1987, its debts are 75% of market capitalization.
- Enron sets up a trading arm, with a financial trading desk and its own traders hired from investment banks.
- It lobbies successfully for exemption from normal US regulatory oversight of derivatives trading. When the New York Mercantile Exchange allows futures trading on gas deliveries, Enron is both supplying the gas and trading the futures.
- By the end of 2000, trading activities accounted for 80% of turnover, which itself had grown fivefold in the previous year.
- Enron's share price grew spectacularly in the 1990s and an increasing amount of activity relied on Enron stock as security. The stock price needed to remain high also as security on debt.
- In 2001, the company experienced a number of difficulties in its international operations. The CEO, Ken Lay, resigned and cashed in $100 million of stock options. Skilling became CEO, then resigned after six months.
- Following the activities of a whistle blower, the firm's auditors advised Enron that its accounts would need to be restated. The firm announced a write-down of $1.2 billion of shareholders' equity and the SEC announced an investigation.
- No one who looked at the accounts would take it over, the debt was downgraded to 'junk', and it went bankrupt in December 2001.

It is a great story and they made a musical out of it. Let us take a closer look at the nexus of contracts.

To feed its pipelines, Enron entered deals with suppliers involving Volumetric Production Payments (VPPs). Enron would pre-pay for long-term gas supplies at a fixed price, with the payment secured on the gas itself, not the supplier's assets. Because of this and the liquidity impact, these were popular with suppliers, and Enron in return had long-term supply. To finance these deals, Enron in effect securitized the future cash flows and sold them off to investors by using 'Special Purpose Entities' (SPEs) which were off-balance-sheet partnerships. The counter-parties were often senior Enron employees. By the end, Enron had over 3000 subsidiaries and SPEs. Increasingly, Enron's reported financial results did not represent its liabilities accurately.

Many of these deals were cash-negative; that is Enron was paying for gas it did not yet have, often above current market rates. To resolve this, Enron adapted its accounting practice. First, it adopted a variant of mark-to-market accounting. This values an asset or security at the current market rate, with the gain or loss taken through the income statement, as opposed to using historic valuation. The variant Enron used is termed 'mark-to-model' accounting.[5] The net effect was to allow Enron to take up front the anticipated profits on their supplier contracts. The approach was simple; a trader would, using a curve of forecast prices, calculate the future cash flows on a (say) ten-year contract, then discount that to generate a net present value for the contract. This NPV was almost always positive and appeared as 'profit'.

As Enron became, in effect, an unregulated bank, it hired more and more traders and accountants. It operated a rigorous performance appraisal system of the 'rank and yank' type discussed in Theme 5 based on short-term performance. Project management skills, traditional in the energy industry, were not valued. What Skilling termed an 'asset-light' strategy focused on trading energy not generating or supplying it, and diversification into weather derivatives and tanker freight rate futures increased trading volumes to the point where supporting 1200 trading books required an electronic trading floor with substantial liquidity requirements.

Ultimately, Enron was in effect a Ponzi scheme with new trading activities attracting investment to fund older liabilities. The collapse, exacerbated by the impact of 9/11 on financial markets, was at the time the biggest bankruptcy in US history. Its legacies include the Sarbanes Oxley Act and the collapse of a major accounting firm, Arthur Andersen, as well as gaol sentences for key Enron players and the ruin of a number of investors, including Enron employees who held their pensions in stock.

Just (Don't) Do It!

Business school thinking had an even more direct impact on Nike than on Enron.[6] Its CEO, Phil Knight, developed the idea while on the Stanford MBA. The idea had two main elements:

1. Radically reduce costs by outsourcing all manufacturing.
2. Spend the money saved on manufacturing on marketing.

---

[5] Mark-to-market accounting requires there to be a current market price against which to value an asset (or liability). Models, and mark-to-model methods, are employed where one needs to value an asset or liability against a *future* price.

[6] This section relies in part on HBS case 9.385.025.

Again, let us look in more detail.

Knight, an athlete himself, saw the need for an *American* running shoe in a market then (1960s) dominated by German companies Adidas and Puma. The name, 'Nike', the distinctive 'swoosh' logo and the expression 'Just do it' were adopted early as elements in the distinctive brand. Growth in the 1970s was rapid, and by the 1980s, Nike had replaced Adidas as the market leader in the USA, become a public company, and was hailed by *Forbes* as the most profitable firm in America. Initially focused on shoes, it moved into the full range of athletic apparel.

The outsourcing approach meant that what looked like a US company was in fact an international one, since pursuing the cost advantage meant subcontracting in low-wage economies. In the 1970s, most Nike shoes were made in South Korea and Taiwan. In the 1980s, as wages there increased partly through union activity, Nike moved operations to Indonesia and China. Subsequently, it has developed operations in Vietnam; it chases cheap labour and switches production. This approach generates a large numerical difference between those who work for and those who make Nike. In the early 2000s Nike employed approximately 25,000 people, mainly involved in the core activities of design, marketing, and distribution. This has the reputation of being a high-commitment culture in which many employees have the brand as a tattoo and make substantial gains from stock options. By contract, over half a million employees around the world make Nike shoes and apparel, often working for establishments that have an arm's-length relationship with the company.

The marketing approach also has clear parameters. Quantitatively, Nike spends about 12% of sales revenue on advertising and promotion. It targets high-profile athletes; Olympic medal winners in general and very high-profile superstars like Michael Jordan and Tiger Woods in particular. From the 1970s to 2000, its non-US revenues went from almost zero to 43%, and it has targeted 'non-US-specific' sports such as football (soccer) and tennis. Arguably, its products sell more as fashion items than as functional ones. Although Nike holds patents on 'functional' innovations such as air soles, its product changes are more to generate sales. The marketing and labour strategies converge in Nike stores (many of which Nike does not own) in which sales assistants often receive a considerable part of their reward in access to Nike product.

Nike is described as a 'vertical architect' or 'value chain organizer' by some commentators (Roberts, 2004: 191). Its strategy may less attractively be described as a huge arbitrage play in which it uses production in low-wage economies to sell product in high-wage ones. Certainly, its investors have a right to be happy, and its producers have shown signs of being unhappy. Nike has shown consistent profitability. The average annual return on equity for the 20 years to 1998 was 28%, approximately the same as the compound average revenue growth. A stock purchase of $100 at flotation would have grown to $4080 by 1999. By contrast, 1998 was also when Nike became involved in serious problems with labour practices and, particularly, wages in its supply chain. These problems were serious enough to threaten its strategy.

In the 1990s, activists began to report instances of alleged unfair labour practices within the supply chain. Pervasively, these concerned wages; Nike experienced a huge gap between the pay of its top employees in the USA and those of its producers in Vietnam. However, there were also concerns about child labour, coercion and bullying, and dangerous working conditions. These did not emerge primarily in countries of manufacture, but paradoxically as violations of California consumer law. In 1998 Nike was accused in San Francisco Superior Court of willfully misleading the public about sweatshop conditions in its Asian manufacturing. Its initial response to revelations—we don't make shoes—was not compelling. However, some figures were. At the time, the average retail cost of a Nike shoe in US was $90, of which the labour cost was $3.37; Nike did not appropriate all of the difference, but the gap was damaging.

In response, the company argued, first, that it brought jobs to these areas and, second, that it could not be expected to pay US wages elsewhere (particularly where its competitors did not), but the brand associated with both 'cool' and athletic success could not simultaneously be associated with labour abuse. More specifically, the California lawsuit demanded return of profits and a 'corrective' advertising campaign, attacking both investor return and consumer perception. The outcome was a commitment from the company on labour practices, primarily addressing child labour, safety, education, and inspection, with rather less to say on wages.

Conclusion: Make or Buy?

In Chapter 7 I quoted Edith Penrose's remark that firms make things but markets don't. The two cases shown here indicate that, where firms seek to organize themselves as a nexus of contracts, they make less. The paradox of the financial conception of the firm addressed at dealing with managerial excesses is that it encourages firms to behave more like financial institutions and, in financial institutions, managerial capitalism remains strong; the recent financial crisis is almost a case study in investor impotence. I shall return to this later.

In both these examples, the core of the strategy, both in success and failure, was to focus on the elements of a value chain that generate the maximum shareholder returns. This was trading rather than production in Enron and marketing rather than production in Nike. Both companies have produced impressive returns to shareholders for a period and impressive salaries for senior managers but, arguably, considerable social costs for employees. In the financial conception of the firm, business strategy collapses into financial strategy. Indeed, academic finance has developed a slightly imperialist tone in its discussion of business practice. In a recent book published *after* the 2008 crash, Shiller remarks:

> At its broadest level, finance is the science of goal architecture—of the structuring of the economic arrangements necessary to achieve a set of goals and of the stewardship of the assets needed for that achievement.
>
> (Shiller, 2012: 6)

Some of the implications of this hubris will be explored in the final chapters, but first we have to turn our attention elsewhere, since business and management schools, and their curricula, are not populated exclusively by Shillers and Jensens. There remains a substantial body of research rooted in very different academic traditions in which rationality is not the gold standard, but a variable. This literature operates at both a micro level (managerial behaviour) and at a macro level (organizational culture), it is descriptive rather than analytical, predominantly (though not exclusively) qualitative, and, arguably, extremely influential for management practice. I turn to it.

Chapter 9

The Anthropology of Management?

Letter from the Duke of Wellington (dispatched from Spain in August 1812).[1]

Gentlemen

Whilst marching from Portugal to a position which commands the approach to Madrid and the French forces, my officers have been complying diligently with your requests which have been sent by H.M. ship from London to Lisbon and thence by dispatch to our headquarters. We have enumerated our saddles, bridles, tents and tent poles, and all manner of sundry items for which His Majesty's Government holds me accountable. I have dispatched reports on the character, wit and spleen of every officer. Each item and every farthing has been accounted for, with two regrettable exceptions for which I beg your indulgence.

Unfortunately the sum of one shilling and nine pence remains unaccounted for in one infantry battalion's petty cash and there has been a hideous confusion as to the number of jars of raspberry jam issued to one cavalry regiment during a sandstorm in western Spain. This reprehensible carelessness may be related to the pressure of circumstance, since we are at war with France.

This brings me to my present purpose, which is to request elucidation of my instructions from His Majesty's Government so that I may better understand why I am dragging an Army across these barren plains. I construe that perforce it must be one of two alternative duties, as given below. I shall pursue either one to the best of my ability, but I cannot do both:

1. To train an army of uniformed British clerks in Spain for the benefit of the accountants and copy-boys in London, or, perchance,

2. To see to it that the forces of Napoleon are driven from Spain.

Your most obedient servant
Wellington.

---

[1] This quote is cited by Norwich (1977). He has his doubts about raspberry jam in the Peninsular War and so do I.

Introduction

In Chapter 4 I traced a lineage from the early human relations movement to the modern management discipline of organizational behaviour. In this chapter, I look at another path of descent from the same source. The Hawthorne studies involved both the business school at Harvard and the anthropology department. The latter, largely transplanted to Chicago, continued the tradition of intensive, observational fieldwork that had characterized the later phases of the Hawthorne studies. To this was added the self-confidence to make interventions based on those observations intended to 'improve' some outcome such as efficiency or group cohesion. The rather oxymoronic term 'Applied Anthropology' was used unselfconsciously (Rose, 1988: 156–8).

The purpose of this chapter is to trace the influence of this approach on more modern academic management thinking. In contrast to the rational expectations approaches discussed in the last chapter and theme, the emphasis of a large body of academic work in the last thirty years has been to avoid modelling or hypothesis testing in favour of intensive field studies designed to understand 'real' management activities, in context. Methods are borrowed primarily from anthropology, in particular the components of ethnography (of which more below). Some concepts are borrowed too, notably the idea of culture. In this process of acquisition, changes to both method and concept have occurred, many of which could be seen to do violence to the anthropological originals. In addition, whereas arguably in classical anthropology the ethnographical ideal was to produce an account of the Nuer or the Kula using methods which were as unobtrusive to the practices described as possible, in modern management use of these ideas (or their derivatives) there is a tendency to move quite quickly from description to prescription, and even consultancy interventions.

The structure echoes that of Chapter 4. I will look at two broad areas of academic work that have borrowed either the techniques or the concepts of anthropology, and examine their findings and implications. The first concerns the nature of managerial work. There is a body of work seeking fieldwork-based understanding of what managers do, why they do it, and how these findings relate to 'theories' of management. Broadly, it finds management to be less rational, more social, and more fragmented as a set of activities than formal theories predict. It raises questions about the extent to which managers are agents or victims. The second concerns the idea of organizational culture. This generated a great deal of academic activity from the early 1980s with the onset of Japanese competition in the West, and quite quickly the idea of culture as some sort of manageable entity with performance consequences supplanted the more holistic anthropological idea of culture as process.

However, by now any anthropologist still hanging on might be a little queasy about my use of terms and about some sweeping generalizations about anthropology as a discipline, so I turn first to describing what has been borrowed and why.

Madness in the Method

There is some highly abstract theory in anthropology, notably that associated with structuralism—in particular the work of Levi-Strauss—and indeed there are structuralists working in the management field (who will not detain us here), but the main impact of anthropology on management has concerned method. A core method of anthropology is ethnography, about which there is much argument; so much so that Bate (1997: 1150) notes with distress in reviewing the literature that there are many more people writing about organizational ethnography than actually doing it.

There are at least two reasons for this. First, it is extremely labour intensive, involving participation and observation of organizational practices over a period of time with meticulous note taking, listening, and questioning; there is bound to be a virility test about how much of this you need (I was up the Amazon longer than you . . .). Second, the account is not immediately verifiable or intersubjectively testable; if I give you my data and show you my regression equation you can replicate it, but in anthropology it is much more difficult; so knowing *how* I got the data becomes important. Here is a recent definition of ethnography in the management field:

> A style of social science writing which draws upon the writer's close observation of and involvement with people in a particular social setting and relates the words spoken and the practices observed or experienced to the overall cultural framework within which they occurred.
>
> (Watson, 2011: 205–6)

So in this definition, ethnography refers both to the practice itself and its output.[2] I would add a third and very practical reason for the absence of masses of management ethnographies—that it is difficult to get access to do it; the very findings of management ethnography, specifically that a manager's life is often hectic, hinder this type of work.

The root notion of empirical anthropology is that thought and behaviour can only be understood in context, and that one needs to see that context from the point of view of the participant; hence the term 'participant observation' and the role of the researcher as 'professional stranger' (Hammersley,

---

[2] This is part of an interesting debate on method; see also Van Maanen, 2011.

1990). These roles were played by the anthropologists involved in the Hawthorne studies, who came armed with the core ideas of the informal system and informal organization. Informal relationships became key objects of interest for industrial sociologists in the 1950s studying manager–worker relationships (e.g. Gouldner, 1954; Roy, 1952) and in 1959 Dalton wrote a highly influential study on 'Men Who Manage', focusing entirely on managers in four factories, looking at interpersonal relationships and conflicts, and using participant observation. Its influence stemmed from the convincing and rich picture it gave of how managers see their world.

More modern business ethnographies have focused on groups such as the LA police force, British HR managers, laboratory scientists, and financial traders (Van Maanen, 1988; Watson, 1994; Latour and Woolgar, 1979; Zaloom, 2006). They have also focused on issues such as sabotage and storytelling (Linstead, 1985; Boje, 1995). It is reasonable to say that, from a purist perspective, none of these would avoid the lip curl of a traditional anthropologist. Even a broadly sympathetic observer refers to 'jet-plane ethnography' (a euphemism for flying visits), and 'a safe and closely chaperoned form of anthropological tourism' (Bate, 1997: 1150). Now, the academic value of a study does not depend on the difficulty of doing it, and if I have done an ethnography of catwalk models (sadly, I have not) this should not be worth less than one on serial killers (?), but it does indicate that the approach of business anthropology is generally thinner, both in duration and the array of methods, than would have been typical of Evans-Pritchard. Generally, the studies of managers we will look at use observation, documentary analysis, and questioning over an extended period of time. They maintain a focus on the root notion of anthropology mentioned in the previous paragraph.

After this preamble, I turn to the evidence, but a few more remarks may be of value. First, academics who use the methods and approach described in the last chapter and theme and those who do this sort of qualitative work do not converse easily; I will return to this point in the conclusion. Second, one of the reasons they do not do so is that the output of this kind of work tends to be rich description, not theory. And the sources of 'rich description' may be not only academic research but also journalism, literature, and film-making.[3] Some of the researchers in this qualitative vein do not regard what they do as social science at all. However, qualitative work tends to be extremely important for those who are studying *in order to become managers* since, as guidance to practice, it may have much to say. And as the prevalence of the

---

[3] Compare for example, Zaloom's book on traders with Michael Lewis's earlier *Liar's Poker*, which is regarded as journalism, or Henry Mintzberg's *Managing* (2009) with Stud's Terkel's (1974) *Working*, after which it is named.

(qualitative) case study method in management education indicates, understanding practice is important.

Just Managing

The classic formulations of what managers do emphasize rationality and hierarchy. Fayol (1916) identified five elements of management: planning, organizing, commanding, coordinating, and controlling. Similar ideas emerged in Barnard's (1938) study of executives and, much later, in Drucker's (1974) ideas about dimensions of managerial work. Now in all cases there may be a substantial experiential basis for these ideas—in that all three were practising managers or acute observers—but they do not rest on research on what managers do. They appear, as Hales (1999: 339) notes, more like answers to the question: what are the functions of management? Fayol's elements have four characteristics. First, autonomy: the manager is seen to be an independent actor, or designer, not a constrained member of a group or network. Second, rationality: the assumption is the pursuit of ends (unspecified) by rational choice. Third, power: that is the ability to coordinate and control. Fourth, universality: these are the key roles in any organization and context is not important. This is management as science or profession. The science analogy relates to the application of previously codified knowledge to a problem. The professional analogy relates to the autonomy of the practitioner to adapt that knowledge to the problem at hand.

Those who sought to analyse what managers actually did were interested in seeing management as a set of practices, to classify them, and to analyse variance (Mintzberg, 2009: 10–11). One of the best summaries of their findings is that:

> Much managerial work involves dealing with problems that are quite interdependent with other parts of the organisation, are specific to this firm, market and industry and not readily reduced to a general, standard syndrome.
>
> (Whitley, 1995: 92)

If this is true, then as Hales (1999: 337) notes, one tends to focus on specifics of the case-study organizations and on variance of management practice between them. If the specifics can only be described, and the variance cannot be explained, then the limitations of a broadly anthropological approach become clear; it was never developed to explain why the Nuer differ from the Azande, so it is unlikely to help in a discussion about effective and ineffective managerial behaviour (indeed these are hardly anthropological categories). The accumulation of academic studies of idiosyncratic managerial practice began to look unattractive, just as the study of market anomalies in

Categories	Roles
Interpersonal	
	Figurehead
	Leader
	Liaison
Informational	
	Monitor
	Disseminator
	Spokesperson
Decisional	
	Entrepreneur
	Disturbance handler
	Resource allocator

Figure C9.1. Mintzberg's managerial activities.

behavioural finance does today, and for the same reason; where could additional studies lead, if theory is not generated?

Enter Henry Mintzberg, whose anthropological credentials are hardly
impeccable, but whose contribution to this debate is central. Primarily by
close observation of a very small sample (five) of executives, he examined
what managers did (Mintzberg, 1973, 1975). Heroically, from this sample, he
sought to generalize about managerial activity. As we have seen from
Chapter 5, he does classifications; this time ten roles under three headings,
as shown in Figure C9.1.

In addition, he found managers work at unrelenting pace; that their actions
are brief, various, and discontinuous; that they have action bias and do not get
involved in much reflection; that they favour oral (he says verbal) communication and meetings over information systems; and that they use judgement
and intuition (1975). His recapitulation forty years on, with a larger (twenty-
nine) sample, finds that despite the arrival of email, the Internet, and huge
advances in information processing capabilities, there need be no fundamental revision of these findings (Mintzberg, 2009).

One could examine these in detail, but much here is self-evidently not
Fayol. First, the social has much more emphasis. The Fayol command and
control model gives way to a more interactive and reactive model. The idea of
autonomy is subsumed in an idea of a social actor involved in interaction and
negotiation, as much with peers as with subordinates in a hierarchy. Second,
rationality gives way to accommodation and coping. Third, power is not so
much exercised as created at some cost. The fourth Fayol idea of standardization is preserved. Mintzberg thought these were generalizable categories and

> **Processes (What)**
>
> Acting as a figurehead; monitoring and disseminating information; networking in a web of contacts; negotiating with subordinates, peers, and superiors; planning and scheduling work; allocating resources; directing and monitoring others; human resource management tasks such as recruitment, training, and appraisal; problem solving; innovating process and product; technical work relating to the manager's functional specialism.
>
> **Areas (Where)**
>
> Daily management of people; of processes and work flow; and of information. Non-managerial activities related to function.
>
> **Characteristics (How)**
>
> Short, fragmented activities; ad hoc reaction to events or requests; collaborative not individual activity; face-to-face verbal interaction; tension, pressure and conflict; competing demands; choice and negotiation over the nature of the job.

Figure C9.2. The what, where, and how of management.
(*Source*: Hales, 1999: 338)

other authors, notably Stewart (1982) in the UK and Europe and Kotter (1982) in the USA, come up with similar categories from similar research.

In an excellent review of this field, Hales (1999: 338) makes the distinction between generic managerial processes, substantive areas in which they are used, and characteristic features of their use; approximately, what, where, and how. His list is paraphrased in Figure C9.2.

Although there is overlap between these categories, the list is useful in several respects. It nicely summarizes the commonalities of managerial work, while indicating how observed variance can be generated. To use an analogy, we can know what ingredients are in a restaurant kitchen but still see variance in what comes onto the plate and, in this recipe analogy, we can get variations in quality of output. The sources of variation may be hierarchical (managers at different levels do different mixes) or organizational (organizations have different work patterns). It may seem strange to have non-managerial activities on the list of processes, but there is a substantial literature on managerial careers that indicates a tension between technical specialism (being an engineer, accountant, market analyst, etc.) and managing people and resources (e.g. Hill, 1992); management activity must be balanced against other things, involving opportunity costs.

At the most general level, the list indicates the problematic social relations that underpin the simplified notions of hierarchy and agency. Two tensions emerge from this literature that are probably central to an understanding of management:

243

1. Rationality vs. Coping. In Hales's (1999: 342) entertaining terminology the manager is both the child of the organization learning to cope with its complexity and an actor of considerable expertise trying to make the organization her playground.

2. Agent vs. Victim. In Drucker's (1974) terms, managers exercise responsibility but are themselves subject to powerful pressures operating within hierarchies which are not only coordinating mechanisms but political and social systems, full of transaction costs.

The first item renders problematic simple notions of agency the second simple notions of hierarchy.

Much of the work on managers discussed so far concerns itself with behaviours, but there is another large stream of management work which borrows a concern from anthropology with the management of myth, symbols, and ceremony. A key proponent of this essentially cognitive view of organizations is Weick, who has argued pithily that 'Managerial work can be viewed as managing myths, images, symbols and labels' and that 'an organization can be viewed as a body of jargon available for attachment to experience' (Weick, 1979: 42). In this approach, managers manipulate symbols and language to 'construct' the organization—in the darker versions (e.g. Reed, 1990) simply in order to retain control of those others—workers, creating value. Management is thus seen as the management of meaning and the appropriate object of analysis is managerial discourse and the use of rhetoric as justification for actions, rather than the actions themselves (Gowler and Legge, 1983). Asserting and maintaining legitimacy are seen to be at the core of managerial behaviour. Stories, told by managers or about them, and the manipulation of their content, become important levers for personal advancement (Mangham, 1986; Gabriel, 2000).

I shall deal at greater length with this type of work when I shift the unit of analysis from the individual manager to the organization in the discussion of culture below, but it is worth noting that this view of management relegates rationality to a minor role and, although few measures of managerial effectiveness or performance appear in this literature, it tends to question the contribution of management to organizational performance.

In summary, then, there is a body of work on management going back at least as far as the 1950s which seeks to apply versions of an anthropological method to understand what managers do. It has unearthed a complex management reality which differs both from the *a priori* generalizations of management 'theorists' and from the simplified conception of hierarchy favoured by economists. Managers are agents and victims, planners and reactors, embedded in enabling and constraining sets of social relationships. The literature tends to emphasize the complexity of management and the range of non-technical skills managers need. This is perhaps why, as we shall see below, some of this work has affected the practice of management consultancy.

In his appraisal of this field, Linstead (1997: 95–6) argues that social anthropology has had a significant impact on the study of management, but that in the process many anthropological concepts and methods have been 'misapplied' or 'trivialized'. This may be a purist view, but the original ideas have certainly been changed; I shall have a similar story to tell in the analysis of organizational culture.

Sophistry and Illusion

> Whenever I hear the word "culture", I release the safety catch on my pistol.

This quote is often attributed (inaccurately) to Goering, but the frustration it embeds might not have been entirely inappropriate in the early 1980s following publication of a book called *In Search of Excellence*. The book was the work of two consultants who worked with McKinsey. Peters and Waterman (1982) presented a one-best-way argument that organizations with a certain type of culture which generated a specific set of practices were 'excellent' and thus successful. The USA was reeling under the impact of Japanese competition; an argument had emerged that the Japanese economy had an inbuilt competitive (cultural) advantage rooted in the way they did business. This was deeply disempowering to US businesses. So the Peters and Waterman idea that the unit of analysis ought to be the firm, and that the firm could manage its organizational culture just like it might manage a product launch, was deeply empowering; excellence was internationally available.

So, one could not be in the set of firms that had no culture or one that was not 'excellent'. The die was cast. Although the authors changed their minds on what culture was, and how important it was, and although many of the cited 'excellent' firms ceased to be so in any publicly visible way, the culture concern became central to the study of management, and remains so still. At the time of writing, press coverage bemoans the safety 'culture' of BP and the risk 'culture' of banks; so it is also part of the discourse that 'culture' can have both positive and negative consequences (Willman and Fenton O'Creevy, 2013).

However, another strand of work emerging at the same time, with approximately the same stimulus, took a different unit of analysis; instead of the firm, national cultural differences were examined (Ouchi, 1981; Hofstede, 1980). Ouchi focused primarily on Japan, Hofstede looked in particular at Europe, and both generated a set of followers. The assertion was that different countries have different cultures; in particular, they do business differently.

Now these two literatures—on corporate and national culture—have similarities and differences. The similarities are that they drive first towards metrics, specifically looking for quantifiable dimensions of culture and, second, towards classification on those dimensions. The prime difference is that many corporate culture writers see culture as a malleable managerial tool; corporate cultures can be analysed and changed. For the national culture writers, who dominate in sub-fields such as international business and cross-cultural management, the key conclusion is about adaptation, by the firm or the individual, to national differences which are regarded as powerful and (relatively) stable.

In the remainder of this chapter, we will look at examples of cultural 'tools' for the analysis of both corporate and national culture. However, first we look at academic antecedents and consequences of the importation of culture as a concept and a set of practices to the study of management. The concept of culture is almost an intellectual case study of what can happen to an innocent social scientific concept that falls into the hands of management academics determined to bring it to market. By the time we look at our two examples—those of Goffee and Jones, and Hofstede—we will have travelled a long way from any concept of culture familiar to the anthropologist, and we need to trace the path. Two key changes need to be borne in mind.

1. Whereas for the anthropologist, culture is a broad and embracing notion, pervasive to the tribe or group in question, for the management academic it is an aspect or characteristic of the object of study. Put more bluntly, for the anthropologist a group *is* a culture but for the management academic a group *has* a culture (Smircich, 1983). The latter perspective is essential for those who wish to analyse the relationship between culture and some dependent variable such as performance. Anthropologists would not tend to do this. Management academics seldom do anything else; to be useful, culture must be analytically separable from other organizational properties. A subsidiary point is that if one is concerned with the performance relationship, one might be tempted to say one culture is 'better' than another if it is associated with higher performance. This is almost the opposite of what anthropology is about, which is to understand societies from the point of view of their members.

2. Methods differ fundamentally. If one wants to pursue the anthropological original, then typically one uses ethnography. If one wishes to compare organizations and societies, one develops standardized measures and dimensions of culture which are independent of the cultures of any one society. This is a minefield we will re-enter below, but for the moment the

trade-off we need to think about is rigour versus practicality. A rigorous idea of culture embraces behaviours, myths, symbols, and meanings. A practical one uses questionnaires that focus on values and behaviours.

Culture Clash

The concept is central to anthropology and therefore, almost by definition, contested (Geertz, 1973; Borowski, 1994), so in the interest of economy let us begin with the definitions of culture offered by those organizational theorists who have tried to adhere to the true faith in importing the concept. Two definitions stress what culture *does*.

> ...the importance for people of symbolism—of rituals, myths, stories and legends—and about the interpretation of events, ideas and experiences that are influenced and shaped by the groups within which they live.
>
> (Frost et al., 1985: 17)

> ...the shared rules governing cognitive and affective aspects of membership in an organisation and the means by which they are shaped and expressed.
>
> (Kunda, 1992: 8)

It is cognitive (inside peoples' heads), social (experienced as an external constraint), and historical (tradition is often a source of legitimacy). In this richer notion, culture is not a variable or sub-system but a 'root metaphor' and a 'manifestation of human consciousness', and the research agenda is to study the intersubjective experience of organizational members (Smircich, 1983: 348). But if culture is not reduced to a variable in this approach, *rationality* certainly is. In fact, several works use the word in the plural (which I cannot bring myself to do). Economic or structural variables are seen as manifestations of culture, not dependent variables, as are accounting variables such as cost, revenue, and margin. For example, organizational size, which is a potent explanatory variable in almost all quantitative work on firms, may be seen as cultural preference (Starbuck, 1993). Strategic decision-making may similarly be seen as a cultural manifestation; both Schein (1985) and Pettigrew (1985) have examined the assumptions and processes of strategic decision-making as cultural phenomena.

The objective of work in this tradition is not to develop hypotheses, but to generate a richer understanding of how organizations, and specifically organizations as cultures, work. Alvesson, (2002: 29–39) has rather heroically attempted a summary, using the notion of eight 'metaphors' of what work on culture—including some of which the purists would disapprove—has discovered.

- *Culture as exchange regulator.* Culture is seen as a set of rules or conventions for handling complex intra-organizational transactions. Typically this embeds notions of fairness, integrity, and community to spell out what should and should not happen. This is entirely consistent with a transaction costs perspective. Culture replaces monitoring by socializing employees into the avoidance of opportunism and helps reduce transaction costs. This notion is most similar to the limited treatment of the idea of culture in organizational economics (Kreps, 1990).

- *Culture as the organization's compass.* This view emphasizes the role of culture as a set of values that guide the organization's ultimate goals and the strategies and processes designed to attain them. Empirically, mission statements and ethical policies provide guidance to this aspect of culture. It is close to the marketing conception of organizational 'brand'.

- *Culture as glue.* This view emphasizes the role of culture as a promoter of social cohesion, helping avoid fragmentation and conflict. Culture here is seen primarily as a set of social norms and values which may emerge spontaneously through interaction or, more sinister, the conscious articulation of such norms by senior managers intent on control.

- *Culture as sacred cow.* This conception emphasizes value commitments that control strategies. Organizations are seen as having an identity which dictates the adoption or rejection of specific strategies and the subordination of rationality to emotional attachment. Strategies then become subordinate to the maintenance of corporate identity, even where there may be economically more beneficial options. Here are two examples. When Apple was a computer company it refused to license its operating system (the 'crown jewels') to other manufacturers. Microsoft gave Windows, its operating system, away and thus became the industry standard. Oxford University maintains an expensive tutorial system, in which very small class sizes (2–4) are maintained, at vast cost, in deference to its commitment to a particular style of education. Harvard does not.

- *Culture as affect regulator.* Organizations control and discipline the display of emotions in order to sustain some valued organizational practice or achieve a business objective. (See Box C9.1 for an example.)

- *Culture as disorder.* Given the evidence of cultural differences *within* organizations, and the ensuing conflict, one needs a metaphor which is in some ways the opposite of culture as exchange regulation to characterize such circumstances (Jelinek et al., 1983). These circumstances include (but are not restricted to) companies which are the result of merger or acquisition, and research exists to show this conflict and tension is a feature both of cross-border merger activity and intra-country mergers

---

Box C9.1 THE SMILE FACTORY

Van Maanen conducted a 'realist ethnography' of Disneyland; he had worked there (and been fired) and he spent a lot of time with employees ('cast members'). In his account, the product of the 'Park' is emotion—laughter and wellbeing—and it is consumed both by customers ('guests') and cast members. Disneyland is a 'smile factory' in a 'feeling business' run according to a tightly defined set of rules about appearance (in 'costumes' not 'uniforms') and behaviour when 'on-stage'. Corporate culture is explicitly to maintain order. It is defined as:

1. The philosophy underlying all business decisions.
2. The commitment of management to that philosophy.
3. The actions taken by individual cast members that reinforce the image.

Cast members tightly manage their emotions in the required way so that the right sentiments can be delivered as commodities for guests. The culture is backed up by close surveillance and tight discipline by 'security hosts'.

(Van Maanen, 1990)

(Olie, 1994; Empson, 2001); that is, it is relevant to studies of both corporate and national culture. Figure C9.3 depicts part of a lexicon I developed in facilitating a merger between a UK and a German law firm. Language differences were generating difficult outcomes, but the language issues had less to do with the spoken mother tongue and more to do with how the common language—English—was used to reflect different cultural assumptions.

- *Culture as blinders* and *Culture as world closure*. I have merged Alvesson's last two metaphors, since they seem close to the same idea that culture acts as a lens making current practice seem like the natural order of things, rather than the outcome of contingencies, and thus blinding organizational members to the possibility of alternate states of things. It is central to the anthropological venture that culture is a concept that enables the reader to understand what might seem to be bizarre tribal practices as part of a consistent world view. Conformism and the inability to question may be features of modern organizations also. To take two examples, in both oil and tobacco companies, the notion that the core product and central purpose of both industries generated harmful outcomes in the form of climate change and cancer respectively was harder for members to address than outsiders. An interesting corollary of this aspect of culture is that companies affected often have to be pressured into changes by external bodies, and debate on the organization's core identity is conducted by non-members.

It is well known that the British do not always say what they really mean. So, with the growing international nature of business, the definitions below may help people from other nations understand their British counterparts better.

What They Say	What They Mean
◆ I hear what you say	◆ I disagree and do not wish to discuss it any further
◆ With the greatest respect	◆ I think you are a fool
◆ Not bad	◆ Good or very good
◆ Quite good	◆ A bit disappointing
◆ Perhaps you would like to think about .../ it would be nice if...	◆ This is an order. Do it or be prepared to justify yourself
◆ Oh, by the way/ Incidentally	◆ This is the primary purpose of our discussion
◆ Very interesting	◆ I don't agree/ I don't believe you
◆ Could we consider the options	◆ I don't like your idea
◆ I'll bear it in mind	◆ I will do nothing about it
◆ Perhaps you could give that some more thought	◆ It is a bad idea. Don't do it
◆ I'm sure it is my fault	◆ It is your fault
◆ That is an original point of view/ brave option to consider	◆ You must be crazy
◆ You must come for dinner sometime	◆ Not an invitation, just being polite; it will not happen
◆ Not entirely helpful	◆ Completely useless
◆ Not unreasonable	◆ Absolutely right

Figure C9.3. What the British really mean.

The vast literature on culture contains other such attempts at classification, but Alvesson's approach is sufficient to illustrate both why some academics feel organizational cultures are sufficiently intrinsically interesting to be studied for their own sake, without any notion of identifying a management tool, and why others are concerned to systematize understanding of cultures into metrics which are the basis for generalization. As noted, such metrics exist, and we look at one for the analysis of corporate culture which, though highly simplified, has clear anthropological roots; and one for national culture, which is one of the most widely cited in social science.

Culture Club

Goffee and Jones (1998) is a very good example of a practitioner-focused diagnostic for understanding corporate culture. The basic model is a 2 x 2, as depicted in Figure C9.4. Two axes, 'sociability' and 'solidarity', characterize the 2 x 2. But in each quadrant there are positive and negative aspects. Sociability refers essentially to dimensions of collaboration and community: how well do we get on? Solidarity refers to focus on performance and

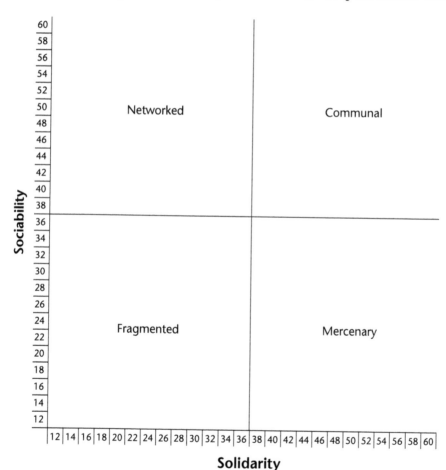

Figure C9.4. The Goffee and Jones framework.

objectives: how well do we work? When we plot them, we get the four 'cultures' in Figure C9.4, each with positive and negative attributes.

Networked cultures put community above results and are extremely difficult to change. Fragmented cultures are poorly coordinated work benches or platforms for individuals to perform. Mercenary cultures are focused, performance-driven tournaments. And communal cultures are intense, arrogant, and self-confident. The iconic examples are respectively a government department, an advertising agency, an investment bank, and a large oil company.

The framework is evaluative in one dimension but not in all. The dominant idea for the quadrants is one of 'fit' between the culture and the environment in which the firm operates (very broadly conceived to embrace both history and industry). *Within* quadrants, the interest is in the balance between positive and negative aspects of the culture; so one can have good and bad network cultures, for example. Cultural change may have one of two features. It may be improvement of the existing culture (within quadrant) or switching culture (movement between quadrants) if there is a misfit between culture and environment. The framework is effective at explaining differences in practices. For example, network cultures will be effective at matrix management (because they search for compromise and consensus) but bad at performance management (because they value relationships and community). Fragmented cultures will be good at permitting individual creativity (because they value autonomy), but less good at sharing knowledge (because they also promote self-interest). Mercenary cultures will be very good at setting and hitting targets (because they set clear rewards for success and penalty for failure) but bad at devising long-term strategies (also because they set clear metrics and do not tolerate ambiguity). Communal cultures will by contrast be good at pursuing long-term strategy (because they have substantial self-belief) but (for the same reason) may not analyse competitors very well.

This is quite a simple approach and its intellectual antecedents are clear. The solidarity/sociability contrast echoes the distinction between task and maintenance behaviours in problem-solving groups which goes back at least as far as Bales (1958). But there are also clear affinities with the main attempt within anthropology itself to move beyond the accumulation of descriptions of cultures onto a typology of cultures using the grid–group approach to cultural theory developed by Mary Douglas and others (Douglas, 1978; Gross and Rayner, 1985). The dimensions of grid and group are different, but the idea of a cultural typology is not.[4] Cultural theory so devised is currently widely used in anthropology, notably to analyse approaches to risk (Adams, 1995). So

---

[4] The grid dimension refers to the presence or absence of externally imposed restrictions on choice. The group dimension is more similar to the sociability idea—it refers to the individualized or collective properties of the group.

the innovative aspect of the Goffee–Jones model is to synthesize ideas about group behaviour from social psychology with the idea of a cultural typology from anthropology to generate a tool with which managers can analyse organizational culture based on a simple metric derived from a questionnaire. Many scholars deplore both the reductionist and eclectic nature of such ventures, but it is almost an ideal type of the way in which management theory has developed.

Observations that different countries appear to do business differently are almost as old as travel literature itself, but in the modern era the first and most influential work on the *classification* of national cultures is that of Hofstede (1980, 1991), which similarly emerged in the 1980s though from work conducted in the 1970s. Hofstede classified national cultures on four bipolar dimensions. These are depicted in Figure C9.5. They related to beliefs about power and how it should be distributed, attitudes towards risk (uncertainty), the individual–collective dimension, and finally one termed 'masculinity-femininity', which actually has nothing to do with gender but concerns two different things: assertiveness and its absence, and a concern with material possessions. Hofstede devised his dimensions in a less politically correct age. As Figure C9.5 also shows, these dimensions can be related to specific organizational practices in areas such as hiring, the exercise of authority, control of HR policies, rewards, and performance evaluation. Incidentally, the approach, if correct, has strong implications for the multinational business; should it adapt to national culture, or develop a strong and centralized organizational culture as a counterweight?

The approach spawned imitators, notably Smith et al. (1990) with a three-factor model and Trompenaars (1993) with a seven-factor one. We will concentrate on Hofstede for two reasons; first, it is the most widely cited and criticized, second, those new to this field would be impressed more by the similarities between these classifications than the differences. I am concerned here with whether the classificatory approach is useful rather than the details of the classification.

1. Power distance
  - *Degree of tolerance for unequal outcomes in wealth, income, power*
  - *Denmark (egalitarian) vs. Panama (non-egalitarian)*
2. Uncertainty aversion
  - *Degree of comfort with ambiguity, uncertainty, lack of structure, risk*
  - *Portugal (uncertainty-averse) vs. Jamaica (uncertainty-seeking)*
3. Individualism
  - *Preference for self-reliance over paternalism, social support networks*
  - *New Zealand (individualist) vs. Ecuador (collectivist)*
4. Masculinity
  - *Goals, tasks, achievement, assertiveness vs. relationships, quality of life*
  - *Germany (task-oriented) vs. Norway (relationship-oriented)*

Figure C9.5. Hofstede's theory of cultural distance.
(Based on Hofstede, 1980)

Hofstede claims that he can 'uncover the secrets of entire national cultures' (1980b: 43), that there are highly significant differences in the work-related behaviours and attitudes of employees from different countries, and that the notion of national culture explains more of the variance in such attitudes than does hierarchical position, profession, age, or gender. Indeed, in later (1991) work, he claims to have identified national culture in its entirety, not just as it relates to work. In social scientific terms, this is asking for it, and he has duly received a range of criticisms of theory, method, and results.

The main ones are as follows.[5]

- *Criticisms of the definition of culture.* He defines culture in highly subjective and individualistic terms as 'software of the mind' (1991); given his data (see below) he could hardly do otherwise, but this is a long way from anthropology. Perhaps related, there is confusion as to whether the notion of national culture refers to a common component of all individuals or a statistical average concealing unobserved heterogeneity; the first is implausible and the second problematic (Schwartz, 1992). He also attributes absolute causality to this notion of culture, to the exclusion of other variables.

- *Criticisms of the idea of 'nation'.* By 'nation', Hofstede means 'country' or 'state'. So Belgium is Belgium, not a mix of Dutch and French, and Great Britain is a nation whereas England, Scotland, and Wales are not. Great Britain does not actually exist, but the United Kingdom does and is really quite young, much younger than the USA (Davies, 1999), so the question naturally arises as to where national culture comes from if it is anchored to recent political fixes. Empirically, it ignores very good anthropological work, for example, on how very *idiosyncratic* the English are (Fox, 2004).

- *Criticisms of the data.* There are essentially three. First, although the sample size is huge (117,000), it covers two surveys and a large number (66) of countries so that in some cases national culture is being defined on the basis of very small samples. Second, the survey was conducted exclusively within one company, IBM. Hofstede argues that this controls for the influence of different organizational cultures, but critics have argued naturally that findings can only be generalized to IBM. Third, the surveys used were not designed for this research project; they were employee attitude surveys mined for this purpose; there is no guarantee that they tapped *all* dimensions of any national culture, which compromises the resulting classification. It is perhaps worth reiterating

---

[5] There is almost an entire literature on Hofstede. This section relies primarily on the excellent article by McSweeney, 2002, which summarizes the most important points.

that individual survey responses tend to lead to a definition of culture as an individual attribute.

- *Criticisms of the argument.* Hofstede does not establish the existence and characteristics of national cultures prior to data analysis. Rather, he stratifies his sample by nation and pronounces that the resulting differences represent national culture. There are problems with this. First, any stratification of the sample would probably have generated variances, some of which might have been larger than the (moderate) inter-nation differences presented. Second, as McSweeney (2002: 100) elegantly puts it, it is hardly 'appropriate' for a study which says it has found national uniformity to assume it in advance.

These are trenchant criticisms, and one might question why Hofstede's work has been so widely cited, discussed, and used. The citation issue is perhaps easier; as a doctoral student I was once advised that I should produce the best article ever or the worst if I wished to be widely cited. The broader impact question remains. McSweeney himself suggests that parts of the management field may have standards about the acceptability of evidence which are too loose. This may be (or have been) true. But I think it is not the full story and offer the following observations.

- In both academic and practitioner circles in the 1980s, there was a keen awareness of different patterns of business conduct in different countries and a perceived need to go beyond the casual empiricism of observations of differences to a classification and, perhaps, a predictive model. Cross-border initiatives within the EU, investments in and competition from Asia, particularly Japan, and the opportunities in emerging markets put a high premium on understanding cultural difference. It was almost more important to know how another culture might differ from one's own than to know what it comprised as a whole.

- Parallel developments discussed above in corporate culture had both raised the salience of the concept and provided a potential performance-enhancing set of tools to manage it. No parallel existed in the national culture arena and a sense of corporate disempowerment in the face of national differences fed a need for understanding and control. One might not be able to change the English but in doing business with them it might help to know what they might do.

- First-mover advantages and Matthew effects abound in academic life, and this classification benefitted from both. Rejecting the *idea* that culture could be classified probably had more appeal to academics than practitioners, so one response to Hofstede's research was to use it as the baseline for future attempts.

Conclusion

The primary purpose of this chapter has been to introduce works on management and organizations which find their inspiration, in different ways, from social anthropology. I have looked at works that study different units of analysis; on the one hand, the work of individual managers and, on the other, the ideas of corporate and national culture. In the former case I have looked at the borrowing of the method of ethnography, and in the latter the concept of culture. In both cases we have seen how management scholars borrow, adapt, and integrate the intellectual property of another discipline. The characteristics of management as a discipline identified at the outset—opportunistic, eclectic, and derivative—are all in evidence here.

But the fourth characteristic, fragmentation, should also be clear. Those who analyse organizations from the perspectives and with the tools described in Chapter 8 and Theme 8 have almost nothing intellectually in common with the researchers described in this chapter. For the former, (hyper-) rationality is an assumption and optimization the objective. For the latter rationality is (at best) a variable, and understanding practice is the objective. The management student needs a tolerance of ambiguity that (perhaps) the student of economics or physics does not.

This chapter has also tried to introduce the next theme, which is the interaction of academic work and business practice. To choose just two, Mintzberg and Hofstede have had enormous currency in the ways in which practitioners see the world. I use the vague term 'currency' deliberately, since it is clear that, although their work may have had an impact on practice, practice has had a substantial impact in the reverse direction. I turn to a more systematic assessment of the relationship between theory and practice in the next theme.

Theme 9

Performativity—Does Life Imitate Art?

'In theory there is no difference between theory and practice. In practice there is.'
(Yogi Berra)

Introduction

The purpose of this theme is to examine the relationship between the academic study of management and its practice. It is less an audit of which parts of academic theory have changed practice and more an argument about how we might think about the relationship, with examples. We have seen that, in the early days of theorizing, practitioners such as Taylor wrote pieces about methods in action, which have entered the academic canon, and that human relations academics engaged closely with industrial practice and developed 'theory' from that. We have also seen how, in the growth of academic finance, ideas were essentially thrown from the tops of ivory towers that subsequently became embedded in financial market practice. Academic theories about the 'M form' organization post-dated its diffusion and, to some extent, rationalized it, influencing the business strategy discipline. One might surmise from these examples that there is variance in the relationship between theory and practice.

What are the sources of this variation? One way of thinking about this is to apply academic ideas to academia. In academic models of business innovation, there are 'technology-push' and 'demand-pull' models of innovation. The former argue that technological innovations occur which allow new products to be developed for which demand subsequently emerges. Television is a good example; there are no data showing mass demand in advance of development. The latter argues that innovations develop in response to market demand. Fuel-efficient cars are a good example. When oil prices went up massively in the 1970s, people shifted to the most efficient cars on the market and new technological developments allowed more fuel-efficient cars to emerge. The same thinking may apply to management theory. In some cases, an idea finds a use; in another, a perceived need for a use generates an idea. Incidentally, this encourages us to think about management ideas as a 'technology', an idea to which we will return.

So, if notions about supply and demand help, we might think about a market for academic ideas. There are incentives for business academics to supply solutions to perceived problems, and there are also incentives to identify problems that might require an academic solution. Similar incentives probably exist in any academic discipline that has a practitioner counterpart, notably medicine, law, and engineering. In all of these disciplines, there is a balance between what academics are prepared to put into the public domain and what they wish to copyright or charge for. An additional consideration is that, over roughly the period in which management theory has developed, the industry of management consultancy has also developed, which has a natural interest in proprietary information which can be translated into billable hours.

This provides context for what follows. In the next section, the intellectual background for the ugly word 'performativity' is presented as a way of thinking about the relationship between theory and practice; we look at the ways in which the idea has been used in economics. Subsequent sections look at the interaction between management theory and practice to promote the argument that the development and current state of management theory is embedded in management experience.

The World's a Stage

The term 'performativity' originates in philosophy; Austin (1970) noted that some words *do* things. If I say, 'I apologize', or 'I thee wed', I am not just saying it but doing it. More relevantly, if I say 'I buy' in a financial market, it is binding. His sets in Figure T9.1 are as follows, from MacKenzie (2006: 17) is a simple classification of how the idea can be applied to economics. MacKenzie is interested in whether economics affects the 'real world', and how. His sets are as follows.

- *Generic performativity* might be the use of the Shiller house price index by banks or realtors lending or trading in the US house market. It may also be regulators using a model of economic value added or return on capital to set energy prices.
- *Effective performativity* might be the design of an auction process by an academic economist, perhaps using game theory.

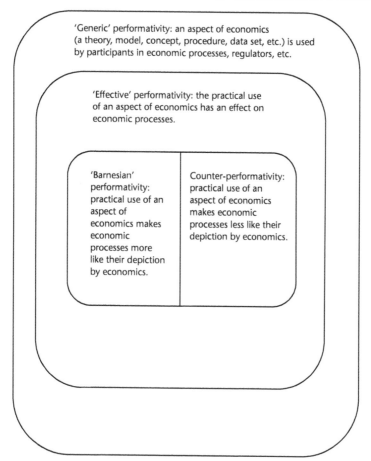

'Generic' performativity: an aspect of economics (a theory, model, concept, procedure, data set, etc.) is used by participants in economic processes, regulators, etc.

'Effective' performativity: the practical use of an aspect of economics has an effect on economic processes.

'Barnesian' performativity: practical use of an aspect of economics makes economic processes more like their depiction by economics.

Counter-performativity: practical use of an aspect of economics makes economic processes less like their depiction by economics.

Figure T9.1. The performativity of economics.
(*Source*: MacKenzie (2006; 17))

The two innermost sets are the strongest versions, and those that I am most interested in here.

- *'Barnesian' performativity*[1] refers to self-validating feedback loops in which, put bluntly, economics changes part of the world, so that life imitates art.
- *Counter-performativity* refers to the opposite, in which unintended consequences of a theory's use make the world less like economics.

MacKenzie's own work gives an example of the former. His study of the use of the Black–Scholes–Merton options pricing formula indicates its impact *both*

---

[1] The reference is to the sociologist who developed the idea.

on options trading practice *and* on the development of more sophisticated derivative instruments. There are some key points to the study.

1. Options trading pre-dated the development of the theory.
2. Initially, the theory did not describe empirical options prices.
3. Use of the theory in specific markets caused prices to move towards the theory's price predictions.
4. Developments of the theory became the standard means of options pricing.

With specific reference to financial markets, he argues that economic theory has affected financial markets in three ways: technical, linguistic, and legitimatory (2006: 250–2). To return to his specific example of Black–Scholes-Merton:

- *Technical*: the model is widely used and embedded in the software subsequently developed to fix options prices.
- *Linguistic*: the model generates the language used in trading. Options are often priced as 'implied volatilities', which is what you get when you run the Black–Scholes–Merton model backwards to determine the volatility of the underlying asset implied by the option price.
- *Legitimatory*: the model provided a rationale to differentiate options trading from (illegal) betting on price movements.

Unfortunately, he does not provide an equally documented example of 'counter-performativity'. I offer as a contender the use of agency theory to address the issue of executive pay. To cover similar territory to MacKenzie:

1. Problems with the separation of ownership and control pre-dated modern agency theory.
2. Initially, the theory did not describe the setting of executive pay.
3. Use of the theory in specific corporations generated the outcome—a mismatch of principals' interests with those of agents, and the massive rise in the costs of executive remuneration (which it was designed to control).
4. The theory became discredited as a standard for executive pay.

The impacts can be considered in the same categories, with opposite signs.

- *Technical*: formulaic links of executive pay with measures of corporate performance are avoided because they are seen as easily gamed.
- *Linguistic*: 'incentivization', 'stock options', and 'shareholder value', among others, became terms to avoid.
- *Legitimatory*: the model provided a rationale to intervene to prevent or control 'excessive' executive rewards.

To summarize in John Kay's words:

> The attempt to structure elaborate incentive schemes to align the interests of managers and shareholders did not eliminate fraud: it provoked it.
>
> (Kay, 2004: 347)

You may not agree with all of this, but this is what a counter-performative argument would need to contain. There are several other candidates, notably the application of free market ideas in post-communist Eastern Europe or the design of broadband spectrum auctions with adverse consequences (Milgrom, 2004). The proposition is the same, namely that one can see economic ideas implemented with negative or at least unforeseen consequences, a probability that arguably increases as economists come to see themselves as social engineers.

The co-existence of technical, linguistic, and legitimatory impact is the strongest case. If, for example, economics was simply a way of describing the world which accorded legitimacy to the describer, we might treat it as rhetoric, not social science. If appeal for legitimacy without common language were the main feature, we might find it weaker still. And opinions differ. Faulhaber and Baumol (1988) tried to assess the impact of major economic and business innovations in economics, with mixed results. They found four different sets of cases:

1. cases where economists had invented something then been involved in its implementation (portfolio theory and beta);
2. cases where economists had helped with implementation (discounted present value);
3. cases where economists provided the formula for an already understood problem (peak load pricing in electricity markets); and
4. cases where economists disseminated the ideas of others (they cite marginal analysis but as we saw in Chapter 6 one might add almost all of game theory).

The relationship between theory and practice proved to be highly variable.

However, operating at a very different level of analysis, Ferraro et al. (2005) argue that it is the core idea of 'self-interest' that economics has made respectable and indeed moved from assumption to a norm. Citing a range of non-economic evidence, they show that exposure to economic ideas generates respectability at two levels; we design institutions (not just firms) on assumptions about the self-interest of institutional members and we accept behaviours as social norms that articulate self-interest as a motive. Their third level is language. They borrow a rather older sociological idea from Wright Mills and argue that with norms come 'vocabularies of motive' with which we articulate our actions in terms of the 'norm' of self-interest (2005: 16). Their analysis thus is similar to that of MacKenzie.

The argument that a social science discipline like economics provides a toolkit to solve practical problems (or not) is one thing. The argument that the discipline's core assumptions mould social action (to exaggerate Ferraro et al. only slightly) is quite another. They remark:

> Contests among theories are typically presumed to be decided by which theories best **explain** the world, not which best **affect** the world and thereby become true as a result of their own influence.

(Ferraro et al., 2005: 10)

However, it is not clear quite what this means. In the following paragraph they refer to the Kuhnian notion of a paradigm in the philosophy of science—a view of the world sustained by consensus that survives until supplanted by a better view (Kuhn, 1970). Arguably all scientific theories are evaluated in terms of their effect, but the unique feature of the social sciences is that they may affect the object they describe. Genes don't give you feedback on the double helix idea. In the rejoinder to their paper, Bazerman notes that economics is both a descriptive and prescriptive field, so if the prescriptions were ignored it would be relatively unsuccessful (Bazerman, 2005: 26). And it is not unsuccessful; it is the most successful social science. We have already cited Shiller in Chapter 7 with a cheerfully megalomaniac view of finance as all goal-directed behaviour. It is a view shared by others. Lazear (2000), for example, exults economic imperialism with a cheerfully Victorian disregard for the views of the natives affected by its expansion; they may not like it but it will be good for them in the end. Economists have invaded not only the business field, but also the study of education, healthcare, and the family. Whatever your discipline, they are coming to a cinema near you.

Back to Business: Rendering Accounts

There are at least two reasons for arguing that the performativity of economics is relevant to understanding the performativity of management theory. The first is that management theory also has descriptive and prescriptive components. There are management theorists who absolutely do not wish to influence practice, but by and large I have protected you from them so far. The second is, as implied, the importance of economics as a component of management theory. A recent report for the AACSB—a business school pressure group—listed the following as 'advances in basic research that have had a substantial impact on practice' (AACSB, 2008: 18): portfolio selection, the irrelevance of capital structure, the CAPM, the efficient markets hypothesis, options pricing, and agency theory. They list few others unconnected with these advances in financial economics. In organizational behaviour, they cite Hofstede's work on culture and Vroom's on motivation. Earlier than 2008, the list may have been different, with representation from other sub-disciplines; in 2013, a similar exercise would probably yield more finance.

Arguably, the different sub-disciplines of management bear different relationships to practice and the idea of 'performativity' is also variable. Using Faulhaber and Baumol's simple classification, one could argue that the dominant approach in academic finance is set 1; where academic invention prompted adoption. Strategy was borne out of Chandler's work on the M form, which arguably falls into set 3, but much academic strategy has disseminated ideas from management consultants (notably McKinsey's and BCG (the Boston Consulting Group)) and may fall into set 4. So there is probably variance within sub-disciplines in this respect, and a general classification does not seem really helpful. In order better to understand the interaction between theory and practice that is central to performativity, we turn to the area of management which, as the oldest documented, has the longest history of interaction: academic accounting.

We have seen already that the practice of accounting predates the firm, going back at least as far as Renaissance Italy. We have also touched on the 'Sombart' arguments about the relationship between the rise of capitalism and the development of double entry bookkeeping, and the dispute about causality. Accounting generally and double entry bookkeeping in particular have 'academic' origins in the church and universities (Hoskin and Macve, 1994; Thompson, 1994). We can thus, over an extended time period unavailable in the study of finance, look at the interaction of theory and practice. In the terms we have used above, accounting is a calculative technology, with its own language and terminology, that creates legitimacy internal to the firm by making the firm externally accountable by practices such as audit (Miller, 1994; Power, 2003). It is performative in that it transforms physical activities and flows within the organization into financial numbers. As Miller puts it:

> To reconfigure an organisation into profit centres, costs centres, investment centres, strategic business units . . . is to change lines of responsibility and the possibilities of action.
>
> It is a singular capacity of accounting to change the world.
>
> (Miller, 1994: 2)

Although accounting is influenced by social and institutional factors, its domain is the organization. Accounting is to the hierarchy what economics is to the market—a set of rules governing transactions and financial flows (Hopwood, 1992). The relationship between accounting practices within the firm and the market transactions in which the firm engages are not straightforward. For example, transfer prices within the firm may be different from a similar pattern of market transactions, and to declare the book value of a firm's assets is very different from declaring the market value. One main difference between the rules of the market and the rules of the hierarchy is that the latter are clearly the subject of constrained choice. Organizations differ not only in the ways in which they allocate costs but also how they define them. There are also different ways of valuing assets, with different consequences for the organization. We look at each in turn.

One of the most widely cited cases in the history of cost accounting is that of Josiah Wedgwood, the eighteenth-century English potter (McKendrick, 1970; Hopwood, 1992). The survival of correspondence and records has enabled academic accountants to reconstruct the extent of his endeavours to explore the costs of production; costing had to be constructed, rather than revealed. He was facing a depression and wanted to drop his prices, but not to below cost; but what was product cost? He explored labour, materials, and sales costs by product, allowed for depreciation and interest charges, and found glaring disparities between his management accounts and financial accounts (Edwards, 1989). Part of the reason was that he had some employees who were defrauding him, but once this was resolved he found himself in possession of a calculative tool to reform the entire production process; in 'creating' costs, he changed not only prices but the production process and the rewards of employees (Hopwood, 1992: 134).

The more general development of cost accounting in the UK was again prompted by a crisis, that of World War I. During the war, government became a major customer of the UK private sector and a regulator, concerned to maximize the productive capacity of the economy for the war effort and to control the prices of scarce goods (Loft, 1988, 1994). Insistence on rigorous cost accounting became a feature of government dealings with manufacturers; it offered control without ownership (which would have meant nationalization) and thus:

> ...helped sustain the uneasy compromise between the principles of the free market and total government control... the attempted alignment was between the practices of individual manufacturers and the overall objectives of controlling war production.
>
> (Loft, 1994: 132)

Moreover, there was a ratchet effect. The concomitant rise in the status of cost accountants was the basis for the growth of the profession of accounting (Loft, 1994) and, in the eyes of some, an unhealthy focus by UK managers on accounts rather than production (Armstrong, 1987).

The final development in costing I examine here is the emergence of standard costing. Miller and others have looked at the growth of standard costing, its link to scientific management and their allied growth in the post-World

War I period (Miller and O'Leary, 1987; Miller and Napier, 1993; Miller, 1994). Standard costing allowed cost accountants to look to the future as well as the past; for example, the cost of labour input for a future product could be calculated from standard times and the price of labour. Individual perform-ance variances could be isolated, and the actions of individuals given financial visibility. 'Efficiency' could be achieved within firms by reducing the oper-ation of individuals, processes, or machines to a standard cost.

These costing examples have a number of significant features. First, there is an interaction between theory and practice; events change accounting practices and accounting practices change events. Second, there are several significant actors; owners like Wedgwood, consultants like Taylor, and governments. Third, developments in one area prompt changes to other areas of the organ-ization, which themselves develop theories; Wedgwood, for example, is seen as a precursor to developments in labour discipline, sales, and marketing, all changes consequent on his cost analysis.

Our (single) example of asset valuation methods illustrates, in particular, the influence of one academic discipline on another; in this case financial economics on accounting, leading to institutional transformation. Tradition-ally, many firms stated the historical value of their assets in financial state-ments; that is an asset would be recorded at the price paid (subject to depreciation or evaluation policies). But this leads to a number of problems. One is that two firms could buy identical assets at different prices, so there could be different balance sheets covering identical assets (or vice versa). A second is that historical values tend to understate current ones, so that any measures of returns are biased in favour of overestimating returns. This in turn encourages many of the managerial agency problems of such concern to finance theorists like Jensen. For example, securitizing (historically) under-valued assets is a way managers can show profit by a financial manoeuvre; this is called 'gains trading' and was an element in the financial crash of 2008 (Laux and Leuz, 2009). It is from finance that an alternate measure of valu-ation has emerged.

This measure, generically termed 'fair value accounting' uses market valu-ations and it is borrowed from practice on futures exchanges. In such exchanges, traders deposit a 'margin' (i.e. cash) with the exchange at the start of trading to cover the exchange against loss. If the trader makes money during the day, she picks up the excess over margin at close; if she makes a loss, she has to top up the margin (a margin call) (MacKenzie, 2006; Duhon, 2012). For this to work, the value of the trader's account has to be 'marked-to-market' at close of trading. This has become an accounting prac-tice since the 1980s, replacing historical, stable costing with more volatile market valuation of a firm's assets. The theoretical underpinnings of this are the efficient markets hypothesis (market prices contain all information) and agency theory (market prices give the principal a measure of firm performance and thus both monitor the agent and show opportunity costs of hiring the agent). Market valuations are underpinned by 'Fair value' regulations (e.g. US GAAP FAS 157) for circumstances where no market valuation is possible, and the possibilities for fraud in this case are substantial, as in the Enron case in Theme 8. In the Enron case, as we saw, the asset valuation involved 'marking-to-model'—that is assessing the value in terms of the firm's own models of future revenues.

A daily trading regulation thus became a widespread accounting practice when academic theories became embedded in an accounting standard. The implications are considerable. Historically, accountants trained in double entry bookkeeping distinguished between *assets* on one side of the balance sheet—meaning the things in which money was invested—and, on the other side of the balance sheet, the invested money itself—that is *shareholders' equity* and other *liabilities*. The valuation methods for the two might differ. However, financial economists tend to identify both as capital to be evaluated in terms of discounted future cash flows. Looking at both sides of the balance sheet in these terms can be transformative (Chiapello, 2008).

Here is an example of what can happen. Figure T9.2 shows the surplus/deficit of UK defined benefit pension funds. A defined benefit pension fund

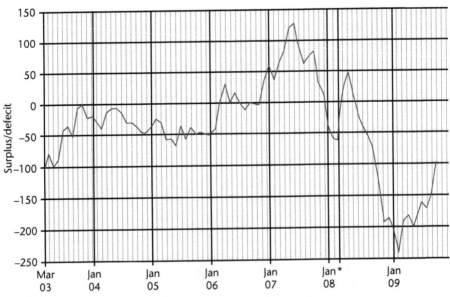

*Figures from 31 March 08 are based on new actuarial assumptions

Figure T9.2. Surplus/deficit of the UK's private sector final salary pension.
(*Source*: Pension Protection Fund)

266

invests the contributions of employers and employees covered by the fund in assets which are thus to cover the liabilities. The liabilities are to pay a proportion of salary for life to those employees covered; the prime uncertainties are about inflation of the benefit payments and longevity of the beneficiaries. The risk-averse investment strategy would be to invest everything in index-linked government bonds, but since salaries have tended to rise faster than inflation, it can be problematic. At the start of the period covered by the Figure, these funds invested over 60% of assets in equities, in order to get better returns; by the end this had halved. Extreme volatility in equity markets has magnified the performance volatility as these funds have had to use mark-to-market valuations to demonstrate that they can cover liabilities that fall some decades away. Many defined benefit pension funds closed to new entrants across the period. The prognosis for such funds in the private sector is dire. Kiosse and Peasnell (2009) go so far as to argue that the introduction of fair value accounting is the cause of this decline.

There is an agency problem at the heart of this. Historically, firms set up defined benefit schemes to retain skilled labour in tight labour markets (Hannah, 1986). They are set up as trusts and one way of evaluating their benefits is to ask: is the cost to the employer of the trust less than the cost of losing the skilled labour in the absence of a retention device? The answer might be different if one looks at the problem from the perspective of managers running the business, or of shareholders; labour retention is a managerial problem, and managers themselves become beneficiaries of the pension scheme.

Financial economics sees the pension fund as a shareholder investment. The assets of the pension fund are a sub-set of shareholder investments in the firm. The firm itself is valued by reference to market. Why not the pension fund? If the pension fund is over-valued, the firm might be an attractive takeover target. If under-valued, it is likely to protect managers (by insulating them from the market for corporate control) but disadvantage shareholders (by requiring them to invest more money in the fund). Either way, fair value accounting

> Enables both shareholders and (scheme) members to distinguish the contribution of the pension fund to the profitability of the firm from the profits arising from the sponsors operations.
>
> Moreover FRS17 (the relevant accounting standard) required deficits to be reflected on the sponsoring firm's balance sheets ...

(Avrahampour, 2008)

The case is of academic theory embedded through standards in an accounting practice. And the theory is from financial economics. Hopwood (1992) has stressed how modern economics works on accounting and accounting standards to operationalize economic theory *within the firm*, ultimately forcing the hierarchy to operate more like a market. Accounting has tended to define capital used by firms in backward-looking terms as money invested in capital goods, or as those goods themselves. Financial economics defines capital as an expectation of revenues. When the latter displaces the former, some forms of organization are no longer viable.

Moreover, the agency problem identified in the pension fund example is more general. Power (2010) has argued that not only does fair value accounting claim to offer an exit valuation method immune to management manipulation, it is also independent of the auditing process, which is increasingly governed by it. Reliability of valuation thus rests in the 'collective judgement of the market' (2003: 200–1) and thus is heavily dependent on the liquidity of the market concerned.

When large firms emerged, as we saw in Chapter 2, models of large-scale organization already existed in church and state. These organizations already had accounting systems, firms adapted them, and accounting as a discipline had a first-mover advantage. This might be a factor in explaining why economics became interested in the internal workings of firms at such a late date; there seemed already to be a technology in place. But with the growth in oversight of firms by financial markets, economic theories have colonized accounting, mainly by suggesting that firms should work like markets.

So, the performativity debate hints that it might not simply be a question of understanding whether theory leads practice, or vice versa, but understanding how changes in theory and changes in practice are intertwined. The accounting story we have told here has multiple agents and varying relationships; it is a story about institutional context as well as firm behaviour.

Management as Technology?

An important consideration here is intent. Many academic management theorists do not simply wish to produce theory, they wish also to influence practice and they write to do so. This is not merely a matter of selling books in airports; although they do that too. Strategy writers such as Porter and Hamel have set up consulting firms. Nobel Prize winners Scholes and Merton became principals in Long Term Capital Management. Fama, who developed the efficient markets hypothesis, is involved in an investment advisory firm, Dimensional, that articulates one proposed link presented here as the feedback loop in Figure T9.3, between academic theory development and practice. It has a clear logic.

Figure T9.3. The Dimensional success model.
(*Source*: Dimensional website)

- Academic leaders in the field of asset pricing find new sources of risk and return in advance of the industry.
- Dimensional engineers strategies and brings client feedback to these financial economists and researchers for further testing and enhancements.
- Empirical research becomes more relevant to practical investing, and practical investing is backed by solid theory and economic knowledge. (Dimensional website.)

The outcome is clear too: investment success. The route is, as one might expect from Fama, to invest in indices, since they proxy the market as a whole.

There are many more (but often less successful) examples. The fact that theory influences practice is thus not realistically considered a by-product of academic management output, it is to a greater or lesser degree a core purpose of it. Now the performativity debate above implies that this feedback loop might be a bit too simple. But it is clearly aspirational; and it shows how, to use MacKenzie's term, finance theory can become an 'engine'—a technology to drive practice.

What happens if we decide to treat the body of management theory in application as a 'technology'?

The most extensive work on this topic appears in a number of papers by Bloom, Van Reenen, and others (Bloom and Van Reenen, 2007, 2010; Bloom et al., 2013). Their underlying concern is with enduring differences in productivity between firms and countries; they argue that the quality of management makes a difference. Using a survey instrument developed jointly with McKinsey, they classify 18 basic management categories into three broad sets.

1. Do firms monitor for improvement?
2. Do they set targets?
3. Do they use performance-based incentives?

Firms that do more of these activities, have 'good' management and those that do less have 'poor' management. The key findings are as follows.

- Firms with better management perform better in terms of survival, size, growth rates, and productivity.
- There is enormous variance in management, both between firms and countries, and much of the inter-country variance is explained by the survival of poorly managed firms. This is much less common in the USA than elsewhere, and the USA has the highest country score.
- There are inter-country variances in style; for example the Americans are good at incentives and the Swedes at monitoring.
- Strong product market competition boosts average management practice by eliminating the laggards.
- Multinationals are managed well and export their management style.
- Exporters are managed better than non-exporters.
- Family-run firms are badly managed.
- State-owned firms are badly managed, particularly compared to publicly-quoted or private-equity-owned firms.
- Firms with more highly educated workers are better managed. This is seen to be because of the importance of human capital.
- Lighter labour market regulation is associated with better use of incentives.

(Bloom and Van Reenen, 2010: 204–5)

The authors are economists and there remains the problem for them that if, as they argue, improving management improves total factor productivity, why is there such heterogeneity between firms? Put simply, if it is so good why doesn't everyone do it?

> The slow evolution of management practices . . . suggests that management practices do have a resemblance to process technologies that diffuse slowly over time . . . New management practices are often complex and hard to introduce without the assistance of employees or consultants with prior experience.

(Bloom and Van Reenen, 2010: 220)

So this is essentially a slow technology diffusion argument. Management is information and can be considered like a software innovation (the authors in separate papers study ICT diffusion). However, you need know how to benefit from adopting management practice. But if you need to call McKinsey to find out how to benefit from a practice your competitors have already adopted, it may not be worth it.

The sample is huge and the survey has been repeated several times. Critics point to data problems, such as the truncation of the firm size distribution (only relatively small firms with <5000 employees), the non-strategic and simple management measures (which clearly owe a lot to agency theory), and the reliance on single respondents to generate firm-level measures (very unpopular with management academics; see Waldman et al., 2012). However, there are two other sets of reservations. First, if management is a diffusing process technology then it should behave like others, with first- and second-mover advantages, contingent benefits, and costs of adoption and interactions with product change (Geroski, 2000; Stoneman, 2002); not only is there no direct data on diffusion, there is no model of the process.[2] The second concerns the implication that the USA is the gold standard; the USA has the best practices (i.e. highest average) and is the most rigorous selection environment (i.e. shortest tail of low performers). Progress in management improvement means becoming more like the USA. This resurgence of a rather old convergence theory argument is, to say the least, curious. The decade of the surveys (2000s) was not one of conspicuous success for the US economy, and the BRIC countries with much higher rates of growth come out as having many badly managed firms on these measures. Could the measures themselves be culturally specific, agency theoretic practices likely to have more impact in the USA than anywhere else?

This body of economic work has not yet had much impact on the teaching of management, even though the core finding that management matters ought to be music in the halls of academia. The core finding of the extent of heterogeneity is highly significant and its pattern, that 'core' management practices are poorly developed in the world's largest and most rapidly growing economies, is one to which I will return.

There's a Brand New Dance...

The logical final set not presented by MacKenzie in Figure T9.1 is 'zero-performativity': no impact on practice. It arguably happened to such eminent academics as Coase and Penrose for several years but it is generally not part

---

[2] For an attempt to study diffusion of a single management practice, see Bryson et al., 2007.

of the plot. Academics often want to influence or change practice and that means occasional over-supply of ideas. So while we have examples of slow-burning theoretical contributions, we also have ideas with a pretty short shelf life, and minimal long-term impact. The final area we need to look at in this theme is management fashion.

Many academic disciplines have fads or fashions. In history, the term 'revisionist' is often used to deal with the fact that there is only so much history, and quite a lot of historians, who go back reinterpreting the same information with a different lens. In economics, topics become fashionable. Some years ago, it was fashionable to study sports, currently it is 'wellbeing'; new areas are 'colonized' by the application of economic reasoning and methods.

There is work in the philosophy of science that addresses non-cumulative change in academic work, notably the Kuhnian ideas referred to above. For Kuhn (1962), scientific activity does not manifest linear progress, but rather a shift between 'paradigms'—a change in the basic assumptions scientists use in looking at the world, like that between Newtonian and quantum mechanics. But in physics this happens once every few hundred years and in management theory it sometimes seems to happen while you make the coffee. Kuhn (1970) himself was not sure whether social sciences could have paradigm shifts as opposed to crises of conscience, but one could point in economics to the shift *to* Keynesian approaches from neoclassicism, and then away again, towards rational expectations as, at least, *major* coffee breaks.

For many in the management field, the absence of a sense of clear progress is problematic. Eccles and Nohria, for example, worry that each generation discovers core management principles anew, and that,

> Even as the fundamental principles of management remain the same, the words used to express them constantly portray them as new.
>
> (Eccles and Nohria, 1992: 5)

Barley and Kunda worried that academic discourse might simply reflect managerial discourse at large and 'our efforts may be neither cumulative or path-breaking' (Barley and Kunda, 1992: 394.) Donaldson (1995) is concerned that, in organizational studies, competing and proliferating 'paradigms' guarantee innovation without progress, and the problem is rooted in the structure of academic activity itself.

Let us look again at management as innovation; arguably, there are a set of supply-side pressures on academics to generate innovation, and a set of demand-side pressures to find answers to perceived problems. As with other technologies, innovation may be technology-push or demand-led.

I will focus the discussion mainly on academic output—but there are a number of other players. If you pick up a book in an airport with a title like

Getting Rich Beyond the Dreams of Avarice or *The Six Characteristics of Immortals*, chances are a working academic did not write it (but don't rule it out). The best-selling business books on Amazon tend to be written by consultants who want to make a living from it. But most business academics have to make a choice between writing for academic journals and citations or writing for airport sales, and the correlation between success in these two fields is not great (Baldridge et al., 2004). In addition, business academia now sits within a set of knowledge intensive industries such as consultancies, the business press, software companies, investment banks, and market research companies that generate output influencing practice *and* academic curricula; for example, most strategy texts over recent years have featured the Boston Consulting Group's growth matrix.

In a series of articles, Abrahamson (1991, 1996, 1997) has looked at fashion-setting and fashion-using actors in the management theory field. Although he defines fashion as a 'transitory collective belief', he sees it as a very serious business for academics competing with the other institutions identified in the last paragraph. By examining fashions such as those for quality circles in the 1970s and 1980s, and for employee stock options repeatedly across the twentieth century, he illustrates how things come and go (1996: 255–9).

What does *not* come and go is fashion itself. By drawing a very sensible comparison with fashion and cultural industries themselves, he argues that, far from the penchant for fads being evidence of some pre-paradigmatic academic adolescence, it is a robust feature of a field embedded in practice, and often led by it. Echoing Barley and Kunda (1992) he argues that performance concerns by fashion users (i.e. managers) generate demands for different types of innovation, which might be supplied by any of the fashion-setting institutions, and the issue for academics is to compete effectively in this market. Galbraith (1980: 162) has argued similarly that there are no innovations in studies of organization that 'emerge from the test tubes of organisation theory'; all come from 'inventive practitioners'. More specifically, Barley et al. (1988) argue that the debates on organizational culture discussed in the previous chapter were practitioner-led.

This approach puts emphasis on the 'client' drivers of fashion. They may be short or long term. Barley and Kunda (1992) stress the importance of the business cycle in fuelling fashion demand in a rather materialist conception of academic production. Other authors (e.g. Mitroff and Mohrman, 1987) reacted to the growing economic power of Asia (specifically Japan) to suggest that academic innovation was a response at the time to the relative decline of Western business. In the next chapter, I will speculate on what continued relative decline might do to the academic study of management in the near future.

Conclusion

This theme has focused on the often complicated relationship between academic theory and managerial practice. There appear to be examples of technology-led developments (finance), as well as demand-pull (culture). In fields such as accounting, there appears to be a complex interplay involving several actors. To return to the language of Chapter 1, finance academics tend to be theologians and organizational scholars chroniclers or preachers. But this is not just a matter of individual preference or disciplinary style; the management field since the outset has seen a close relationship between academic theory and managerial practice, and we need to understand what this might look like in the future.

Chapter 10

In Search of a Better Past?

Introduction

In this final chapter, I look backwards and forwards. The story so far has tried to balance genealogy and content; to give an account of the development of management disciplines and to explain what their primary concerns are. Core concepts bind these disciplines, but loosely. I argued at the outset that the fragmentation of the management field is stated as a problem throughout its development. Key events, such as the growth of the firm, the separation of ownership and control, the rise of labour power, and the development of the M form, have caused academics to engage with practical problems and to develop theories and concepts in response. In turn, and in different ways, we can see how these theories and concepts shaped the practical world of management. In this final chapter I will attempt to provide some thematic unity in summary form and will also look at some prospects for the corpus of academic activity called management.

Coase and Effect?

The broad argument may be summarized in a set of (rather sweeping) generalizations.

- The large firm in the West rose without academic trace. Economics did not develop any theory to guide the activities of those managing large firms.

- Managers found solutions to the central problems of coordination, control, and efficiency in hierarchies by borrowing ideas from large organizations in church and state. Ideas borrowed from military engineering were particularly important.

- Lacking the punitive sanctions of church and state, managers had to address the problem of consummate cooperation and did so by borrowing ideas from social psychology and anthropology.
- The success of these tools allowed managers to develop substantial independence of action; specifically, independence from control by investors or by governments.

These four generalizations are concerned with the management of hierarchy. And the principles established for the management of hierarchy have proved robust. They have been brilliantly summarized by Hamel, presented here as Figure C10.1. These tools are embedded in the managerial sub-disciplines of operations management, organizational behaviour and design, and management accounting. Hamel cites them to bemoan their legacy in constraining the thought processes of managers several generations after their development. Here, I cite them to indicate their success as a toolkit for control and independence. The net effect is that the large managerial firm looked *nothing like* a market. Efficiency is not on the list of principles.

But failure to control markets could substantially undermine the ability to control hierarchies; hence our next two generalizations.

- Once the problems of coordination and control had been rendered tractable within hierarchies, managerial thinking turned to the development of tools and techniques to extend control into markets. The most basic tool was to turn a market into a hierarchy by vertical integration.
- Where markets remained, hierarchy could best be protected by the avoidance of competition, particularly on price.

These two generalizations are concerned with the management of markets. The tools to do so are embedded in the managerial sub-disciplines of marketing and strategy. The essence of both is the creation and protection of rents through differentiation of product or service. Again, they are not primarily concerned with efficiency.

These generalizations take us, both chronologically and intellectually, to a point just before the rise of finance as the dominant academic sub-discipline. Some broad observations need to be made. These intellectual developments had two necessary conditions; first, that rents existed and, second, that hierarchies could appropriate them. Growth of hierarchy could be associated with profitability. Put more prejudicially, more managers mean more profit. These managers needed also to have sufficient autonomy to use the tools described above and indeed as the tools became more complicated, managers specialized around the sub-disciplines in firm sub-units called operations, human resources, marketing, and so on.

Principle	Application	Goal
Standardization	Minimize variance from standards around inputs, outputs, and work methods.	Pursue scale economies, manufacturing efficiency, reliability, and quality.
Specialization of tasks and functions	Group like activities together in modular organisational units.	Reduce complexity and accelerate learning.
Goal alignment	Establish clear objectives through a cascade of subsidiary goals and supporting metrics.	Ensure individual efforts are congruent with top-down goals.
Hierarchy	Create a pyramid of authority based on a limited span of control.	Maintain control over a broad scope of operations.
Planning and control	Forecast demand, budget resources, and schedule tasks, then track and correct deviations from plan.	Establish regularity and predictability in operations and conformity to plans.
Extrinsic rewards	Provide financial rewards to individuals and teams for achieving specified outcomes.	Motivate effort and ensure compliance with policies and procedures.

Figure C10.1. Hamel: Principles of management.
(*Source*: Hamel, 2007)

Throughout the development of this field, the dominant unit of analysis has been the firm. We have noted the paradox that, in the early part of the twentieth century, firms dominated developed economies yet there was an intellectual gap in the absence of a theory of the firm. Generally in social science, a unit of analysis is only interesting if it can be seen to have independence of action; we do not like to sample on dependent variables. In the

277

history of management studies, this has had three implications. First, assumptions about firm independence have tended to be strong, and often untested. Second, analysis has been overly interested in large firms with market power; that is where the assumption was safest. Third, other forms of institution, such as governments, have tended to remain peripheral, that is studied as a constraint. Too much of the earlier work in management is about oligopoly and the intra-firm structures supported by it.

Even after Coase, economics could not be of much assistance because his theory of the firm was a theory of market failure; that is it was a theory of why markets might not work rather than how firms did work. The internal operations of the firm were dealt with by assumption, namely that an 'entrepreneur' could unproblematically coordinate and control. It did not adequately deal with the question of *why* there was so much market failure that modern economies were dominated by large firms. Later work by economists such as Williamson did not break out of the intellectual straitjacket of seeing hierarchies as second best to markets in efficiency terms.

The implications of this line of thought for managers are both substantial and severe. From this viewpoint, managers are either trying to escape market disciplines by protecting rents, and thus need to have those disciplines imposed, or they are acting rationally in following the dictates of the market. As Fligstein (1990: 303) puts it 'The market is the final arbiter of efficiency and managers who are successful are efficient because the market is efficient.' There is no room here for Chandler's 'visible hand', that is the idea that managerial action might be *better than* the market. It is time for our final generalizations, which are about the financial view of the firm.

- The emergence of the large diversified M form required financial performance measures to evaluate dissimilar divisions and product lines.
- Financial measures, such as return on assets, became not simply a measure of past performance but a resource allocation tool.
- The ultimate allocation tool became the stock price of the firm, which was assumed to contain all information about future cash flows.
- The firm could be imagined as a market, a nexus of contracts for delivery of shareholder value.

These four generalizations are concerned with management of hierarchies *by* markets. As Davis has eloquently argued, Chandler's golden age of the firm, of managerial capitalism, gave way to the substantial intrusion of markets, or market thinking, into the study of the firm. Management accounting yielded to financial reporting. Rent secretion yielded to shareholder value. Internal labour markets yielded to performance pay. Vertical integration yielded to outsourcing.

The development of the finance sub-discipline has been a very important ingredient in all of this. Standardized measures of asset valuation allow closer oversight of managerial performance. Markets for corporate control could eliminate sub-standard management performance. The efficient markets hypothesis in particular downgraded managerial strategizing from the selection of firm goals to the selection of means for the pursuit of shareholder value. Financial skills became central to management success. As Fligstein notes, efficiency, or more precisely the definition of efficiency, is the issue. Manufacturing efficiency is about maximizing throughput and has largely firm-internal measures. Sales and marketing efficiency is about margins and market share and has demand-side measures. Both of these forms of efficiency rest on techniques requiring managerial knowledge of process and product. Financial efficiency is about return on assets; it does not.

The development of finance has introduced substantial changes to the management field. First, it is intellectually very strong on modelling and prescription. As an accurate or even plausible *description* of managerial practice, it is not at the races. Arguably it has accelerated a split between those academics interested in describing what managers do and those interested in prescribing it. Second, it questions the firm as the unit of analysis; a nexus of contracts can be a firm or a network of firms. It subordinates the firm to the capital market, but the capital market to nothing.

Even in its manifestation as organizational economics, the rational expectations approach still defaults to a view of the firm as a physically challenged market. But as a candidate for the approach that might provide a unifying approach to the study of management, it is the only game in town; Shiller's quote above may be wrong, but nobody else is even saying it. Finance is the most prestigious discipline within the management field, and we know for sure after 1987, 2001, and 2008 that it is not because it can *predict*. It cannot even predict the past.

In summary, then, I have argued that the development of the academic body of work called 'management' and specifically its six sub-disciplines—Accounting, Operations Research and Management, Organizational Behaviour, Marketing, Strategy, and Finance—can be understood in terms of a few broad concepts. Managers seek techniques to control hierarchies and markets. They seek to assert control in markets dominated by efficiency and to introduce efficiency into hierarchies dominated by control. Historically this curriculum developed first the tools to control hierarchy. It then turned to the control of markets; first labour markets, then product markets, then capital markets. It powerfully emphasized managerial agency. The quest for financial performance measures then led to the development of tools to introduce market efficiency into the firm; rational managers become agents of the

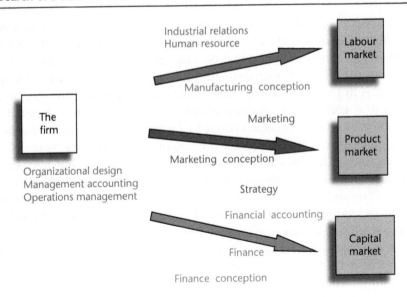

Figure C10.2. Control in hierarchies and markets.

market. An attempt is made to summarize this in Figure C10.2, which elaborates the opening Figure C1.1 in this book.

The Bigger Picture?

It is beyond the scope of this text to outline a theory of management or even a curriculum for the future, but some observations on this field of study are relevant, particularly in light of recent events, such as the fall of Enron and the financial crisis.

It is very fashionable at the time of writing to be sceptical about business management in general and the business curriculum in particular. Let us start by retaining the baby not the bathwater. As Hamel puts it:

> If you have two cars in the garage, a television in every room, and a digital device in every pocket, it is thanks to the inventors of modern management.

> (Hamel, 2007: 5)

He argues that management was the trigger turning scientific discovery and enlightened policy into global prosperity. Now, I would argue that prosperity is not global, and that if you have absolutely none of the things he lists above, that might be down to the activities of modern management too, but let us accept the point that, in the material terms he cites, it has worked for many. So the starting point here is that, to adopt the extreme words of Mintzberg

(2009), managing might be the world's most important job. If it works in the aggregate, what are the main issues? Let us first look at what the corpus of the management curriculum leaves aside.

Despite the importance of the firm to modern society, no other field treats the firm as its primary unit of analysis. Most of our understanding of how the firm works comes out of the traditional business curriculum. This is both a strength and a weakness. The strength is that looking *inside* the firm generates understanding of the context in which many of us will spend much of our lives. The disadvantage is that other actors in the business scene are ignored. Davis, for example, stresses the very peculiar institutional context, originating in the Great Depression in the USA, in which our approaches to the managerial firm developed. This level of autonomy from state control is likely to prove unusual. Specifically, how much business activity in the twenty-first century is likely to take place in elective democracies?

In fact, the absence of the state even for this period is illusory. Managerial capitalism flourished in a period where Western governments pursued full employment in labour markets and regulation of capital markets. It died when governments ceased to do either. Management of firms by markets emerged, but in the aftermath of the financial crash, as with the Great Depression of the 1930s, the institutional context currently being developed will have an impact on managerial practices in future.

The short twentieth century was important for another aspect of state activity: war. War, particularly large-scale war, severely impacts business. It creates international trade barriers, limits capital and labour mobility, and generates labour shortage. On the other hand, it has tended to boost demand for certain products, develop technologies that have commercial use, and create markets for government debt. Our pattern of understanding of the firm has developed primarily by examination of circumstances where hot or cold war was a constant state of affairs, impacting the practice of management and thus theories about its role. We have seen how academic disciplines such as operations research, accounting, and organizational behaviour have been influenced directly by knowledge transfer from military activity or the demands of a wartime economy. There is also evidence of the re-importation of management techniques into government work, most notably the role of firms in wartime and specifically of DuPont in the Manhattan Project (Weatherall, 2013). But it is perhaps surprising that having borrowed models of organization from government precedent, the activity of government itself should cease to be of interest.

The final aspect of state activity that has had a substantial impact on the practice of management concerns law. Let us begin with examples, from macro to micro. Dobbin et al. (1993) have linked the emergence of the personnel function in the USA to equal rights legislation. At the industry level,

McKenna (2006) has shown how the development of the entire management consulting industry in the USA was prompted by a restriction on the activities of banks in analysing companies to which they would lend. At the micro level, individual management style is influenced by the development of law around the employment contract (Conway and Briner, 2005). The relevant law is thus not only that specifically designed to regulate business, but also that which reflects larger social change (for example on discrimination). Some legislative change brings the very idea of an imperatively coordinated hierarchy into question; where the legitimacy of management becomes problematic, the comparative advantage of approaches that *assume* management control (such as organizational economics) erodes in favour of those that *investigate* it (such as those rooted in anthropology).

If state activity becomes important, so does its avoidance. At the time of writing, governments of the G8 countries are considering collaboration over increasing tax avoidance by large companies, many of whom use a combination of transfer pricing and internet technology to root accountability in low-tax jurisdictions. Many firms—including some of the biggest brands in the world—are actually *networks* of companies in which individual governments might find it difficult to locate accountability for a particular managerial practice. A recent work on the twenty-first-century firm described a pervasive 'migration of agency from firms to networks', and raised questions over three issues:

- Strategy—can a network have a single objective function?
- Valuation—can capital markets evaluate a network where assets are spread across legal entities and jurisdictions?
- Accountability—how can it be regulated? (DiMaggio, 2001: 225–7).

Put simply, it may be impossible to analyse the strategy or structure of an international business without detailed knowledge of its attitude towards governments and the likely response of those governments to avoidance.

So, arguably, silence about government is a risky option for any future management curriculum. Another major exogenous consideration is technology. Early contributors to management thought were often engineers with a good understanding of (mainly manufacturing) technologies. They produced the thinking behind Figure C10.1. But in the Anglo-Saxon curriculum which has come to be so influential in the study of management, one does not study technology, and generalizations are often made about management behaviour which are intended to be, if not universal, then not dependent on technology. For example, in Figure C10.1, how are spans of control affected by information technology? Does it affect the optimal management style?

Let us use the dot-com boom as a case study. Academics, but *not* business academics, originated the Internet. It generated changes in both business and society comparable to an industrial revolution. New industries emerged. Firms grew faster than was thought possible. The landscape of large firms changed completely. Financial services were automated to a degree that, arguably, changed their nature. It changed executive pay massively. Rents in the sector proved to be transient. Industries relocated to low-wage economies. Then the bubble burst. How did the academic management curriculum respond?

The answer is; largely by controlling its distress. Many studies (and case studies) of Internet business emerged, as did studies of e-commerce and information technology adoption. But this industrial revolution did not have the same impact on management thinking as that which produced the large firm at the start of the twentieth century. In Chapter 9, we saw that Mintzberg's replication of his 1970s study in the twenty-first century did not lead to any fundamental revision of his views. He remarks 'the internet is not changing the practice of management fundamentally; rather, it is reinforcing characteristics that we have been seeing for decades' (Mintzberg, 2011: 39).

This is intriguing, since a lost tradition associated with the Tavistock Institute and Joan Woodward held that technology was a defining dimension of organization, with profound implications for managerial and non-managerial work (Chapter 4). Major changes to technology could be expected to generate major changes in what managers do, but it has not shown up in academic theory about management.

Or, at least, not in the core. One measure of the resilience of the core concepts of management is that change generates curriculum addition rather than transformation. What I mean by this is that with the globalization of business, cross-cultural management courses are added to the curriculum; with the emergence of ethical concerns after Enron, ethics and corporate social responsibility are added, and so on. More disturbingly, after the financial crisis, courses on financial crises have been added to many curricula while Finance 1 stands unmoved in its commitment to normal distributions. There is resilience to the core management curriculum that might be a cause for concern.

Another cause for concern is the corollary of the fragmentation we identified at the outset. There is still no overarching and widely accepted theory of the firm. The management disciplines do not sum to one and it remains 'one of the less developed and agreed upon areas of economics' (Hart, 2011: 102). Despite outsourcing and downsizing, economic activity within firms is still at least as great as that within markets (Lafontaine and Slade, 2007). But within economics—which remains the only candidate discipline for the production of a theory of the firm—the production function view of the firm simply as a combination of inputs with a single objective function remains influential.

This view has nothing to say about five vital things, all of which have been examined by the growing discipline of organizational economics.

1. Governance. The modern business landscape includes public companies, entrepreneurially or family owned businesses, cooperatives and mutually owned businesses, and government-owned firms. So, in the European airline industry British Airways (publicly owned) competes with Air France (government) and Virgin (entrepreneurially owned). In UK retailing, Tesco (publicly owned) competes with John Lewis (partnership). Should a theory of the firm embrace different ownership types? Or, in examining these sets of competitors, do we need a theory for each governance form? Much of the core curriculum rests on ideas developed under managerial capitalism and the joint stock company.

2. Boundaries. The main contribution of Coase and Williamson was to examine the boundary issue ignored in the production function approach. Boundaries are set at the point at which the cost of using the price mechanism exceeds the cost of ownership. But in the early twenty-first century the worldwide value of acquisitions and mergers was over \$4 trillion.[1] What explains this? And why do vertically integrated firms often compete against those who are not; for example, in mobile telephony, some firms own networks and others rent network usage?

3. Authority. For Coase and Williamson, once you move a transaction inside a hierarchy, authority works unproblematically; that is hierarchy is a solution, not a problem. For agency theorists, authority *is* problematic; agents may pursue divergent interests. So bargaining may not be eliminated by bringing a transaction into a hierarchy. What are the conditions under which authority, which is in turn the basis for most of the efficiency properties of the firm, work or not?

4. Capital Structure. As we have seen, the Modigliani–Miller model sees capital structure as irrelevant in the absence of taxes, but an agency approach might see it differently. Imagine a manager is an owner (100%). He will not buy a corporate jet he does not really need. Then imagine he needs to raise capital. He could issue equity, and reduce his stake to 50%. Now he shares the jet cost with other stakeholders, but enjoys the whole jet. If he borrows the same amount, he bears the full cost of the jet against his equity if he goes broke. Capital structure may impact managerial behaviour. Since it is often senior managers who make the debt equity decision, how do investors control this?

---

[1] *Economist*, 13 January 2007.

5. Incentives. There is a vast literature on managerial incentives and firm performance, but it is often conducted on the unrealistic assumption that investors make the decision about the design of the incentive scheme. Often they do not, and if managers are making decisions both about capital structure and about incentives, then incentive issues and governance issues become closely intertwined. I venture that there is no area of economics that has done more damage in recent years than that which led to the development of high-powered incentives. What should be the set of principles governing the design of incentives for senior managers?

There is much resistance to the perceived imperialism of economic (including finance) approaches, much of it based on the view that economics rests on unrealistic assumptions about managerial rationality. However, those who take this view are themselves highly varied in their intellectual approaches to both managerial processes and the tools at managers' disposal. Figure C10.3 attempts a summary of some of the issues at stake. It uses the broad categorization of management scholars presented in the opening chapter.

The figure should be thought of as a simple heuristic to help the reader integrate the materials in this book, but also to understand why many management scholars with different approaches find it hard to talk to each other. The columns distinguish those studying managerial behaviour who treat rationality as an assumption from those who treat it as a variable. The rows distinguish those who think that management tools 'work' and those who do not. It is a caricature, but I hope a useful one. Theologians build models of the

| | Management Process | |
	Rational	Irrational
Performative	Organizational and financial economics, e.g. Jensen, game theorists.	Managerial decision making, e.g. Simon, Kahneman.
Management Tools	Theologians	Chroniclers
Not performative	Process and tool builders, e.g. Taylor, Kaplan, Hamel.	Management as ritual, e.g. anthropologists, critical management theorists.
	Preachers	Sceptics

Figure C10.3. Thinking about management, management process and tools.

process and tools of management but, with few notable exceptions, do not test them empirically. Chroniclers begin with observations of, mostly, managerial behaviour (Kahneman uses experiments with a variety of subjects) and then try to build theory or at least generalization from that. This author's view is that this approach has generated much (though not all) of what is distinctively managerial 'theory'. Preachers tend to assume rational behaviour, but often with much weaker assumptions than theologians, and build analytical or forensic tools such as work study, balanced scorecards, and competence analysis. This is the box where the money is to be had and a fuller list of contributors would have to include several consultancies and accounting firms since this approach is the engine of marketable knowledge about management. Finally comes the very large set of critics, only a few of whom have made it into this book, primarily in Chapter 9. They may see management in a negative or neutral light, but not as a rational process, and not with any measureable impact on firm performance. For some, management is more about power and domination than efficiency; for others, simply an interesting anthropological topic. The idea of building a managerial tool does not arise.

The figure may be of assistance in trying to assess what a particular author is trying to do. It manifestly does not distinguish academics in terms of *what* they study. To take the example of organizational culture discussed in Chapter 9, one may see the most 'authentic' approach as taken by anthropologists, but putting metrics in place (Goffee and Jones, for example) builds a managerial tool, while both economists (effective coordination device) and decision theorists (useful set of social decision heuristics) can see culture as performative. Thus, students of culture could be in any box. This example allows a further broad generalization. Academic dialogue on management is perhaps richer within the columns of the figure than across the rows. If one believes management to be fundamentally a rational activity then, through modelling it or improving it, one can generalize and seek to optimize. Lacking this view, building theories about management proves harder, but understanding the complexity of management activity more likely.

The figure may be seen as an attempt to add content to the opening proposition that the field has four characteristics; it is derivative, opportunistic, eclectic, and fragmented. I would argue that most managerial scholars study roughly the same things—and I have listed my version of the main concerns in Chapter 1—but that they do so with such a variety of assumptions, methods, and purposes that these four characteristics of the field are likely to be enduring. The figure also indicates the variance in the performativity of management theory. In different ways, theologians and preachers seek to change the practice of management and some theologians have been known to preach (Jensen). If such scholars come to dominate the field, it will lose several of its four characteristics.[2] However, much that affects management practice involves chroniclers, who document and then disseminate views of what is seen as best practice, or at least worthy of imitation, and chronicles are dependent upon events. The rise of the Western managerial firm and its reaction to Asian competition and the dot-com boom, were all documented rather than predicted by management academics and, barring the unlikely outcome that economics will mould the business world in its own image, the field is likely to maintain its key features.

---

[2] Since economics imports game theory and portfolio theory, arguably it would remain derivative.

A Short Guide to Texts

This book has a long reference list and the reader might appreciate some guidance about the specific sub-disciplines covered here. All of the books mentioned below appear in the reference list except where specified. In each case I have included one 'standard' text that seeks to encompass the field and one or more works that seek to criticize or evaluate the state of the relevant field. Others may make a different choice. Many of the standard texts go through several editions, so check when you read this which is the most up to date.

Accounting

Standard Text
In accounting, one needs to distinguish between management and financial accounting. For the former, a seminal text is Johnson and Kaplan (1991), the subtitle of which is 'the rise and fall of management accounting'. For the latter, a good if rather dry text is Weetman (2006).

Criticism
A vast body of work exists that sees accounting as performative and as a set of socially constructed rules. A good introduction to this style of thought is the set of readings by Hopwood and Miller (1994). For further elaboration of this line of reasoning see the majestic book by Power (1997).

Finance

Standard Text
Successive editions of Brealey et al. (2008) offer accessible routes into the main theories and practices of financial economics, often with amusing examples.

Criticism
One of the most influential social science books of recent years is MacKenzie (2006) who describes the history and development of finance. MacKenzie is a mathematician who explains in non-technical terms why assumptions about normal distributions are risky.

Marketing

Standard Text

Over many years, Philip Kotler has dominated the text market for marketing theory and marketing management. The second area is the most relevant here, and the latest edition is Kotler et al. (2009).

Criticism

A comprehensive set of readings that examine the strengths and weaknesses of modern marketing is Weitz and Wensley (2002).

Operations Management

Standard Text

The works by Abernathy and Utterback cited in the references give a good flavour of the revival of interest in operations that followed from the impact of Japanese competition.

Criticism

Criticism of the operational efficiency often concerns the impact it has on employees. The classic work here which is a Marxist critique of scientific management in general and Taylor in particular is Braverman (1974).

Organizational Behaviour

Standard Text

For a flavour of how core micro-level OB courses are taught today (i.e. as applied psychology), particularly in USA, see Colquitt et al. (2009).

Criticism

For an appraisal of the entire field, including organizational theory, the best on offer is still Pfeffer (1997). Rose (1988) is invaluable as an account of how the field developed.

Strategy

Standard Text

Core strategy texts are often barely liftable, never mind readable, but Grant (2005) is probably the best written comprehensive guide. Rumelt (2012) is a very good illustration of where the field is today. For the very distinctive approach of Organizational Economics there are a variety of texts, but for the undiluted version, go to Jensen (1998).

Criticism

Henry Mintzberg has written extensively criticizing many of the assumptions of the strategy field but the best book evaluating it critically is Whittington (2001). The title is 'What is Strategy and does it Matter?' and you get an answer to both.

References

AACSB (2008); *Final Report of the AACSB International Impact of Research Task Force*, Tampa, Florida.

Abernathy, W. J. (1978); *The Productivity Dilemma*, Baltimore, Johns Hopkins.

Abernathy, W. J., Clark, K. B., Kantrow, A. M. (1983); *Industrial Renaissance: Producing a Competitive Future for America*, New York, Basic Books.

Abernathy, W. J. and Utterback, J. M., (1982); 'Patterns of Industrial Innovation', in Tushman, M. and Moore, W. (eds), *Readings in the Management of Innovation*, London, Pitman.

Abolafia, M. Y. (1996); *Making Markets: Opportunity and Restraint on Wall Street*, Cambride, MA, Harvard University Press.

Abrahamson, E. (1991); 'Managerial fads and fashion: The diffusion and rejection of innovations', *Academy of Management Review*, 16, pp. 586–612.

Abrahamson, E. (1996); 'Management fashion', *Academy of Management Review*, 24, pp. 254–85.

Abrahamson, E. (1997); 'The emergence and prevalence of employee-management rhetoric: Long and short-run determinants', *Academy of Management Review*, 30, 3, pp. 491–533.

Adams, J. (1995); *Risk*, London, Routledge.

Albrow, M. (1969); *Bureaucracy*, London, Pall Mall Press.

Alchian, A. A. and Demsetz, H. (1972); 'Production, information costs and economic organisation', *American Economic Review*, 62, pp. 777–95.

Altman, E. I. (1968); 'Financial ratios, discriminant analysis and the prediction of bankruptcy', *Journal of Finance*, 23, 4, pp. 589–609.

Alvesson, M. (2002); *Understanding Organizational Culture*, London, Sage.

Amihud, Y. and Lev, B. (1981); 'Risk reduction as a managerial motive for conglomerate mergers', *Bell Journal of Economics*, 12, pp. 605–17.

Amit, R. and Shoemaker, P. J. H. (1993); 'Strategic assets and organisational rent', *Strategic Management Journal*, 14, pp. 33–46.

Anderson, E. and Coughlan, A. T. (2002); 'Channel management: structure, governance and relationship management', pp. 223–47 in Weitz, B. and Wensley, R., *Handbook of Marketing*, London, Sage.

Anderson, G. M, Tollison, R. D., and McCormack, R. E. (1983); 'The economic organisation of the English East India Company', *Journal of Economic Behaviour and Organisation*, 4, pp. 221–38.

Ansoff, I. (1965); *Corporate Strategy*, London, Penguin.

Appelbaum, E., Bernhardt, A. D., and Murnane, R. J. (2003); *Low-Wage America: How Employers are Reshaping Opportunity in the Workplace*, New York, Russell Sage Foundation.

Argyris, C. (1960); *Understanding Organizational Behavior*, Oxford, Dorsey.

Armour, H. and Teece, D. (1978); 'Organisational structure and economic performance: A test of the M-form hypothesis', *Bell Journal of Economics*, 9, pp. 106–22.

Armstrong, P. (1987) 'The rise of accounting controls in British capitalist enterprises', *Accounting, Organisations and Society*, 12, 5, pp. 415–36.

Arrow, K. J. (1974); *The Limits of Organization*, New York, Norton.

Arrow, K. J. (2004); 'Is bounded rationality unboundedly rational?' in Augier, M. and March, J. (eds), *Essays in Honor of Herbert Simon*, pp. 47–56, Cambridge MA, MIT Press.

Austin, J. (1962); *How to do Things with Words*, Oxford, Clarendon Press.

Avrahampour, Y. (2008); 'A relational account of the valuation and management of UK defined benefit pension funds', *Academy of Management Annual Meeting Proceedings*, 8, 1, pp. 1–39.

Axelrod, R. (1984); *The Evolution of Co-operation*, Princeton NJ, Princeton University Press.

Axelrod, R. (1997); *The Complexity of Co-operation: Agent Based Models of Competition and Collaboration*, Princeton NJ, Princeton University Press.

Bain, G. S. (1970); *The Growth of White Collar Unionism*, Oxford, Oxford University Press.

Bain, J. S. (1956); *Barriers to New Competition*, Cambridge MA, Harvard University Press.

Baldridge, D., Floyd, S and Markoczy, L. (2004); 'Are managers from Mars and academics from Venus?' *Strategic Management Journal*, 25, pp. 1063–74.

Bales, R. F. (1958); 'Task roles in problem solving groups', pp. 437–42 in Maccoby, E., Newcome, T., and Horsley, E. *Social Psychology*, New York, Holt, Rinehart and Winston.

Barley, S. and Kunda, G. (1992); 'Design and devotion: Surges of rational and normative ideologies of control in managerial discourse', *Administrative Science Quarterly*, 37, 363–99.

Barley, S., Meyer, G. and Gash, D. (1988); 'Culture of cultures: Academics, practitioners and the pragmatics of normative control', *Administrative Science Quarterly*, 33, pp. 24–60.

Barnard, C. (1938, 1962 edition); *The Functions of the Executive*, Cambridge MA, Harvard University Press.

Barney, J. B. (1991); 'Firm resources and sustained competitive advantage', *Journal of Management*, 17, 1, pp. 99–120.

Bass, (1985); *Leadership and Performance Beyond Expectations*, New York, Free Press.

Bate, S. R. (1997); 'Whatever happened to organizational anthropology?', *Human Relations*, 50, 9, pp. 1147–75.

Batt, R. and Moynihan, L. (2002); 'The viability of alternative call centre production models', *Human Resource Management Journal*, 12, 4, pp. 14–34.

Bazerman, M. (2002); *Judgment in Managerial Decision Making* (5th edition), New York, Wiley.

Bazerman, M. (2005); 'Conducting influential research: the need for prescriptive implications', *Academy of Management Review*, 30, 1, pp. 25–31.

References

Becker, B. and Gerhard, B. (1996); 'The impact of human resource management on organisational performance: progress and prospects', *Academy of Management Journal*, 39, 4, pp. 779–801.

Beer, M. Spector, B, and Lawrence, P. R. (1984); *Managing Human Assets*, New York, Free Press.

Berg, M. (1980); *The Machinery Question and the Making of Political Economy*, Cambridge, Cambridge University Press.

Berle, A. and Means, G. C. (1932); *The Modern Corporation and Private Property*, New York, Macmillan.

Bernstein, P. L. (1996); *Against the Gods: The Remarkable Story of Risk*, New York, Wiley.

Binmore, K. G. (1991); *Fun and Games: A Text on Game Theory*, London, Macmillan.

Black, F. and Scholes, M. (1972); 'The valuation of options contracts and a test of market efficiency', *Journal of Finance*, 27, pp. 399–417.

Black, F. and Scholes, M. (1973); 'The pricing of options and corporate liabilities', *Journal of Political Economy*, 81, pp. 637–54.

Blanchflower, D. and Bryson, A. (2003); 'Changes over time in union relative wage effects in the UK and the US Revisited', chapter 7 in *International Handbook of Trade Unions*, Addison, J. T. and Schnabel, C. (eds), Cheltenham, UK and Northampton MA, USA, Edward Elgar.

Blanchflower, D. and Bryson, A. (2004); 'What effect do unions have on wages now?' *Journal of Labor Research*, 25, 3, pp. 383–414.

Blau, P. (1955); *The Dynamics of Bureaucracy*, Chicago, Chicago University Press.

Blau, P. (1964); *Exchange and Power in Social Life*, New York, Wiley.

Blinder, A. S., Canetti, E. R., Lebow, D. E., and Rudd, J. B. (1998); *Asking About Prices: A New Approach to Understanding About Price Stickiness*, New York, Russell Sage Foundation.

Bloom, N. and Van Reenen, J. (2007); 'Measuring and explaining management practices across countries', *Quarterly Journal of Economics*, 122, 4, pp. 1341–48.

Bloom, N. and Van Reenen, J. (2010); 'Why do management practices differ across firms and countries', *Journal of Economic Perspectives*, 24, 1, pp. 203–24.

Bloom, N., Saddun, R. and Van Reenen, J. (2013); 'Management as a Technology?' Centre for Economic Performance, LSE.

Boje, D., (1995); 'Stories of the storytelling organisation: A postmodern analysis of Disney as "Tamara-Land"', *Academy of Management Journal*, 38, pp. 997–1035.

Borowski, R. (1994); ed. *Assessing Cultural Anthropology*, New York, McGraw-Hill.

Boston Consulting Group, (1975); Strategy Alternatives for the British Motorcycle Industry, London, Her Majesty's Stationery Office.

Braverman, H. (1974); *Labor and Monopoly Capital*, New York, Monthly Review Press.

Brealey, R. A, Myers, S.C. and Allen, F. (2008); *Principles of Corporate Finance*, McGraw-Hill.

Bromiley, P. (2005); *The Behavioral Foundations of Strategic Management*, Oxford, Blackwell.

Bryer, R. A. (1993); 'Double entry book-keeping and the birth of capitalism: Accounting for the commercial revolution in medieval northern Italy', *Critical Perspectives on Accounting*, 4, 2, pp. 113–40.

Bryer, R. A (2000); 'The history of accounting and the transition to capitalism in England. Part 2: Evidence', *Accounting, Organisations and Society*, 25, pp. 327–81.

Bryson, A., Gomez, R., Kretschmer, T., and Willman, P. (2007); 'The diffusion of workplace voice and high-commitment human resource management practices in Britain, 1984–1998', *Industrial and Corporate Change*, 16, 3, pp. 395–426.

Burns, T. and Stalker, G. S. (1959); *The Management of Innovation*, London, Tavistock.

Buroway, M. (1979); *Manufacturing Consent*, Chicago, Chicago University Press.

Burrell, G. and Morgan, G. (1979); *Sociological Paradigms and Organisational Analysis: Elements of the Sociology of Corporate Life*, London, Gower.

Camerer, C. (1991); 'Does strategy research need game theory?' *Strategic Management Journal*, 12, Winter, pp. 137–52.

Cappelli, P. (1999); *The New Deal at Work*, Cambridge MA, Harvard Business School Press.

Carruthers, B. G. and Espeland, W. N. (1991); 'Accounting for rationality: Double-entry bookkeeping and the rhetoric of economic rationality', *American Journal of Sociology*, 97, 1, pp. 31–69.

Cassis, Y. (2007); 'Big Business', pp. 171–94 in Jones, G. and Zeitlin, J. (eds), *The Oxford Handbook of Business History*, Oxford, Oxford University Press.

Chandler, A. (1962); *Strategy and Structure: Chapters in the History of American Enterprise*, London, MIT Press.

Chandler, A. (1971); 'Business history as institutional history', in Taylor and Ellsworth (eds), *Approaches to American Economic History*, Charlottesville VA, University of Virginia Press.

Chandler, A. (1977); *The Visible Hand: The Managerial Revolution in American Business*, Cambridge MA, Harvard University Press.

Chandler, A. (1990); *Scale and Scope: The Dynamics of Industrial Capitalism*, Cambridge MA, Belknap Press/Harvard University Press.

Channon, D. (1973); *The Strategy and Structure of British Enterprise*, Cambridge MA, Harvard University Press.

Charlwood, A. (2003); 'Willingness to unionise among non-union workers', pp. 51–72 in Gospel, H. and Wood, S. (eds), *Representing Workers: Union Membership and Recognition in Britain*, London, Routledge.

Chiapello, E. (2008); 'Accounting at the heart of performativity in economics', *Economic Sociology, The European Electronic Newsletter*, 10, 1, pp. 12–15.

Chung, C. and Kaiser, H. (2000); 'Distribution of generic advertising across participating firms', *American Journal of Agricultural Economics*, 84, pp. 659–64.

Coase, R. H. (1937); 'The nature of the firm', *Economica*, 4, pp. 386–405.

Coase, R. H. (1988); *The Firm, the Market and the Law*, Chicago, University of Chicago Press.

Cohen, D. M. and Levinthal, W. A. (1990); 'Absorptive capacity: A new perspective on learning and innovation', *Administrative Science Quarterly*, 35, 1, pp. 128–52.

Colquitt, J. A., LePine, J. A., and Wesson, M. T. (2009); *Organisational Behaviour; Improving Performance and Commitment in the Workplace*, New York, McGraw Hill.

Commons, J. R. (1909); 'American shoemakers, 1648–1895, A sketch of industrial evolution', *The Quarterly Journal of Economics*, 24, 1, pp. 39–84.

References

Conway, N. and Briner, R. (2005); *Understanding Psychological Contracts at Work*, Oxford, Oxford University Press.

Cooper, L. G. and Inoue, A. (1996); 'Building market structures from consumer preferences', *Journal of Marketing Research*, 33, pp. 293–306.

Crouch, C. (1982); *Trade Unions: The Logic of Collective Action*, London, Fontana.

Crowley, M. (2011); *City of Fortune: How Venice Won and Lost an Empire*, London, Faber.

Cusumano, Michael A. (1985); *The Japanese Automobile Industry*, Cambridge MA, Harvard University Press.

Cyert, R. M., Simon, H. A., and Trow, D. B. (1956); 'Observation of a business decision', *Journal of Organisational Behaviour*, 29, pp. 237–43.

Cyert and March (1963); *A Behavioural Theory of the Firm*, Englewood Cliffs, NJ, Prentice Hall.

Dalton, M. (1959); *Men Who Manage*, Wiley, New York.

Davies, N. (1999); *The Isles: A History*, London, Macmillan.

Davis, G. (2009); *Managed by the Markets*, Oxford, Oxford University Press.

Davis, G. and Cobb, J.A. (2010); 'Corporations and economic inequality around the world: The paradox of hierarchy', *Research in Organizational Behavior*, 30, pp. 35–53.

Davis, G., Diekmann, K.A., and Tinsley, C.H. (1994); 'The decline and fall of the conglomerate firm in the 1980's: The deinstitutionalisation of an organisational form', *American Sociological Review*, 59, 4, pp. 547–70.

Di Maggio, Paul (ed.) (2001); *The Twenty-first Century Firm: Changing Organisation in International Perspective*, Princeton NJ, Princeton University Press.

Dietrich, M. (1994); *Transaction Cost Economics and Beyond*, London, Routledge.

Dixit, A. K. and Nalebuff, B. J. (1991); *Thinking Strategically*, New York, Norton.

Dobbin, F., Sutton, J. R., Meyer, J. W., and Scott, W. R. (1993); 'Equal Opportunity Law and the Construction of Internal Labor Markets', *American Journal of Sociology*, 99, 2, pp. 396–427.

Doeringer, P. and Piore M. (1971); *Internal Labour Markets and Manpower Analysis*, Lexington DC, Heath.

Donaldson, L. (1985); *In Defence of Organisational Theory*, Cambridge, Cambridge University Press.

Donaldson, L. (1995); *American Anti-management Theories of Organisation: A Critique of Paradigm Proliferation*. Cambridge, Cambridge University Press.

Dore, R. (1983); 'Goodwill and the spirit of market capitalism', *British Journal of Sociology*, 34, pp. 439–82.

Dorfman, R. and Steiner, P. O. (1954); 'Optimal advertising and optimal quality', *The American Economic Review*, 44, 5, pp. 826–36.

Douglas, M. (1978); *Cultural Bias*, London, Royal Anthropological Institute.

Drucker, P. F. (1954); *The Practice of Management*, New York, Harper and Row.

Drucker, P. F. (1974); *Management: Tasks, Responsibilities, Practices*, Heinemann, London.

Duhon, T. (2012); *How The Trading Floor Really Works*, London, Wiley.

Durkheim, E. (1933); *The Division of Labor in Society*, New York, Free Press.

Durkheim, E. (1951); *Suicide*, London, Routledge and Kegan Paul.

Dutta, S., Zbaracki, M., and Bergen, M., (2003); 'Pricing process as a capability: A resource-based perspective', *Strategic Management Journal*, 24, pp. 615–30.

Dyas, G. P. and Thanheiser, H. T. (1976); *The Emerging European Enterprise: Strategy and Structure in French and German Industry*, London, Macmillan.

Eccles, R. and Nohria, N. (1992); *Beyond the Hype*, Cambridge, HBS Press.

Edwards, J. R. (1989) *A History of Financial Accounting*, Routledge, London.

Eisenhardt, K. M. (1989); 'Agency theory: An assessment and review', *Academy of Management Review*, 14, 1, pp. 57–74.

Eisenhardt, K. M. and J. A. Martin (2000); 'Dynamic capabilities: What are they?' *Strategic Management Journal*, 21, pp. 1105–21.

Elster, J. (1989); *The Cement of Society*, Cambridge, Cambridge University Press.

Empson, L. (2001); 'Fear of exploitation and fear of contamination: Impediments to knowledge transfer between professional service firms', *Human Relations*, 54, 7, pp. 839–62.

Fama, E. F. (1970); 'Efficient capital markets: A review of theory and empirical work', *Journal of Finance*, 25, 2, pp. 383–428.

Fama, E. F. (1991); 'Efficient capital markets: II', *Journal of Finance*, 46, 5, pp. 1575–617.

Fama, E. F. (1998); 'Market efficiency, long-term returns, and behavioral finance', *Journal of Financial Economics*, 49, pp. 283–306.

Farber, H. and Western, B. (2002); 'Ronald Reagan and the politics of declining union organisation', *British Journal of Industrial Relations*, 40, 3, pp. 385–401.

Faulhaber, G. and Baumol, W. (1988); 'Economists as innovators: Practical products of theoretical research', *Journal of Economic Literature*, 26, pp. 577–600.

Fayol, H. (1916); *General and Industrial Management*, London, Pitman.

Feldman, M. S. and March, J. G. (1981); 'Information in organisations as signal and symbol', *Administrative Science Quarterly*, 26, 2, pp. 171–86.

Fenton O'Creevy, M., Nicholson, N., Soane, E., and Willman, P. (2003); 'Trading on illusions: Unrealistic perceptions of control and trading performance', *Journal of Organisational and Occupational Psychology*, 76, pp. 53–68.

Fenton O'Creevy, M., Nicholson, N., Soane, E., and Willman, P. (2005); *Traders: Risks, Decisions, and Management in Financial Markets*, Oxford, Oxford University Press.

Ferraro, F., Pfeffer, J., and Sutton, R. (2005); 'Economics Language and Assumptions: How theories can become self fulfilling', *Academy of Management Review*, 30, 1, pp. 8–24.

Fligstein, N. (1985); 'The spread of the multi-divisional form 1919–1979', *American Sociological Review*, 50, pp. 987–1008.

Fligstein, N. (1990); *The Transformation of Corporate Control*, Cambridge, Harvard University Press.

Fox, A. (1974); *Beyond Contract: Work, Power and Trust Relations*, London, Faber.

Fox, K. (2004); *Watching the English*, London, Hodder and Stoughton.

References

Francis, A. (1983); 'Markets and hierarchies: efficiency or domination?' pp. 105–16 in Francis, A., Turk, J., and Willman, P., *Power, Efficiency and Institutions*, London, Heinemann.

Frank, R. H. and Cook, P. J. (1995); *The Winner Take All Society*, New York: Random House.

Freeman, R. and Medoff, J. (1984); *What Do Unions Do?* New York: Basic Books.

Freeman, R. and Rogers, J. (1999); *What Workers Want*, Ithaca NY, ILR Press.

Friedman, M. (1953); *Essays in Positive Economics*, University of Chicago Press.

Frost, P. J., Moore, L., Louis, M. R., Lundberg, C., and Martin, J. (1985); *Organizational Culture*, Sage, London.

Gabriel, Y. (2000); *Storytelling in Organizations*, Oxford: Oxford University Press.

Galbraith, J. K. (1968); *The New Industrial State*, Princeton NJ, Princeton University Press.

Galbraith, J. R. (1980); 'Applying theory to the management of organisations', pp. 151–67 in Evan, W. M. (ed.), *Frontiers in Organisation and Management*, New York, Praeger.

Geertz, C. (1973); *The Interpretation of Culture*, New York, Basic Books.

Geroski, P. (2000); 'Models of technology diffusion', *Research Policy*, 29, 4–5, pp. 603–25.

Ghoshal, S. and Moran, P. (1996); 'Bad for practice: A critique of the transaction cost theory', *Academy of Management Review*, 21, 1, pp. 13–47.

Giddens, A. (1971); *Capitalism and Modern Social Theory*, Cambridge, Cambridge University Press.

Gigerenzer, G. (2004); 'Striking a blow for sanity in theories of rationality', pp. 389–409 in Augier, M. and March, J. (eds), *Essays in Honor of Herbert Simon*, Cambridge MA, MIT Press.

Gigerenzer, G. (2008); *Rationality for Mortals*, Oxford, Oxford University Press.

Goffee, R. and Jones, G. (1998); *The Character of a Corporation: How your Company's Culture can Make or Break your Business*, New York, Harper.

Gomez, R., Bryson, A., and Willman, P. (2010); 'Voice in the wilderness? the shift from union to non-union voice in Britain', pp. 383–406 in *Oxford Handbook of Participation in Organizations* Wilkinson, A. et al. (eds), Oxford, Oxford University Press.

Goold, M. and Campbell, A. (1987); *Strategies and Styles*, Oxford, Blackwell.

Gospel, H. (2007); 'The management of labor and human resources', pp. 420–47 in Jones, G., and Zeitlin, J. (eds), *The Oxford Handbook of Business History*, Oxford, Oxford University Press.

Gouldner, A. (1954); *Patterns of Industrial Bureaucracy*, Glencoe IL, The Free Press.

Gowler, D. and Legge, K. (1983); 'The meaning of management, the management of meaning: a view from social anthropology', 197–233 in Earl, M. (ed.) *Perspectives on Management*, Oxford, Oxford University Press.

Granovetter, M. (1985); 'Economic action and social structure: A theory of embeddedness', *American Journal of Sociology*, 91, 3, pp. 481–510.

Grant, R. M. (2005); *Contemporary Strategy Analysis*, Oxford, Blackwell.

Greiner, L. (1972); 'Evolution and revolution as organisations grow', *Harvard Business Review*, 50, 4, pp. 73–86.

Gross, J. L. and Rayner, S. (1985); *Measuring Culture: A Paradigm for the Analysis of Social Organization*, New York, Columbia University Press.

Guest, D. (1998); 'Is the psychological contract worth taking seriously?' *Journal of Organisational Behaviour*, 19, 7, pp. 649–64.

Guillen, M. F. (1994); *Models of Management: Work, Authority and Organisation in a Comparative Perspective*, Chicago, Chicago University Press.

Hackman, J. R. and Oldham, G. (1976); 'Motivation through the design of work: Test of a theory' *Organisational Behaviour and Human Decision Processes*, 16, 2, pp. 250–79.

Hales, C. (1999); 'Why do managers do what they do? Reconciling evidence and theory in accounts of managerial work', *British Journal of Management*, 10, 4, 335–50.

Hall, R. C. and Hitch, L. J. (1939); 'Price theory and business behaviour', *Oxford Economic Papers*, 2, pp. 12–45.

Hamel, G. (2007); *The Future of Management*, Boston MA, Harvard Business Review Press.

Hamel, G. and Prahalad, C. K. (1996); *Competing for the Future*, Boston MA, Harvard Business School Press.

Hammersley, M. (1990); *Reading Ethnographical Research: A Critical Guide*, London, Longman.

Hancock, D. (1995); *Citizens of the World: London Merchants and the Integration of the British Atlantic Community, 1735–1785*, Cambridge, Cambridge University Press.

Hannah, L. (1986); *Inventing Retirement*, Cambridge, Cambridge University Press.

Hart, O. (2011); 'Thinking about the firm', *Journal of Economic Literature*, 49, 1, pp. 101–13.

Haveman, H.A. (2009); 'The Columbia School and the study of bureaucracies: why organizations have lives of their own' In Adler, P. (ed.) *The Oxford Handbook of Sociology and Organization Studies: Classical Foundations*, pp. 585–606.

Hayes, R. H., Wheelwright, S. C., and Clark, K. B. (1988); *Dynamic Manufacturing: Creating the Learning Organization*, New York, The Free Press.

Heath, A. (1976); *Rational Choice and Social Exchange: A Critique of Exchange Theory*, Cambridge, Cambridge University Press.

Hill, L. (1992); *Becoming a Manager: Mastery of a New Identity*, Cambridge MA, Harvard University Press.

Hirschman, A. (1970); *Exit, Voice and Loyalty*, Cambridge MA, Harvard University Press.

Hite, R. and Fraser, C. (1988); 'Meta-analyses of attitudes toward advertising by professionals', *Journal of Marketing*, 52, 3, pp. 95–103.

Hobsbawm, E. (1994); *The Age of Extremes: The Short Twentieth Century, 1914–1991*, London, Michael Joseph.

Hofstede, G. (1980); *Culture's Consequences: International Differences in Work-Related Values*, Beverley Hills CA, Sage.

Hofstede, G. (1980); 'Motivation, leadership and organization: Do American theories apply abroad?' *Organizational Dynamics*, 9, 1, pp. 42–63.

Hofstede, G. (1991); *Cultures and Organisations: Software of the Mind*, London, McGraw-Hill.

Holt, D. and Cameron, D. (2010); *Cultural Strategy*, Oxford, Oxford University Press.

Holweg, M. (2007); 'The genealogy of lean production.' *Journal of Operations Management*, 25, 2, pp. 420–37.

Homans, G. (1961); *Social Behaviour: Its Elementary Forms*, London, Routledge and Kegan Paul.

Hopwood, A. (1992); 'Accounting, calculation and the shifting sphere of the economic' *European Accounting Review*, 1, 125–43.

Hoskin, K. and Macve, R. (1994); 'Writing, examining, disciplining: the genesis of accounting's modern power' pp. 67–98 in Miller, P. and Hopwood, A. (eds) *Accounting as Social and Institutional Practice*, Cambridge, Cambridge University Press.

Hotelling, H. (1929); 'Stability in competition', *Economic Journal*, 39, pp. 41–57.

Hudson, M. (1999); *Managing Without Profit*, London, Penguin.

Huselid, M. A. (1995); 'The impact of human resource management practices on turnover, productivity, and corporate financial performance', *Academy of Management Journal*, 38, 3, pp. 635–72.

Jelinek, M., Smircich, L., and Hirsch, P. (1983); 'A code of many colors', *Administrative Science Quarterly*, 28, 3, pp. 331–8.

Jensen, M. C. (1972); 'Capital markets: theory and evidence,' *Bell Journal of Economics*, 3, 2, pp. 357–98.

Jensen, M. C. (1989); 'Eclipse of the public corporation', *Harvard Business Review*, 67, 5, pp. 61–74.

Jensen, M. C. (1993); 'The Modern industrial revolution, exit and the failure of internal control systems', *Journal of Finance*, 48, 3, pp. 831–80.

Jensen, M. C. (1998); *Foundations of Organisational Strategy*, Cambridge MA, Harvard University Press.

Jensen, M. C. and Meckling, W. H. (1976); 'The theory of the firm: Managerial behaviour, agency costs and ownership structure,' *Journal of Financial Economics*, 3, pp. 305–60.

Johnson, H. T. and Kaplan, R. S. (1991); *Relevance Lost: The Rise and Fall of Management Accounting*, Boston MA, Harvard Business Review Press.

Jones, D. G. B. and Shaw, E. H., (2002); 'A history of marketing thought', pp. 39–65 in Weitz, B. and Wensley, R. *Handbook of Marketing*, London, Sage.

Jurgens, U., Malsch, T., and Dohse, K. (1993); *Breaking from Taylorism*, Cambridge, Cambridge University Press.

Kahneman, D. and Tversky, A. (1979); 'Prospect theory: An analysis of decision under risk', *Econometrica*, 47, 2, 263–91.

Kahneman, D. and Tversky, A. (1983); 'Extensional versus intuitive reasoning: The conjunction fallacy in probability judgement', *Psychological Review*, 90, 4, pp. 439–50.

Kaplan, R. (1984); 'The evolution of management accounting', *Accounting Review*, LIX, 3, pp. 390–418.

Kaplan, R. and Norton, D. (1992); 'The balanced scorecard-measures that drive performance', *Harvard Business Review*, 70, 1, pp. 70–5.

Kaplan, R. and Norton, D. (1996); *The Balanced Scorecard: Translating Strategy into Action*, Boston MA, Harvard Business School Press.

Kaplan, R. and Norton, D. (2000); *The Strategy-Focused Organisation*, Boston MA, Harvard Business School Press.

Kay, J. (2004); *The Truth About Markets*, London, Penguin.

Keen, M. (1984); *Chivalry*, New Haven, Yale University Press.

Kelly, J. (1992); 'Does job redesign theory explain job redesign outcomes?' *Human Relations* 45, 8, pp. 753–74.

Kelly, J. (1998); *Rethinking Industrial Relations*, London, Routledge.

Kendall, M. (1953); 'The analysis of economic time series – Part 1: Prices', *Journal of the Royal Statistical Society*, A, 116, pp. 11–25.

Kerr, C. (1962); *Industrialism and Industrial Man: The Future of Industrialized Societies*, London, Heinemann.

Kersley, B., Alpin, C., Forth, J., Bryson, A., Bewley, H., Dix, G., and Oxenbridge, S. (2006); *Inside the Workplace: Findings from the 2004 Workplace Employment Relations Survey* (WERS 2004), London: Routledge.

King, T. A. (2006); *More than Just a Numbers Game: A Brief History of Accounting*, New Jersey, Wiley.

Kiosse, V. and Peasnell, K. V. (2009); 'Have changes in pension accounting changed pension provision? A review of the evidence', *Accounting and Business Research*, 39, 3, pp. 255–67.

Knoke, D. (1990); *Organizing for Collective Action: The Political Economics of Associations*, New York, Aldine de Gruyter.

Kogut, B. and Parkinson, D. (1998); 'Adoption of the multi-divisional structure: Analysing history from the start', *Industrial and Corporate Change*, 7, 2, 249–73.

Kotler, P. (2004); *Principles of Marketing*, London, Prentice Hall.

Kotler, P. et al. (2009); *Marketing Management*, Pearson.

Kotter, J. (1982); *The General Managers*, Free Press, New York.

Kotter, J. (1990); 'What leaders really do.', *Harvard Business Review*, 68, 3, 103–11.

Kreps, D. (1990); 'Corporate culture and economic theory' in Alt, J. and Schepsle, K. (eds) *Perspectives on Positive Political Economy*, Cambridge, Cambridge University Press.

Krippner, G. (2005); 'The financialization of the American Economy', *Socio-Economic Review*, 3, 2, 173–208.

Kuhn, T. S. (1962; 1996 edition); *The Structure of Scientific Revolutions*, Chicago, University of Chicago press.

Kuhn, T. S. (1970, September); 'Reflections on my critics'. In *Criticism and the Growth of Knowledge: Volume 4: Proceedings of the International Colloquium in the Philosophy of Science, London, 1965* (Vol. 4, p. 231), Cambridge, Cambridge University Press.

Kunda, G. (1992); *Engineering Culture: Control and Commitment in a High-Tech Corporation*, Philadelphia, Temple University Press.

Lafontaine, F. and Slade, M. (2007); 'Vertical integration and firm boundaries: the evidence' *Journal of Economic Literature*, 45, 3, pp. 629–85.

Lambkin, M., and Day, G. S. (1989); 'Evolutionary processes in competitive markets: Beyond the product life cycle', *The Journal of Marketing*, 53, 3 pp. 4–20.

Landes, D. S. (1969); *The Unbound Prometheus*, Cambridge, Cambridge University Press.

Landsberger, H. A. (1958); *Hawthorne Revisited*, Ithaca NY, Cornell University Press.

Langer, E. J. (1975); 'The illusion of control', *Journal of Personality and Social Psychology*, 32, 2, pp. 311–28.

Latour, B. and Woolgar, S. (1979); *Laboratory Life: The Construction of Scientific Facts*, Beverly Hills, Sage.

References

Laux, C. and Leuz, C. (2009); 'The Crisis of Fair Value Accounting: Making Sense of the Recent Debate' CFS Working Paper 2009/09, Frankfurt.

Lazear, E. (2000); 'Economic imperialism' *Quarterly Journal of Economics*, 115, 1, pp. 99–146.

Lee, C. M. C. (2001); 'Market efficiency and accounting research: A discussion of "capital market research in accounting" by S. P. Kothari', *Journal of Accounting and Economics*, 31, 2, pp. 233–53.

Lee, R. (1998); *What is an Exchange?*, Oxford, Oxford University Press.

Leonard-Barton, D. (1995); *Wellsprings of Knowledge*, Boston MA, Harvard Business School Press.

Lewchuk, W. (1983); 'Fordism and British motor car employees, 1896–1932', in Gospel, H. and Littler, C. (eds), *Managerial Strategies and Industrial Relations*, London, Heinemann.

Linstead, S. A. (1985); 'Breaking the purity rules: Industrial sabotage and the symbolic process', *Personnel Review*, 14, pp. 3–11.

Linstead, S. A. (1997); 'The social anthropology of management', *British Journal of Management*, 8, 1, pp. 85–98.

Locke, E. and Latham, G. (1990); *A Theory of Goal Setting and Task Performance*, Englewood Cliffs, Prentice Hall.

Loft, A. (1988); *Understanding Accounting in its Social and Historical Context*, New York, Garland.

Loft, A. (1994); 'Accountancy and the First World War', pp. 116–38 in Miller, P. and Hopwood, A. (eds), *Accounting as Social and Institutional Practice*, Cambridge, Cambridge University Press.

Lukes, S. (1974); *Power: A Radical View*, London, Macmillan.

MacDuffie, J. P. (1995); 'Human resource bundles and manufacturing performance: Organizational logic and flexible production systems in the world auto industry', *Industrial & Labor Relations Review*, 48, 2, pp. 197–221.

MacKenzie, D. (2006); *An Engine, Not a Camera: How Financial Models Shape Markets*, Cambridge MA, MIT Press.

Mahajan, V., Sharma, S., and Bettis, R. (1988); 'The adoption of the M-form organisational structure: A test of imitation hypothesis,' *Management Science*, 34, 10, pp. 1188–1201.

Maister, D. H. (2003); *Managing the Professional Service Firm*, New York, Simon and Schuster.

Mangham, I. (1986); *Power and Performance in Organisations*, Blackwell, Oxford.

March, J. G. and Simon, H. (1958); *Organizations*, New York: John Wiley & Son.

Marglin, S. (1974); 'What do bosses do?' *Review of Radical Political Economy*, 6, pp. 33–60.

Markowitz, H. (1956); 'The optimization of a quadratic function subject to linear constraints', *Naval Research Logistics Quarterly*, 3, pp. 111–33.

Markowitz, H. (1952); 'Portfolio selection', *Journal of Finance*, 17, pp. 77–91.

Marsden, D. and Belfield, R. (2006); 'Pay for performance where output is hard to measure: The case of performance pay for school teachers'. *Advances in Industrial and Labor Relations*, 15, pp. 1–34.

Mayo, E. (1933); *Human Problems of an Industrial Civilisation*, New York, Macmillan.

Mazower, M. (1998); *The Dark Continent: Europe's Twentieth Century*, London, Allen Lane.

McKendrick, N. (1970); 'Josiah Wedgewood and cost accounting in the industrial revolution', *Economic History Review*, 23, 1, pp. 45–67.

McKenna, C. D. (2006); *The World's Newest Profession: Management Consulting in the Twentieth Century*, New York, Cambridge University Press.

McSweeney, B. (2002); 'Hofstede's model of national cultural differences and their consequences: A triumph of faith, a failure of analysis,' *Human Relations*, 55, 1, pp. 89–118.

de Menezes, L. M., Wood, S. J., and Gelade, G. (2010); 'The integration of human resource and operation management practices and its link with performance: A longitudinal latent class study' *Journal of Operations* Management, 28, 6, pp. 455–71.

Merton, R. (1940); 'Bureaucratic structure and personality', *Social Forces*, 18, pp. 560–8.

Merton, R. C. (1973); 'Theory of rational option pricing,' *Bell Journal of Economics*, 4, 1, pp. 141–83.

Metcalf, D., Hansen, K., and Charlwood, A (2001); 'Unions and the sword of justice', *National Institute Economic Review*, 176, pp. 61–75.

Meyer, M. W. (2002); *Rethinking Performance Measurement: Beyond the Balanced Scorecard*, Cambridge University Press.

Michels, R. (1915, reprinted 1962); *Political Parties*, New York, Dover.

Michie, R. C. (2006); *The Global Securities Market*, Oxford, Oxford University Press.

Milgrom, P. (2004); *Putting Auction Theory to Work*, New York, Cambridge University Press.

Miller, M. H. and Modigliani F. (1961); 'Dividend policy, growth and the valuation of shares', *Journal of Business*, 34, 4, pp. 411–33.

Miller, P. (1994); 'Introduction', pp. 1–40 in P. Miller and A. Hopwood (eds), *Accounting as Social and Institutional Practice*, Cambridge, Cambridge University Press.

Miller, P. and Napier, C. (1993); 'Genealogies of calculation', *Accounting, Organisations and Society*, 18, 7, pp. 631–74.

Miller, P. and O'Leary, T. (1987); 'Accounting and the construction of the governable person', *Accounting, Organisations and Society*, 12, 3, pp. 235–65.

Mintzberg, H. (1973); *The Nature of Managerial Work*, Harper and Row, New York.

Mintzberg, H. (1975); 'The manager's job: folklore and fact', *Harvard Business Review*, 53, 2, pp. 100–110.

Mintzberg, H. (1978); 'Patterns in strategy formation', *Management Science*, 24, 9, pp. 934–48.

Mintzberg, H. (1983); *Structure in Fives: Designing Effective Organisations*, Englewood Cliffs, NJ, Prentice Hall, pp. 1–25.

Mintzberg, H. (1985); 'Of strategies, deliberate and emergent', *Strategic Management Journal*, 6, 3, pp. 257–72.

Mintzberg, H. (1994); *The Rise and Fall of Strategic Planning: Reconceiving Roles for Planning, Plans, Planners*, New York, Free Press.

Mintzberg, H. (2009); *Managing*, London, Pearson.

References

Mirowski, P. (2002); *Machine Dreams: Economics Becomes a Cyborg Science*, Cambridge, Cambridge University Press.

Mitroff, I. and Mohrman, S. (1987); 'The slack is gone: How the United States lost its competitive edge in the world economy', *Academy of Management Executive*, 1, 1, pp. 65–70.

Modigliani F. and Miller, M. H. (1958); 'The cost of capital, corporation finance and the theory of investment', *American Economic Review*, 48, 3, pp. 261–97.

Morrison, A. D. and Wilhelm, W. J. (2007); *Investment Banking: Institutions, Politics, and Law*, Oxford, Oxford University Press.

Nelson, D. (1980); *Frederick W. Taylor and the Rise of Scientific Management*, Madison, University of Wisconsin Press.

Nelson, R. and Winter, S. (1982); *An Evolutionary Theory of Economic Change*, Cambridge MA, Belknap Press.

Nicholson, N. (2000); *Managing the Human Animal*, London, Texere.

Norwich, J. J. (1977); *A History of Venice*, London, Allen Lane.

O'Connor, E. S. (1999); 'The politics of management thought: A case study of the Harvard Business School and the Human Relations School', *Academy of Management Review*, 24, 2, pp. 117–31.

Ofir, C., and Winer, R. S. (2002); 'Pricing: economic and behavioural models', pp. 267–81 in Weitz, B. and Wensley, R., *Handbook of Marketing*, London, Sage.

Olie, R. (1994); 'Shades of culture and institutions in international mergers', *Organisation Studies*, 15, 3, pp. 381–405.

Olson, M. (1971); *The Logic of Collective Action*, Cambridge MA, Harvard University Press.

Osterman, P. (1996); *Broken Ladders: Managerial Careers in the New Economy*, Oxford, Oxford University Press.

Ouchi, W. (1981); *Theory Z*, Reading, Addison-Wesley.

Overy, R. (1995); *Why the Allies Won*, London, Norton.

Padmanabhan, V. and Pang, I. P. (1997); 'Manufacturer's return policies and retail competition', *Marketing Science*, 16, 1, pp. 81–94.

Palmer, D., Friedland, R., Devereux-Jenings, P., and Powers, M. (1987); 'The economics and politics of structure: the multi-divisional form and the large US corporation' *Administrative Science Quarterly*, 32, 1, pp. 25–48.

Parsons, T. (1969); *Politics and Social Structure*, New York, Free Press.

Pascale, R. and Athos, A. G. (1981); *The Art of Japanese Management: Applications for American Executives*, New York, Simon and Schuster.

Pencavel, J. (1971); 'The demand for union services: An exercise', *Industrial and Labor Relations Review*, 24, 2, pp. 180–90.

Penrose, E. (1959); *The Theory of the Growth of the Firm*, (2009 edition), Oxford, Oxford University Press.

Peters, T. J. and Waterman, R. H. (1982); *In Search of Excellence*, New York, Harper and Row.

Pettigrew, A. (1985); *The Awakening Giant: Continuity and Change in Imperial Chemical Industries*, Oxford, Blackwell.

Pfeffer, J. (1994); *Competitive Advantage through People*, Boston, HBS Press.

Pfeffer, J. (1995); 'Producing sustainable competitive advantage through the effective management of people', *Academy of Management Executive*, 9, 1, pp. 55–72.

Pfeffer, J. (1997); *New Directions for Organizational Theory*, Oxford, Oxford University Press.

Piketty, T. (2014); *Capital in the Twenty-First Century*, Cambridge MA, Belknap Press.

Pine, B. J. and Gilmore, J. H. (1998); 'Welcome to the experience economy' *Harvard Business Review*, 76, 4, pp. 97–105.

Pitelis, C. (2009); 'Edith Penrose's "Theory of the Growth of the Firm" Fifty years later', in Penrose, E. (1959), *The Theory of the Growth of the Firm*, (2009 edition), Oxford, Oxford University Press.

Pollard, S. (1965); *The Genesis of Modern Management: A Study of the Industrial Revolution in Great Britain*, London, Penguin.

Porter, M. E. (1980); *Competitive Strategy: Techniques for Analysing Industries and Firms*, New York, Macmillan.

Porter, M. E. (1991); 'Towards a dynamic theory of strategy', *Strategic Management Journal*, 12, pp. 95–117.

Porter, M. E. (2008); 'The five competitive forces that shape strategy', *Harvard Business Review*, 86, 1, pp. 78–93.

Postrel, S. (1991); 'Burning your britches behind you: Can policy scholars bank on game theory?' *Strategic Management Journal*, 12, pp. 153–55.

Power, M. (1997); *The Audit Society: Rituals of Verification*, Oxford, Oxford University Press.

Power, M. (2003); 'Auditing and the production of legitimacy', *Accounting, Organisations and Society*, 28, 4, pp. 379–94.

Power, M. (2010); 'Fair value accounting, financial economics and the transformation of reliability', *Accounting and Business Research*, 40, 3, pp. 197–210.

Prahalad, C. K. and Hamel, G. (1990); 'The core competence of the corporation'. *Harvard Business Review*, 68, 3, pp. 79–91.

Prais, S. J. (1976); *The Evolution of Giant Firms in Britain*, Cambridge, Cambridge University Press.

Priem, R. L. and Butler, J. E. (2001); 'Is the resource based 'view' a useful perspective for strategic management research?', *Academy of Management Review*, 26, 1, pp. 22–40.

Pugh, D. S., Hickson, D. J., Hinings, C. R., McDonald, K. M., Turner, C., and Lupton, T. (1964); 'A conceptual scheme for organisational analysis,' *Administrative Science Quarterly*, 8, 3, pp. 289–315.

Pugh, D. S., Hickson, D. J., Hinings, C. R., and Turner, C. (1968); 'Dimensions of organization structure.' *Administrative Science Quarterly*, 13, 1, pp. 65–91.

Putnam, R., (2000); *Bowling Alone; The Collapse and Revival of American Community*, New York, Touchstone.

Quattrone, P. (2004); 'Accounting for God: Accounting practices in the Society of Jesus', *Accounting, Organizations and Society*, 29, 7, pp. 647–83.

Reed, M. (1989); *The Sociology of Management*, Harvester, Wheatsheaf, Hemel Hempstead.

Roberts, J. (2004); *The Modern Firm; Organizational Design for Performance and Growth*, Oxford, Oxford University Press.

References

Robertson, J. and Funnell, W. (2012); 'The Dutch East India Company and accounting for social capital at the dawn of modern capitalism 1602–1623', *Accounting, Organisations and Society*, 37, 5, pp. 342–60.

Roethlisberger, F., and Dickson, W. (1939); *Management and the Worker*, Cambridge MA, Harvard University Press.

Rose, M. (1988); *Industrial Behaviour* (2nd edition), London, Penguin.

Rousseau, D. M. (1995); *Psychological Contract in Organisations; Understanding Written and Unwritten Agreements*, Newbury Park, Sage.

Rousseau, D. M. (2005); 'Developing psychological contract theory', pp. 190–211 in Smith, K. G. and Hitt, M. A. (eds), *Great Minds in Management*, Oxford, Oxford University Press.

Roy, D. (1952); 'Quota restriction and goldbricking in a machine shop', *American Journal of Sociology*, 57, 52, pp. 427–42.

Rumelt, R. P. (1974); *Strategy, Structure and Economic Performance*, Cambridge MA, Harvard Business School Press.

Rumelt, R. P. (1984); 'Towards a strategic theory of the enterprise' in Lamb, R. (ed.), *Competitive Strategic Management*, Englewood Cliffs, Prentice Hall.

Rumelt, R. P. (2011); *Good strategy/bad strategy; The difference and why it matters*, London, Profile Books.

Sabel, C. (1982); *Work and Politics*, Oxford, Oxford University Press.

Sako, M. (1992); *Prices, Quality and Trust*, Cambridge, Cambridge University Press.

Salaman, G. (1981); *Class and the Corporation*, London, Fontana.

Schein, E. H. (1970); *Organizational Psychology* (3rd edition) Englewood Cliffs NJ, Prentice Hall.

Schein, E. (1985); *Organisational Culture and Leadership*, San Francisco, Jossey-Bass.

Schutz, A. (1972); *The Phenomenology of the Social World*, Evanston Il, Northwestern University Press

Schwartz, S. H. (1992); 'Universals in the content and structure of values', pp. 1–65 in M. Zanna (ed.), *Advances in Experimental Social Psychology*, London, Academic Press.

Selznick, P. (1943); 'An approach to a theory of bureaucracy', *American Sociological Review*, 8, 1, pp. 47–54.

Selznick, P. (1957); *Leadership in Administration*, New York, Harper and Row.

Sen, A. (1977); 'Rational fools: A critique of the behavioural foundations of economic theory' *Philosophy and Public Affairs*, 4, pp. 317–44.

Sharpe, W. F. (1964); 'Capital asset prices: A theory of market equilibrium under risk', *Journal of Finance*, 19, 3, pp. 425–52.

Shefrin, H. (2000); *Beyond Greed and Fear: Understanding Behavioral Finance and the Psychology of Investing*, Cambridge, HBS Press.

Shenhav, Y. (1999); *Manufacturing Rationality: The Engineering Foundations of the Managerial Revolution*, Oxford and New York, Oxford University Press.

Shiller, R. (2000); *Irrational Exhuberance*, Princeton NJ, Princeton University Press.

Shiller, R. (2003); 'From efficient markets theory to behavioral finance', *Journal of Economic Perspectives*, 17, 1, pp. 83–104.

Shiller, R. (2012); *Finance and the Good Society*, Princeton NJ, Princeton University Press.

Shleifer, A. (2000); *Inefficient Markets: An Introduction to Behavioral Finance*, Oxford, Oxford University Press.

Shocker, A. D. (2002); Determining the structure of product markets', pp. 106–25 in Weitz, B. and Wensley, R., *Handbook of Marketing*, London, Sage.

Shoonhoven, C. B. (1981); 'Problems with contingency theory: testing assumptions hidden within the language of contingency theory', *Administrative Science Quarterly*, 26, 3, pp. 349–77.

Simon, H. A. (1947); *Administrative Behaviour*, New York, Macmillan (1997 edition, New York, Free Press).

Simon, H. A. (1955); 'A behavioural model of rational choice', *Quarterly Journal of Economics*, 69, pp. 99–118.

Simon, H. A. (1991); 'Organisations and markets', *Journal of Economic Perspectives*, 5, 1, pp. 25–44.

Sloan, A. P. (1963); *My Years with General Motors*, London, Sidgwick and Jackson.

Smircich, L (1983); 'Concepts of culture and organisational analysis', *Administrative Science Quarterly*, 28, 3, pp. 339–58.

Smith, A. (1776); *An Inquiry into the Nature and Causes of The Wealth of Nations* (1976 edition), Oxford, Clarendon Press.

Smith, C., Child, J., and Rowlinson, M. (1990); *Reshaping Work: The Cadbury Experience*, Cambridge, Cambridge University Press.

Smith, P. B., Dugan, S., and Trompenaars, F. (1996); 'National culture and the values of organisational employees: A dimensional analysis across 43 nations', *Journal of Cross-Cultural Psychology*, 27, pp. 231–64.

Spear, S. and Bowen, H. K. (1999); 'Decoding the DNA of the Toyota production system', *Harvard Business Review*, 77, 5, pp. 96–108.

Starbuck, W. (1993); 'Keeping a butterfly and an elephant in a house of cards', *Journal of Management Studies*, 30, 6, pp. 885–921.

Stern, L. W. and Weitz, B. A. (1997); 'The revolution in distribution: challenges and opportunities', *Long Range Planning*, 30, 6, pp. 823–9.

Stewart, D. W. and Kamins, M. A. (2002); 'Marketing Ccmmunications', pp. 282–309 in Weitz, B. and Wensley, R., *Handbook of Marketing*, London, Sage.

Stewart, R. (1982); *The Reality of Management*, Heinemann, London.

Stigler, G. J. (1951); 'The division of labor is limited by the extent of the market', *Journal of Political Economy*, 59, 3, pp. 185–93.

Stoneman, P. (2002); *The Economics of Technological Diffusion*, Oxford, Blackwell Publishers.

Taylor, F. W. (1923); *The Principles of Scientific Management*, New York, Harper.

Taylor, S. M. and Tekleab, A. (2005); 'Taking stock of psychological contract research', pp. 253–84 in J. Coyle-Shapiro et al. (eds), *The Employment Relationship: Examining Psychological and Contextual Perspectives*, Oxford, Oxford University Press.

Teece, D. J. (1982); 'Towards an economic theory of the multiproduct firm' *Journal of Economic Behaviour and Organisation*, 3, 1, pp. 39–63.

Teece, D. J. (2007); 'Explicating dynamic capabilities: The nature and microfoundations of (sustainable) enterprise performance', *Strategic Management Journal*, 28, pp. 1319–50.

Teece, D. J. (2010); 'Alfred Chandler and 'capabilities' theories of strategy and management', *Industrial and Corporate Change*, 19, 2, 13, pp. 297–316.

Teece, D. J., Pisano, G., and Shuen, A. (1997); 'Dynamic capabilities and strategic management', *Strategic Management Journal*, 18, 7, pp. 509–33.

Terkel, S. (1974); *Working*, New York, Pantheon.

Thompson, E. P. (1968); *The Making of the English Working Class*, London, Penguin.

Thompson, G. (1994); 'Early double entry bookkeeping and the rhetoric of accounting calculation' pp. 40–67 in Miller, P. and Hopwood, A. (eds), *Accounting as Social and Institutional Practice*, Cambridge, Cambridge University Press.

Trist, E. L. and Bamforth, K. W. (1951); 'Some social and psychological consequences of the longwall method of coal getting', *Human Relations*, 4, 1, pp. 3–38.

Trompenaars, F. (1993); *Riding the Waves of Culture*, London, Nicholas Brealey.

Tucci, U. (1973); 'The psychology of the Venetian merchant in the sixteenth century', pp. 346–78 in Hale, J. R. (ed.), *Renaissance Venice*, London, Faber and Faber.

Tuchman, B. (1962); *The Proud Tower*, London, Macmillan.

Turnley, W. H. and Feldman, D. C. (1999); 'The impact of psychological contract violations on exit, voice, loyalty and neglect', *Human Relations*, 52, 7, pp. 895–922.

Ulrich, D. (1997); *Human Resource Champions*, Boston MA, Harvard Business Review Press.

Ulrich, D. (2005); *The Human Resource Proposition*, Boston MA, Harvard Business Review Press.

Useem, M. (1996); *Investor Capitalism: How Money Managers are Changing the Face of Corporate America*, New York, Basic Books.

Utterback, J. M. and Abernathy, W.J. (1975); 'A dynamic model of product and process innovation', *Omega*, 3, 6, pp. 639–56.

Van Maanen, J. (1988); *Tales of the Field: On Writing Ethnography*, Chicago, University of Chicago Press.

Van Maanen, J. (1990); 'The smile factory: work at Disneyland', pp. 58–76 in Frost et al. (eds), *Reframing Organisational Culture*, Thousand Oaks, Sage.

Van Maanen, J. (2011); 'Ethnography as work: some rules of engagement', *Journal of Management Studies*, 48, 1, pp. 218–34.

Von Neumann, J., and Morgenstern, O. (1944); *Theory of Games and Economic Behaviour*, Princeton NJ, Princeton University Press.

Vroom, V.H. (1964); *Work and Motivation*, New York, Wiley.

Waldman, D. A., De Luque, M. S., and Wang, D. (2012); 'What can we really learn about management practices across firms and countries?', *Academy of Management Perspectives*, 26, 1, pp. 12–33.

Walking, R. A. and Long, M. S. (1984); 'Agency theory, managerial welfare, and takeover bid resistance', *Rand Journal of Economics*, 15, 1, pp. 54–68.

Wall, T., Clegg, C., Davies, R., Kemp, N., and Mellor, W., (1987); 'Advanced manufacturing and work simplification,' *Journal of Organisational Behaviour*, 8, 3, pp. 233–54.

Wall, T. D. and Wood, S. J. (2005); 'The romance of human resource management and business performance, and the case for big science', *Human Relations*, 58, 4, pp. 429–62.

Watson, A. J. (1994); *In Search of Management: Culture, Chaos and Control in Managerial Work*, London, Routledge.

Watson, A. J. (2011); 'Ethnography, reality, and truth: the vital need for studies of "how things work" in organizations and management' *Journal of Management Studies*, 48, 1, pp. 202–17.

Weatherall, J.O. (2013); *The Physics of Wall Street*, Boston MA, Houghton Miflin Harcourt.

Weber, K., Davis, G., and Lounsbury, M. (2009); 'Policy as myth and ceremony? The global spread of stock exchanges 1980–2005', *Academy of Management Journal*, 52, 6, pp. 1319–47.

Weber, M. (1947); *The Theory of Social and Economic Organisation*, Glencoe, Free Press.

Webster, F. E. (2002); 'The role of marketing and the firm', pp. 66–84 in Weitz, B. and Wensley, R., *Handbook of Marketing*, London, Sage.

Weetman, P. (2006); *Financial Accounting; An Introduction*, Pearson.

Weick, K. (1979); *The Social Psychology of Organizing*, Reading MA, Addison-Wesley.

Weitz, B. and Wensley, R. (2002); *Handbook of Marketing*, London, Sage.

Wiener, M. J. (1985); *English Culture and the Decline of the Industrial Spirit, 1850–1980*, London, Penguin.

Whitley, R. (1986); 'The transformation of business finance into financial economics', *Accounting, Organisations and Society*, 11, 2, pp. 171–92.

Whitley, R. (1995); 'Academic knowledge and work jurisdiction in management', *Organization Science*, 16, 1, pp. 81–105.

Whittington, R. (2001); *What is Strategy—and Does it Matter?* (2nd Edition) London, Thomson International.

Whittington, R., Mayer, M., and Curto, F. (1999); 'Chandlerism in post-war Europe: strategic and structural change in France, Germany and the UK, 1950-1993', *Industrial and Corporate Change*, 8, 3, pp. 519–51.

Williamson, O. E. (1964); *The Economics of Discretionary Behaviour: Managerial Objectives in a Theory of the Firm*, Englewood Cliffs NJ, Prentice Hall.

Williamson, O. E. (1975); *Markets and Hierarchies, Analysis and Anti-Trust Implications*, New York, Free Press.

Williamson, O. E. (1985); *The Economic Institutions of Capitalism*, New York, Free Press.

Williamson, O. E. (ed.) (1995); *Organization Theory: From Chester Barnard to the Present and Beyond*, Oxford, Oxford University Press.

Williamson, O. E. (1999); 'Strategy research: Governance and competence perspectives', *Strategic Management Journal*, 20, pp. 1087–1108.

Williamson, O. E. (2005); 'Transaction cost economics: The process of theory development', pp. 485–508 in Smith, K. G. and M. A. Hitt (eds), *Great Minds in Management*, Oxford, Oxford University Press.

Willman, P. (1982); *Fairness, Collective Bargaining and Incomes Policy*, Oxford University Press.

Willman, P. (1982); 'Opportunism and labour contracting: An application of the organisational failures framework', *Journal of Economic Behaviour and Organisation*, 2, 1, pp. 83–98.

Willman, P. (1986); *Technological Change, Collective Bargaining, and Industrial Efficiency*, Oxford University Press.

References

Willman, P. (2000); 'Risk, greed, sound and fury' *Business Strategy Review*, 11, 2, pp. 71–4.

Willman, P. and Fenton O'Creevy, M. (2013); 'Cultures of risk?' In Shojai, S. and Feiger G., (eds) *Risk in Financial Institutions*, London, Euromoney Publications.

Willman, P., Fenton O'Creevy, M., Nicholson, N., and Soane, E. (2006); 'Noise trading and trader behaviour', *Journal of Management Studies*, 43, 6, pp. 1357–75.

Willman, P., Morris, T. J., and Aston, B. (1993); *Union Business: Trade Union Organisation and Financial Reform in the Thatcher Years*, Cambridge, Cambridge University Press.

Willman, P. and Winch, G. (1985); *Innovation and Management Control*, Cambridge, Cambridge University Press.

Witzel, M. (2002); *Builders and Dreamers: The Making and Meaning of Modern Management*, London, Prentice Hall.

Woodward, J. (1958); *Management and Technology*, London, Her Majesty's Stationery Office.

Wren, D. A. (2005); *The History of Management Thought*, New York, Wiley.

Wright, P. M., and McMahan, G. C. (1992); Theoretical perspectives for strategic human resource management, *Journal of Management*, 18, 2, pp. 295–320.

Yukl, G. A. (2006); *Leadership in Organizations*, Upper Saddle River, NJ: Pearson/Prentice Hall.

Zaloom, C. (2006); *Out of the Pits: Traders and Technology from Chicago to London*, Chicago, University of Chicago Press.

Zambon, S. and Zan, L. (2007); 'Controlling expenditure, or the slow emergence of costing at the venice arsenal, 1586–1633,' *Accounting, Business & Financial History*, 17, 1, pp. 105–28.

Zan, L. (2004); 'Accounting and managerial discourse in proto–industrial settings: the Venice Arsenale in the turn of the 16th century', *Accounting and Business Research*, 32, 2, pp. 145–75.

Zbaracki, M. and Bergen, M. (2010); 'When truces collapse: a longitudinal study of price adjustment routines', *Organization Science*, 21, 5, pp. 955–72.

Zbaracki, M., Ritson, M., Levey, D., Dutta, S., and Bergen, M. (2004); 'Managerial and customer costs of price adsjustment: Direct evidence from industrial markets', *Review of Economics and Statistics*, 86, 2, pp. 514–33.

Zey, M. (1998); *Rational Choice and Organizational Theory: A Critique*, Thousand Oaks, Sage.

Index

ethics 248
ethnography 238–40, 246, 249, 256
Europe 8, 17–18, 23, 26, 39, 48–50, 57, 62, 115,
    123, 141, 165, 176, 220, 230, 245
    Eastern 261
    Western 9, 53, 207
European Union 10, 255
Evans-Pritchard, E.E. 240
exit 68–70
exit-voice model 96
expectancy theory 139
expenditure 204
    military 16
expenses 19, 168 *see also* costs

factory system 6, 24–5, 40, 48
Fama, Gene 109, 215, 219
Fayol, H. 4, 41, 116–17, 241–2
feedback 81–2
fieldwork 238
finance 1, 8, 27, 99, 210–11, 223–4, 228, 235,
    274, 279–80
    academic 4, 104, 129, 211, 217, 219, 223,
        225, 231, 236, 257, 269
    'behavioural' 109, 217, 223, 242
    'financialization' 10, 228
    global 22
    theory 43, 229, 269
financial control 169–70, 227
financial domain 136
financial management 220
financial statements 130–1
Financial Times 143–4, 150
firms 36, 98, 102–103, 129, 155, 161, 179,
    183, 230, 264, 268, 270, 275, 277, 287
    attributes of 180
    capabilities of 188
    conglomerate 227, 230
    dynamic capabilities of 186–7
    economics of 6, 29
    family run 270
    Fortune 500 165, 227
    governance of 4, 43, 284
    independence of 278
    industrial 40, 150
    inequality in 44
    investors 47
    management controlled 44
    measuring size of 50
    mechanistic 118
    multi-divisional 32, 162, 226 *see also*
        divisionalization
    multi-product 179
    operation of 44, 154, 178
    organic 118, 120
    owner controlled 44
    performance of 4, 225

relationship with employees 56
state owned 270
strategy of 113
structure of 113, 125, 278–9 *see also*
    organizations, structure of
theories of 7, 29, 122, 181, 187, 229,
    278, 283
first mover advantage 271
Fitch and Moody rankings 141
'Five Forces' framework 150–3
Flora 202
Forbes Magazine 234
Ford 24, 28, 42, 74, 76, 199
Fox, Alan 2
fragmentation 8, 225, 238, 251, 256, 283, 286
    of management field 46, 275
France 52, 165, 254
franchises 57, 170, 172, 175, 207–208
free trade arrangements 10
Frescobaldi 16
Friedman, Milton 103, 213
'functional specialization' 119
funding 24

G8 countries 282
Galbraith, J.K. 149
Gauntlett, Victor 206
game theory 154–61, 187, 191, 205, 207, 258,
    261, 287
games 46, 49, 141, 190
General Electric 28, 167
    'rank and yank' system 138, 233
General Motors 74, 131, 147–9, 199
Germany 26, 50, 52, 63, 79, 86, 92, 123, 165,
    234, 249
Giddens, Anthony 2
Gigerenzer, G. 103, 106, 109, 111, 122
Gini coefficients 230
globalization 220
Goering, Hermann 245
Goethe,Johann Wolfgang von 19
Goffee, R. and G. Jones 246
Goldman Sachs 218, 222
Goldthorpe, John 2
Gouldner, A. 116
government 6, 40, 50, 123, 145, 265,
    267, 278
    involvement in business 26, 264, 270,
        281–2
Great Depression 50, 193, 281
Gritti 16
groups 129, 253
    cohesion of 238
    peer 140
    self-selecting 81
growth (of businesses) 3, 169, 180, 270,
    273, 275